Betty Crocker

Spend 30 Minutes or Less in the Kitchen

Come Home to DINNER

350 Delicious Recipes for the SLOW COOKER, BREAD MACHINE, and OVEN

RODALE

This edition published by arrangement with Wiley, Inc.

Printed in the United States of America

Material in this book has previously been published by Wiley Inc. as *Betty Crocker's More Slow Cooker Recipes* (© 2003 by General Mills, Inc.), by Hungry Minds, Inc. as *Betty Crocker's Easy Slow Cooker Dinners* (© 2001 by General Mills, Inc.) and by IDG Books Worldwide, Inc. as *Betty Crocker's Cookbook* (© 2000 by General Mills, Inc.), and by Macmillan Publishing USA as *Betty Crocker's Slow Cooker Cookbook* (© 1999 by General Mills, Inc.) and *Betty Crocker's Best Bread Machine Cookbook* (© 1999 by General Mills, Inc.) and as *Betty Crocker's Good and Easy Cookbook* (© 1996 by General Mills, Inc.).

General Mills, Inc.
Betty Crocker Kitchens
Director, Book and Online Publishing: Kim Walter
Manager, Book Publishers: Lois Tlusty
Recipe Development and Testing: Betty Crocker Kitchens
Food Styling: Betty Crocker Kitchens Food Stylists
Photography: General Mills Photo Studios

Cover Designer: Christina Gaugler
Interior design from *Betty Crocker More Slow Cooker Recipes*

Library of Congress Cataloging-in-Publication Data
Crocker, Betty.
    Betty Crocker come home to dinner : 350 delicious recipes for the slow cooker, bread machine, and oven.
        p.   cm.
    Includes index.
    ISBN 1–59486–017–3 hardcover
    1. Electric cookery, Slow.   2. Automatic bread machines.
I. Title.
TX827.C7297   2004
641.5'884—dc22   2004010672

Distributed in the book trade by Holtzbrinck Publishers

2   4   6   8   10   9   7   5   3   1   hardcover

For more great ideas, visit www.bettycrocker.com.

Contents

Dear Friends,

It's already dinnertime and everyone's home and hungry! Thank goodness for slow cookers, bread machines and oven-baked casseroles because you're welcomed with a delicious aroma wafting from the kitchen. Instead of last-minute scrambling through the refrigerator or piling into the car for take-out food, your simple preparations in the morning give a big payoff! Just mix together a salad, cut up some bread and spoon out plates of steamy homemade stew. Then sit down with your family and catch up with the happenings of the day over a delicious meal.

Sounds too good to be true? *Betty Crocker Come Home to Dinner* was created to help you make easy, delicious dinners, just like this—more than 350 of them. In just a few minutes in the morning or at your convenience, you can toss some ingredients into the slow cooker, a casserole dish or the bread machine; turn it on and walk away.

You'll discover new favorites along with classic dishes, from hearty main-course soups and zesty chilies to fork-tender roasts and stews chock-full of vegetables, herbs and savory spices. Your family will delight in homemade breads, rolls, coffee cakes and sweet breads. There are even special tip pages filled with great ideas to **Celebrate Summer** and make casual get-togethers a breeze with **Potluck Pointers.** And there's no need to bake every day with the easy ideas from **Keeping Bread Fresh** and **Freezing Breads.**

You'll find the book divided into three parts to make your meal preparations a breeze. Look for slow-cooker recipes in *Sensational Slow Cooker Recipes*, casseroles and oven dinners in *Relax While It Cooks* and bread machine recipes in *The Very Best Bread Machine Recipes*.

With *Betty Crocker Come Home to Dinner*, it's easy to have homemade meals on *your* schedule. Savor the possibilities!

Warmly,

Part 1
Sensational Slow Cooker Recipes

Here's a simple way to make a delicious, homemade meal, without having to spend a lot of time in the kitchen. Preparing dinner in a slow cooker is easy—and convenient—because the meal you're making requires little to no attention while it cooks. Some of the recipes in this section make many servings, as many as 10—providing plenty of leftovers—so look for *Leftovers . . . What a Great Idea* for simple suppers that come together in minutes using these leftovers.

◄ **Beef Roast with Shiitake Mushroom Sauce**

Slow Cooking Made Simple

In these days of drive-through dinners, fast food and canned convenience, the idea of slow cooking appears to be out of touch with the times. In reality, that couldn't be further from the truth. Slow cookers can save you time, money and energy. They allow you to "fix it and forget it," so you can spend precious time with family and friends, instead of in the kitchen. And if the simplicity of slow cooking doesn't convince you of its merits, the inviting aromas it sends throughout your house quickly will. Check out these slow-cooker secrets to help you make your recipes their slow-simmered best.

Secrets to Slow-Cooked Success

Like any other kitchen appliance, slow cookers come with a variety of options and features. Before you begin using your cooker, it's best to become familiar with how your model works.

As the name implies, continuous slow cookers cook food continuously by using a very low wattage. The heating coils, located in the outer metal shell of the cooker, remain on constantly to heat the crockery liner. Continuous slow cookers have two or three fixed settings: low (about 200°), high (about 300°) and in some models, auto, which shifts from high to low automatically. Some models feature removable ceramic liners. All recipes in this book were tested using continuous slow cookers. If you have an intermittent cooker (see box on this page), you'll need to follow the manufacturer's instructions.

Slow cookers come in a variety of sizes. One-quart cookers work well for dips and spreads, and 6-quart cookers are ideal for large cuts of meats and crowd-

Intermittent Cookers

Intermittent cookers have a heating element in the base and a separate cooking container that is placed on the base. The heat cycles on and off to maintain a constant temperature. Also, some intermittent cookers have a dial with numbers or temperatures rather than low, medium and high. The recipes in this cookbook have not been tested in an intermittent cooker. If you have an intermittent cooker, please follow the manufacturer's instructions for layering ingredients and selecting a temperature.

size recipes. For best results, make sure to use the slow-cooker size recommended in the recipe. Slow cookers tend to work most efficiently when between two-thirds and three-fourths full of food.

Slow-Cooker Tips and Tricks

These suggestions will help ensure that all your slow-cooker meals are successful:

- Spray the inside of your slow cooker with cooking spray to make cleanup easier.

- Food in the bottom of the slow cooker will often be moister (from being in the cooking liquid), and meat, such as ribs, roasts and chicken, will fall off the bones sooner. Rotate meats halfway through cooking to help them cook evenly.

- Root vegetables, such as potatoes and carrots, take longer to cook, so cut them into smaller pieces and place them closest to the heat source, at the bottom of the cooker.

- Remove skin from poultry and trim excess fat from meats before cooking to keep fat and calories to a minimum.

- Cook and drain ground meats before adding them to the slow cooker.

- Brown meats and poultry in a skillet before placing them into the slow cooker. Although this isn't necessary, browning can enhance the finished flavor and appearance of your dish.

- Use dried leaf herbs instead of ground because they retain their flavor better during long cook times.

- For more flavor in soups and stews, substitute broth for the water or add bouillon cubes with the water.

- Ground red pepper (cayenne) and red pepper sauce tend to become bitter during long, slow cooking. Use small amounts, and taste during the last hour of cooking to decide whether you need to add more.

Watching the Clock

Slow cookers require little to no clock watching. For the most part, you can prepare the recipe, turn on the cooker and then forget about it until you're ready to eat. Here are some timely tips:

- A low setting is often suggested in recipes because longer cooking times fit best into workday schedules. You can fast-forward the cooking time by turning the slow cooker to high for 1 hour, which counts as 2 hours on low.

- Smaller isn't always faster. Baby-cut carrots, for example, take longer to cook than some other veggies. Remember to check for doneness.

- Slow cookers offer flexibility. Most cooked food can be held up to an hour on the low setting without overcooking. Some recipes, such as dips and spreads, can be kept on low for several hours. Be sure to stir occasionally if needed.

- Don't peek! Removing the cover allows heat to escape and adds 15 to 20 minutes to the cooking time. If you absolutely can't wait to see inside, try spinning the cover until the steam clears.

The Perfect Ending

When it comes to preparing meals in your slow cooker, the phrase "save the best for last" often applies. To get the most flavor from your slow-cooker foods, try these helpful hints:

- Develop flavors in the juices by removing the lid and cooking on the high setting for the last 20 to 30 minutes. This evaporates the water so the flavors become more intense.

- Stir in fresh herbs during the last hour of cooking so they stay flavorful. Some herbs, such as oregano and basil, change flavor with an extended cooking time.

- Fish and seafood fall apart during long hours of cooking, and some seafood, such as shrimp, becomes very tough. Add these ingredients during the last hour of cooking.

- Add tender vegetables, such as fresh tomatoes, mushrooms and zucchini, during the last 30 minutes of cooking so they don't become overcooked and mushy.

- Frozen vegetables that have been thawed will keep their bright color and crisp-tender texture if you add them during the last 30 minutes of cooking.

- Dairy products, such as milk, sour cream and cheese have a tendency to curdle. Keep sauces and gravies from "breaking down" by adding these ingredients during the last 30 minutes of cooking.

- For more texture and a little extra flavor, sprinkle the top of your slow-cooker meal with chopped fresh herbs, grated cheese, crushed croutons or corn chips, chopped tomatoes or sliced green onions just before serving.

Adapting Your Own Recipes

Want to convert a favorite range-top recipe to a slow-cooker recipe? Consider the following:

- Find a recipe in this cookbook similar to the recipe you want to adapt, and use it as a guide for quantities, amount of liquid and cooking time.

- Reduce the liquid in your recipe by about half unless you are making a soup. Liquids don't boil away as much in the slow cooker as they do in other cooking methods.

- Less-expensive meats work well in the moist heat and low temperatures of the slow cooker. Trim as much visible fat as possible from the meat before cooking so there is less to remove from the finished dish.

- Fresh dairy products, such as cheese and milk, can curdle. Add these near the end of cooking, or substitute canned condensed soups, nonfat dry milk powder or canned evaporated milk.

- Allow enough time. Most soups, stews and one-dish meals require 8 to 10 hours on the low setting.

High-Altitude Tips

Cooking at high altitudes (3,500 feet and above) presents certain challenges, and slow cooking is no exception. Because no set rules apply to all recipes, trial and error is often the best way to make improvements.

- Longer cooking is necessary for most foods, particularly meats cooked in boiling liquid. The time may be up to twice as long as the recipe suggests for meats to become tender. To shorten the cooking time, try cooking meats on the high setting instead of on low.

- Cut vegetables into smaller pieces than the recipe suggests to help them cook more quickly.

- Call your local USDA (United States Department of Agriculture) Extension Service office, listed in the phone book under "county government," with questions about slow cooking at high altitudes.

Simple Sides and Desserts

Many dishes prepared in a slow cooker are meals in and of themselves. But variety, as the saying goes, is the spice of life, so it never hurts to offer a simple salad or side dish to make a slow-cooker meal more complete. Not sure where to start? Here are some ideas to help make your dinner well rounded.

Simple Salads

Peach and Plum Salad

Divide 3 sliced peaches and 3 sliced plums among 6 serving plates. Sprinkle with ½ cup chopped walnuts. Drizzle with raspberry vinaigrette.

Honey-Lime Fruit Salad

Mix ½ cup honey, ½ cup frozen (thawed) limeade concentrate and 1 tablespoon poppy seed in large bowl. Add 12 cups cut-up fresh fruit (cantaloupe, kiwifruit, pink grapefruit) to honey mixture; carefully toss. Sprinkle with toasted slivered almonds.

Black Bean and Corn Salad

Mix 1 can (15 ounces) black beans, rinsed and drained; 1 can (about 8 ounces) whole kernel corn, drained; 1 can (4 ounces) chopped green chile peppers, drained; ½ cup medium salsa; ¼ cup chopped onion; and 2 tablespoons chopped fresh cilantro in large bowl. Cover and refrigerate 15 minutes.

Satisfying Sides

Pesto Vegetables

Cook and drain a 1-pound bag of frozen vegetables (such as broccoli, cauliflower and carrots) as directed on package. Toss vegetables with ⅓ cup basil pesto. Sprinkle with 1 tablespoon grated Parmesan cheese.

Caesar Vegetable Medley

Heat 2 tablespoons olive oil in 10-inch nonstick skillet over medium-high heat. Add two 1-pound bags of frozen vegetables (such as cauliflower, carrots and snow pea pods) and 1 envelope (1.2 ounces) Caesar salad dressing mix. Cover and cook 5 to 7 minutes, stirring frequently, until vegetables are crisp-tender.

Asparagus with Mustard

Cover and cook 12 to 16 asparagus spears in boiling water until crisp-tender, about 8 minutes; drain. Shake 3 tablespoons honey, 2 tablespoons Dijon mustard, 4 teaspoons lemon juice and 2 teaspoons olive oil in tightly covered container; drizzle over asparagus.

Delectable Desserts

Honey-Chocolate Sundaes

Mix ½ cup honey and ¼ cup apricot brandy or apricot nectar. Spoon over chocolate ice cream in each of 4 dessert dishes. Sprinkle each dish with about ½ teaspoon baking cocoa.

Brown Sugar Strawberries

Place 2 pints (4 cups) unhulled strawberries in serving bowl. Place ⅔ cup each plain yogurt and brown sugar in separate bowls. Dip strawberries into yogurt, then into brown sugar.

Rice and Raisin Pudding

Heat 1 cup uncooked instant rice, 1 cup milk, ¼ cup raisins, 3 tablespoons sugar, ¼ teaspoon each salt and ground cinnamon to boiling in saucepan, stirring constantly; remove from heat. Cover, let stand 5 minutes.

Soups, Stews & Chilies

Meatball Stone Soup

6 servings

SLOW-COOKER SIZE:
3½- to 4-quart

PREP:
10 min

COOK:
Low 9 to 11 hours

FINISHING COOK TIME:
High 1 hour

Betty's Success Tip

This delicious soup borrows its name from *Stone Soup,* a children's book about a group of townspeople who share ingredients from their cupboards—including a stone!—to make a pot of soup. This slow-cooker version doesn't include the stone, but you may have all the ingredients in your freezer and pantry for those times when you don't have time to shop.

Serving Suggestion

Kids will love this soup based on the name alone! Enjoy it as an easy dinner with whole-grain rolls or bread, a large glass of cold milk and a juicy red apple.

1 Serving: Calories 425 (Calories from Fat 190); Fat 21g (Saturated 8g); Cholesterol 125mg; Sodium 1930mg; Carbohydrate 36g (Dietary Fiber 7g); Protein 30g

1 bag (16 ounces) frozen Italian-style meatballs

2 cans (14 ounces each) beef broth

2 cans (14½ ounces each) diced tomatoes with Italian herbs, undrained

1 medium potato, chopped (1 cup)

1 medium onion, chopped (½ cup)

¼ teaspoon garlic pepper

1 bag (1 pound) frozen mixed vegetables

Shredded Parmesan cheese, if desired

Mix frozen meatballs, broth, tomatoes, potato, onion and garlic pepper in 3½- to 4-quart slow cooker.

Cover and cook on low heat setting 9 to 11 hours or until vegetables are tender.

Stir in frozen mixed vegetables. Cover and cook on high heat setting 1 hour. Serve with Parmesan cheese.

Multi-Bean Soup

12 servings

SLOW-COOKER SIZE:
5- to 6-quart

PREP:
10 min

COOK:
High 8 to 10 hours

FINISHING COOK TIME:
High 15 min

Betty's Success Tip

The shredded carrots are added at the end so they don't over-cook and disappear into the soup. Also, the tomatoes are added after the beans are tender because the acid in the tomatoes can prevent the beans from becoming tender during the long, slow cooking.

Ingredient Substitution

Do you have small amounts of various leftover dried beans in your cupboard? Mix them together to make 2¼ cups of beans, and use them instead of purchasing a package of bean soup mix. Or use a 16-ounce package of dried beans for the bean soup mix, but use only 8 cups of water and ¾ teaspoon salt.

1 package (20 ounces) 15- or 16-dried bean soup mix, sorted and rinsed

½ pound smoked beef sausage ring, cut into ¼-inch slices

1 large onion, chopped (1 cup)

10 cups water

1½ teaspoons dried thyme leaves

1 teaspoon salt

½ teaspoon pepper

2 medium carrots, shredded (1⅓ cups)

1 can (14½ ounces) diced tomatoes, undrained

Mix all ingredients except carrots and tomatoes in 5- to 6-quart slow cooker.

Cover and cook on high heat setting 8 to 10 hours or until beans are tender.

Stir in carrots and tomatoes.

Cover and cook on high heat setting about 15 minutes or until hot.

1 Serving: Calories 210 (Calories from Fat 55); Fat 6g (Saturated 3g); Cholesterol 10mg; Sodium 660mg; Carbohydrate 35g (Dietary Fiber 6g); Protein 10g

Pork Tortilla Soup

6 servings

SLOW-COOKER SIZE:
3½- to 4-quart

PREP:
15 min

COOK:
Low 6 to 8 hours

Ingredient Substitution

Great Northern beans add a distinctive, delicate flavor to this Mexican-inspired soup, but you can substitute any canned beans you have on hand.

Serving Suggestion

Serve wedges of lime to squeeze a little fresh flavor into this hearty soup. Pass bowls of shredded Cheddar or Monterey Jack cheese, chopped fresh cilantro and sliced radishes to top each serving.

1 pound pork, boneless sirloin or loin, cut into 1-inch cubes

1 envelope (1¼ ounces) taco seasoning mix

3 corn tortillas (5 or 6 inches in diameter), cut into 1-inch squares

1 can (14½ ounces) diced tomatoes with jalapeños, undrained

2 cans (15½ ounces each) great Northern beans, drained

1 carton (32 ounces) chicken broth

4 corn tortillas (5 or 6 inches in diameter), cut in half, then cut into ½-inch strips

Mix all ingredients except tortilla strips in 3½- to 4-quart slow cooker.

Cover and cook on low heat setting 6 to 8 hours or until pork is tender. Stir gently before serving. Place some tortilla strips into bottom of each of 6 bowls. Ladle soup over tortilla strips.

1 Serving: Calories 365 (Calories from Fat 45); Fat 5g (Saturated 1g); Cholesterol 40mg; Sodium 1180mg; Carbohydrate 56g (Dietary Fiber 11g); Protein 35g

Soup's On!

Tired of serving the same old saltines with your soup? For a finishing burst of flavor, serve one of these tasty tidbits the next time you serve soup from your slow cooker.

- **Melt** slices of Brie cheese on crackers or on thin slices of French bread, and top with toasted sliced almonds.
- **Blend** whipped cream cheese with finely chopped green onions and parsley to spread on crackers or dollop on soup.
- **Sprinkle** shredded mozzarella cheese (or thin slices of Monterey Jack or hot pepper Jack) on flour or corn tortillas, and add a spoonful of salsa. Roll up and microwave on High for 20 to 30 seconds or until cheese is melted.
- **Dust** sesame seed over slices of buttered bread and broil briefly (or use a toaster oven's "top brown" feature) until the butter is melted and sesame seed is golden. Cut into triangles to serve.

Oriental Pork Soup

6 servings

SLOW-COOKER SIZE:
3½- to 6-quart

PREP:
15 min

COOK:
Low 7 to 9 hours; High 3 to 4 hours

FINISHING TIME:
1 hour

Betty's Success Tip

Julienne carrots are matchlike sticks of carrots that add an interesting shape to this soup. But to save a little time, you can cut the carrots into ¼-inch slices.

Ingredient Substitution

Coarsely ground fresh pork is sometimes labeled "chow mein meat." If it isn't available at your store, use regular ground pork, chicken or turkey. Drained canned sliced mushrooms and bean sprouts come in handy when you don't have fresh ones on hand.

Finishing Touch

Spoon a mound of hot cooked rice into each bowl of soup before serving, and sprinkle with some sliced green onion tops.

1 pound chow mein meat

2 medium carrots, cut into julienne strips (1 cup)

4 medium green onions, cut into 1-inch pieces (¼ cup)

1 clove garlic, finely chopped

¼ cup soy sauce

½ teaspoon finely chopped gingerroot

⅛ teaspoon pepper

1 can (48 ounces) ready-to-serve chicken broth

1 cup sliced mushrooms

1 cup bean sprouts

Cook chow mein meat in 10-inch skillet over medium heat 8 to 10 minutes, stirring occasionally, until brown; drain.

Mix meat and remaining ingredients except mushrooms and bean sprouts in 3½- to 6-quart slow cooker. Cover and cook on low heat setting 7 to 9 hours (or high heat setting 3 to 4 hours).

Stir in mushrooms and bean sprouts. Cover and cook on low heat setting about 1 hour or until mushrooms are tender.

1 Serving: Calories 220 (Calories from Fat 115); Fat 13g (Saturated 4g); Cholesterol 50mg; Sodium 1720mg; Carbohydrate 6g (Dietary Fiber 1g); Protein 21g

Oriental Pork Soup

Bayou Gumbo

6 servings

SLOW-COOKER SIZE:
3½- to 4-quart

PREP:
30 min

COOK:
Low 7 to 9 hours

FINISHING COOK TIME:
Low 20 min

Betty's Success Tip

Okra is a signature ingredient for gumbo. The vegetable, which is popular in the South, adds flavor and helps thicken the sauce. The name *gumbo* actually is a derivation of the African word for "okra."

Serving Suggestion

Bake your favorite corn bread muffins, and serve them hot from the oven with plenty of creamy honey-butter. They're ideal companions to this spicy Creole specialty. Serve with a pitcher of cool and refreshing iced tea and slices of whipped cream–topped pecan pie for dessert.

3 tablespoons all-purpose flour

3 tablespoons vegetable oil

½ pound smoked pork sausage, cut into ½-inch slices

2 cups frozen cut okra

1 large onion, chopped (1 cup)

1 large green bell pepper, chopped (1½ cups)

3 cloves garlic, finely chopped

¼ teaspoon ground red pepper (cayenne)

¼ teaspoon pepper

1 can (14½ ounces) diced tomatoes, undrained

1½ cups uncooked regular long-grain white rice

3 cups water

1 package (12 ounces) frozen cooked peeled and deveined medium shrimp, rinsed

Mix flour and oil in 1-quart heavy saucepan. Cook over medium-high heat 5 minutes, stirring constantly; reduce heat to medium. Cook about 10 minutes, stirring constantly, until mixture turns reddish brown.

Place flour-oil mixture in 3½- to 4-quart slow cooker. Stir in remaining ingredients except rice, water and shrimp.

Cover and cook on low heat setting 7 to 9 hours or until okra is tender.

About 25 minutes before serving, cook rice in the 3 cups water, as directed on package. Meanwhile, stir shrimp into gumbo. Cover and cook on low heat setting 20 minutes. Serve gumbo over rice.

1 Serving: Calories 500 (Calories from Fat 180); Fat 20g (Saturated 5g); Cholesterol 140mg; Sodium 720mg; Carbohydrate 54g (Dietary Fiber 4g); Protein 26g

Bayou Gumbo

Savory Cabbage and Pork Soup

8 servings

SLOW-COOKER SIZE:
3½- to 6-quart

PREP:
20 min

COOK:
Low 8 to 9 hours; High 4 to 5 hours

Betty's Success Tip

Trimming the extra fat from the pork before cutting into pieces will give you a soup that is rich in flavor but not in fat.

Ingredient Substitution

If you like a slightly thicker soup, use two 14½-ounce cans of ready-to-serve chicken broth instead of the water and bouillon cubes. If beef is your preference, use a pound of lean beef stew meat, cut into 1-inch pieces, and beef bouillon or broth instead of the pork and chicken broth.

Finishing Touch

Top each serving with a dollop of sour cream for a nice touch of creamy flavor.

1 pound boneless country-style pork ribs, cut into 1-inch pieces

4 medium carrots, cut into ¼-inch slices (2 cups)

2 medium stalks celery, chopped (1 cup)

1 medium potato, peeled and cut into ½ × ¼-inch pieces

1 medium onion, chopped (½ cup)

4 cups chopped cabbage (about 1 medium head)

¼ cup packed brown sugar

4 cups water

1 teaspoon crushed red pepper

½ teaspoon salt

½ teaspoon pepper

4 chicken bouillon cubes

1 can (28 ounces) crushed tomatoes, undrained

Mix all ingredients in 3½- to 6-quart slow cooker.

Cover and cook on low heat setting 8 to 9 hours (or high heat setting 4 to 5 hours) or until pork and vegetables are tender.

1 Serving: Calories 215 (Calories from Fat 65); Fat 7g (Saturated 2g); Cholesterol 35mg; Sodium 920mg; Carbohydrate 21g (Dietary Fiber 4g); Protein 14g

www.bettycrocker.com

Split Pea and Ham Soup

8 servings

SLOW COOKER SIZE:
4- to 6-quart

PREP:
20 min

COOK:
High 3 to 4 hours

Betty's Success Tip

Split peas are a variety of pea grown specifically for drying. They are found with dried beans and lentils in the supermarket.

2¼ cups dried split peas (1 pound), sorted and rinsed

7 cups water

¼ teaspoon pepper

1 large onion, chopped (1 cup)

2 medium stalks celery, finely chopped (1 cup)

1 ham bone, 2 pounds ham shanks or 2 pounds smoked pork hocks

3 medium carrots, cut into ¼-inch slices (1½ cups)

Mix all ingredients in 4- to 6-quart slow cooker. Cover and cook on high heat setting 3 to 4 hours or until peas are tender.

Remove ham bone; let stand until cool enough to handle. Remove excess fat from ham; cut ham into ½-inch pieces.

Stir ham into soup.

1 Serving: Calories 195 (Calories from Fat 45); Fat 5g (Saturated 2g); Cholesterol 15mg; Sodium 220mg; Carbohydrate 34g (Dietary Fiber 12g); Protein 16g

Transportation Tips and Tricks

To ensure your slow-cooker dish arrives in good shape:

- **Use rubber bands** or kitchen string around the handles and lid to keep the lid in place during the trip.
- **Wrap your slow cooker** in several layers of towels to keep it warm.
- **Keep the slow cooker level** when traveling to avoid spilling.
- **Plug in the slow cooker** as soon as you arrive, and set it on Low to keep the food warm until serving time.

- **Mark your name** or an identifiable sign somewhere on your slow cooker. At a potluck, many slow cookers look alike, so it's easy to grab the wrong one.
- **Minimize spills** during transporting by placing the slow cooker inside a large box. Stabilize the cooker with kitchen towels tucked between the cooker and box.

Potato and Ham Chowder

5 servings

SLOW-COOKER SIZE:
3½- to 4-quart

PREP:
10 min

COOK:
Low 7 hours

FINISHING COOK TIME:
Low 1 hour

Serving Suggestion

This heartwarming chowder can be enjoyed as a meal when paired with warm biscuits. Or serve it as a starter with grilled cheese sandwiches on rye bread.

1 package (5 ounces) Betty Crocker® scalloped potatoes

1 cup diced fully cooked ham

4 cups chicken broth

2 medium stalks celery, chopped (1 cup)

1 medium onion, chopped (½ cup)

⅛ teaspoon pepper

2 cups half-and-half

⅓ cup all-purpose flour

Mix potatoes, sauce mix from potatoes, ham, broth, celery, onion and pepper in 3½- to 4-quart slow cooker.

Cover and cook on low heat setting 7 hours.

Mix half-and-half and flour. Gradually stir half-and-half mixture into chowder until blended.

Cover and cook on low heat setting 1 hour, stirring occasionally, until thickened and vegetables are tender.

1 Serving: Calories 340 (Calories from Fat 145); Fat 16g (Saturated 9g); Cholesterol 50mg; Sodium 1840mg; Carbohydrate 35g (Dietary Fiber 2g); Protein 16g

Savory Lentil and Canadian Bacon Soup

8 servings

SLOW-COOKER SIZE:
3½- to 6-quart

PREP:
20 min

COOK:
Low 8 to 9 hours; High 3 to 5 hours

Betty's Success Tip

Lentils are ideal for cooking in a slow cooker because they don't require soaking as do most dried beans and peas. The grayish green lentils are most familiar, but look for other colors such as white, yellow and red for something a little different.

Ingredient Substitution

Canadian-style bacon is a closer kin to ham than it is to regular bacon. It's taken from the lean, tender eye of the loin so it is also lower in fat, and it is fully cooked. If you have leftover ham, go ahead and use 1½ cups of it for the package of Canadian-style bacon.

1 package (16 ounces) dried lentils (2¼ cups), sorted and rinsed

2 cans (14½ ounces each) ready-to-serve vegetable broth

1 package (6 ounces) sliced Canadian-style bacon, coarsely chopped

2 medium carrots, cut into ½-inch pieces (1 cup)

1 medium potato, peeled and cut into ½-inch pieces (1 cup)

1 medium onion, chopped (½ cup)

1 medium stalk celery, cut into ½-inch pieces (½ cup)

4 cups water

1 teaspoon dried thyme leaves

½ teaspoon salt

¼ teaspoon pepper

Mix all ingredients in 3½- to 6-quart slow cooker.

Cover and cook on low heat setting 8 to 9 hours (or high heat setting 3 to 5 hours) or until lentils are tender. Stir well before serving.

1 Serving: Calories 200 (Calories from Fat 20); Fat 2g (Saturated 1g); Cholesterol 10mg; Sodium 880mg; Carbohydrate 39g (Dietary Fiber 13g); Protein 19g

Cuban Black Bean Soup

8 servings

SLOW-COOKER SIZE:
3½- to 6-quart

PREP:
20 min

COOK:
High 6 to 8 hours

2 tablespoons vegetable oil

1 large onion, chopped (1 cup)

3 cloves garlic, finely chopped

2⅔ cups dried black beans (1 pound)

1 cup finely chopped fully cooked ham

3 cups beef broth

1¾ cups water

¼ cup dark rum or apple cider

1½ teaspoons ground cumin

1½ teaspoons dried oregano leaves

1 medium green bell pepper, chopped (1 cup)

1 large tomato, chopped (1 cup)

Chopped hard-cooked eggs, if desired

Chopped onions, if desired

Mix all ingredients except hard-cooked eggs and additional chopped onions in 3½- to 6-quart slow cooker. Cover and cook on high heat setting 6 to 8 hours or until beans are tender.

Serve soup with eggs and onions.

1 Serving: Calories 240 (Calories from Fat 55); Fat 6g (Saturated 1g); Cholesterol 10mg; Sodium 640mg; Carbohydrate 40g (Dietary Fiber 10g); Protein 17g

Senate Bean Soup

8 servings

SLOW-COOKER SIZE:
4- to 6-quart

PREP:
20 min

STAND:
1 hour

COOK :
High 8 to 9 hours

FINISHING TIME:
15 min

2 cups dried navy beans (1 pound)

8 cups water

1 ham bone, 2 pounds ham shanks or 2 pounds smoked pork hocks

1½ teaspoons salt

¼ teaspoon pepper

1 large onion, chopped (1 cup)

2 medium stalks celery, chopped (1 cup)

1 clove garlic, finely chopped

2½ cups mashed cooked potatoes

Mix all ingredients except mashed potatoes in 4- to 6-quart slow cooker. Cover and cook on high heat setting 8 to 9 hours or until beans are tender.

Remove ham bone; let stand until cool enough to handle. Remove excess fat from ham; cut ham into ½ inch pieces.

Stir ham and mashed potatoes into soup. Cover and cook on high heat setting 15 minutes.

1 Serving: Calories 285 (Calories from Fat 80); Fat 9g (Saturated 3g); Cholesterol 15mg; Sodium 930mg; Carbohydrate 45g (Dietary Fiber 9g); Protein 15g

Helpful Cleanup Tips

To make cleanup as effortless as possible:

- **Spray the slow cooker** with cooking spray (or lightly rub the interior with a paper towel sprinkled with vegetable oil) before cooking.
- **A removable ceramic liner** is easy to soak, and you won't have to worry about the power cord getting wet. It can even go into the dishwasher.
- **Completely cool** the slow cooker before adding water for cleanup to prevent cracking the ceramic interior.
- **Timing is key.** The sooner you start cleanup, the less chance food has of sticking permanently to your appliance.

Dill Turkey Chowder

6 servings

SLOW-COOKER SIZE:
4- to 5-quart

PREP:
15 min

COOK:
Low 6 to 8 hours

FINISHING COOK TIME:
High 20 min

Serving Suggestion

Serve this creamy chowder with French bread slices and a large, crisp green salad tossed with your favorite vinaigrette.

1 pound uncooked turkey breast slices, cut into 1-inch pieces

¾ teaspoon garlic pepper

½ teaspoon salt

6 to 8 new potatoes, cut into 1-inch pieces

1 medium onion, chopped (½ cup)

2 medium carrots, sliced (1 cup)

2 teaspoons dried dill weed

2½ cups chicken broth

1 can (15¼ ounces) whole kernel corn, drained

1 cup half-and-half

3 tablespoons cornstarch

Place turkey in 4- to 5-quart slow cooker; sprinkle with garlic pepper and salt. Stir in remaining ingredients except half-and-half and cornstarch.

Cover and cook on low heat setting 6 to 8 hours or until vegetables are tender.

Mix half-and-half and cornstarch; gradually stir into chowder until blended. Cover and cook on high heat setting about 20 minutes, stirring occasionally, until thickened.

1 Serving: Calories 265 (Calories from Fat 65); Fat 7g (Saturated 3g); Cholesterol 55mg; Sodium 840mg; Carbohydrate 33g (Dietary Fiber 3g); Protein 21g

Black-Eyed Pea and Sausage Soup

6 servings

SLOW-COOKER SIZE:
3½- to 4-quart

PREP:
15 min

COOK:
Low 8 to 9 hours

FINISHING COOK TIME:
Low 15 min

Ingredient Substitution

For those who enjoy other greens as well as spinach, use the greens solo or in combination with the spinach. Swiss chard, mustard greens and turnip greens are all good choices. Also, andouille sausage, a Cajun favorite, would give this soup even more of a kick.

Serving Suggestion

Black-eyed peas and sausage give this soup a Southern flair. To spike it with even more flavor, offer Dijon mustard and prepared horseradish to stir in.

2 cans (15 to 16 ounces each) black-eyed peas, rinsed and drained

1 package (16 ounces) smoked turkey kielbasa sausage, cut lengthwise in half and then sliced

4 medium carrots, chopped (2 cups)

4 cloves garlic, finely chopped

½ cup uncooked wheat berries

1 cup water

3 cans (14 ounces each) beef broth

2 cups shredded fresh spinach

1 teaspoon dried marjoram leaves

Mix all ingredients except spinach and marjoram in 3½- to 4-quart slow cooker.

Cover and cook on low heat setting 8 to 9 hours or until wheat berries are tender.

Stir in spinach and marjoram. Cover and cook on low heat setting about 15 minutes or until spinach is tender.

1 Serving: Calories 275 (Calories from Fat 70); Fat 8g (Saturated 2g); Cholesterol 40mg; Sodium 1400mg; Carbohydrate 37g (Dietary Fiber 11g); Protein 25g

Chicken and Rice Gumbo Soup

6 servings

SLOW-COOKER SIZE:
3½- to 6-quart

PREP:
30 min

COOK:
Low 7 to 8 hours

FINISHING COOK TIME:
Low 20 min

Betty's Success Tip

Forgot to put the okra in the refrigerator to thaw? No problem. To quickly thaw it, rinse under cold running water until it is separated and thawed.

Ingredient Substitution

We like the heartier flavor of the chicken thighs in this gumbo, but you can use the same amount of skinless, boneless chicken breast.

Finishing Touch

The red pepper sauce will lose its punch if it is added to the gumbo at the beginning of cooking. Pass the bottle of pepper sauce at the table instead, so everyone can add just the right amount to satisfy his or her taste buds.

¾ pound skinless, boneless chicken thighs, cut into 1-inch pieces

¼ pound fully cooked smoked sausage (two 5-inch sausages), chopped

2 medium stalks celery (with leaves), sliced (1¼ cups)

1 large carrot, chopped (¾ cup)

1 medium onion, chopped (½ cup)

1 can (14½ ounces) stewed tomatoes, undrained

5 cups water

2 tablespoons chicken bouillon granules

1 teaspoon dried thyme leaves

1 package (10 ounces) frozen cut okra, thawed and drained

3 cups hot cooked rice, for serving

Hot red pepper sauce

Mix all ingredients except okra, rice and pepper sauce in 3½- to 6-quart slow cooker.

Cover and cook on low heat setting 7 to 8 hours or until chicken is no longer pink in center.

Stir in okra. Cover and cook on low heat setting 20 minutes.

Spoon rice into individual soup bowls; top with gumbo. Serve with pepper sauce.

1 Serving: Calories 270 (Calories from Fat 80); Fat 9g (Saturated 3g); Cholesterol 35mg; Sodium 1750mg; Carbohydrate 35g (Dietary Fiber 3g); Protein 15g

Chicken and Rice Gumbo Soup

Creamy Chicken and Wild Rice Soup

8 servings

SLOW-COOKER SIZE:
3½- to 4-quart

PREP:
12 min

COOK:
Low 7 to 8 hours

FINISHING COOK TIME:
High 15 to 30 min

Betty's Success Tip

Love this soup but want to trim the fat and calories? Reduce the calories to 230 and the fat to 7 grams per serving by using a 12-ounce can of evaporated low-fat milk instead of the half-and-half.

Ingredient Substitution

If you prefer, use a pound of boneless, skinless chicken breasts instead of the thighs. And if your chicken broth doesn't have roasted garlic, just stir ¼ teaspoon garlic powder into the regular chicken broth.

1 pound boneless, skinless chicken thighs (5 thighs), cut into 1-inch pieces

½ cup uncooked wild rice

¼ cup fresh or frozen chopped onions (from 12-ounce bag)

2 cans (10¾ ounces each) condensed cream of potato soup

1 can (14 ounces) chicken broth with roasted garlic

2 cups frozen sliced carrots (from 1-pound bag)

1 cup half-and-half

Place chicken in 3½- to 4-quart slow cooker. Mix wild rice, onions, soup, broth and carrots; pour over chicken.

Cover and cook on low heat setting 7 to 8 hours or until chicken is no longer pink in center.

Stir in half-and-half. Cover and cook on high heat setting 15 to 30 minutes or until hot.

1 Serving: Calories 240 (Calories from Fat 90); Fat 10g (Saturated 4g); Cholesterol 50mg; Sodium 840mg; Carbohydrate 24g (Dietary Fiber 3g); Protein 17g

Grandma's Chicken Noodle Soup

6 servings

SLOW-COOKER SIZE:
3½- to 4-quart

PREP:
30 min

COOK:
Low 6½ to 7 hours

FINISHING COOK TIME:
Low 10 min

Ingredient Substitution

We love the old-fashioned flavor of the home-style noodles, but if they aren't available, use 1 cup uncooked fine egg noodles or instant rice.

1 Serving: Calories 215 (Calories from Fat 65); Fat 7g (Saturated 2g); Cholesterol 45mg; Sodium 1260mg; Carbohydrate 20g (Dietary Fiber 4g); Protein 22g

¾ pound boneless, skinless chicken thighs, cut into 1-inch pieces

2 medium stalks celery (with leaves), sliced (1¼ cups)

1 large carrot, chopped (¾ cup)

1 medium onion, chopped (½ cup)

1 can (14½ ounces) diced tomatoes, undrained

1 can (14½ ounces) chicken broth

1 teaspoon dried thyme leaves

1 package (10 ounces) frozen green peas

1 cup frozen home-style egg noodles (from 12-ounce package)

Spray 10-inch skillet with cooking spray; heat over medium heat. Cook chicken in skillet 5 minutes, stirring frequently, until brown.

Mix chicken and remaining ingredients except peas and noodles in 3½- to 4-quart slow cooker.

Cover and cook on low heat setting 6½ to 7 hours or until chicken is no longer pink in center. Stir in peas and noodles; cook about 10 minutes longer or until noodles are tender.

Peppery Fish Chowder with Rice

10 servings

SLOW-COOKER SIZE:
3½- to 6-quart

PREP:
15 min

COOK:
Low 7 to 9 hours; High 3 to 4 hours

FINISHING COOK TIME:
High 30 to 45 min

Betty's Success Tip

Cutting the fish into 1-inch pieces will be a snap if you use fish steaks that are 1 inch thick or use thicker cuts of fish fillets. Any firm-fleshed fish, such as halibut, haddock, swordfish, pollack, tuna or red snapper, works well in this soup. If fish is frozen, thaw it in the refrigerator or under cold running water before cutting it into pieces and adding it to the soup.

Ingredient Substitution

The red cayenne pepper in this chowder packs a little punch, but if you prefer a chowder that's a little more tame, use black pepper instead. If you like really fiery chowder, pass a bottle of red pepper sauce at the table!

2 medium stalks celery, chopped (1 cup)

1 medium bell pepper, chopped (1 cup)

1 medium onion, chopped (½ cup)

2 cloves garlic, finely chopped

2 cans (14½ ounces each) diced tomatoes, undrained

½ cup uncooked instant rice

2 cups eight-vegetable juice

1 cup dry white wine or vegetable broth

1 tablespoon Worcestershire sauce

1 teaspoon salt

¼ teaspoon ground red pepper (cayenne)

1 pound firm-fleshed fish steak, cut into 1-inch pieces

3 tablespoons chopped fresh parsley

Mix all ingredients except fish and parsley in 3½- to 6-quart slow cooker.

Cover and cook on low heat setting 7 to 9 hours (or high heat setting 3 to 4 hours) or until rice is tender.

Stir in fish and parsley.

Cover and cook on high heat setting 30 to 45 minutes or until fish flakes easily with fork.

1 Serving: Calories 90 (Calories from Fat 10); Fat 1g (Saturated 0g); Cholesterol 20mg; Sodium 540mg; Carbohydrate 13g (Dietary Fiber 2g); Protein 9g

Two-Bean Minestrone

6 servings

SLOW-COOKER SIZE:
3½- to 4-quart

PREP:
10 min

COOK:
Low 8 to 10 hours

FINISHING COOK TIME:
Low 15 min

Betty's Success Tip

Traditional pesto is a mixture of basil, garlic, olive oil and pine nuts, but any variation, such as sun-dried tomato or roasted bell pepper and spinach pesto, would also make a delicious topping for this veggie-filled soup.

1 can (15½ ounces) dark red kidney beans, drained

1 can (15 ounces) garbanzo beans, drained

1 bag (1 pound) frozen mixed vegetables

1 can (14½ ounces) diced tomatoes with basil, garlic and oregano, undrained

1 large vegetarian vegetable bouillon cube

1 can (11½ ounces) vegetable juice

1 cup water

½ cup uncooked elbow macaroni or other short-cut pasta

1 container (7 ounces) refrigerated basil pesto

Mix all ingredients except macaroni and pesto in 3½- to 4-quart slow cooker.

Cover and cook on low heat setting 8 to 10 hours or until vegetables are tender.

Stir in macaroni. Cover and cook on low heat setting about 15 minutes or until macaroni is tender. Top each serving with spoonful of pesto.

1 Serving: Calories 425 (Calories from Fat 180); Fat 20g (Saturated 4g); Cholesterol 5mg; Sodium 1040mg; Carbohydrate 56g (Dietary Fiber 15g); Protein 20g

---

Get a Head Start

Relax and enjoy the festivities by preparing the basics a few days ahead.

- **Veggies:** Cut or chop vegetables such as carrots and onions; wrap them in plastic wrap or put into plastic containers and refrigerate. Keep bags of baby-cut carrots and frozen vegetables on hand for last-minute additions to your meal.
- **Seasonings:** Mix together herbs and spices and keep in a small bowl or plastic storage bag. Keep ready-to-use jars of minced garlic and canned chopped chile peppers on hand for extra flavor without extra chopping.
- **Liquids:** Measure out broth, juices or wine; cover and refrigerate.

- **Meats:** Stock your freezer with diced cooked chicken, cooked meatballs and ground beef and sausage so you can start an easy slow-cooker dinner anytime during busy holidays.
- **Cheese:** Buy shredded cheese in lots of flavors to make easy, creamy dips to tide everyone over before dinner.
- **Sides:** Keep frozen rolls or biscuits on hand so you can pop them into the oven to heat while your slow-cooker dinner finishes cooking.

Autumn Vegetable Minestrone

7 servings

SLOW-COOKER SIZE:
3½- to 6-quart

PREP:
20 min

COOK:
Low 6 to 8 hours

FINISHING COOK TIME:
Low 15 min

Ingredient Substitution

You can use either vegetable or chicken broth to prepare this great-tasting soup. If you are vegetarian, go ahead and use the vegetable broth. But if you're simply looking for a meatless soup, we prefer the richer flavor of chicken broth.

2 cans (14½ ounces each) vegetable broth

1 can (28 ounces) crushed tomatoes, undrained

3 medium carrots, chopped (1½ cups)

3 small zucchini, cut into ½-inch slices

1 medium yellow bell pepper, cut into ½-inch pieces

8 medium green onions, sliced (½ cup)

2 cloves garlic, finely chopped

2 cups shredded cabbage

2 teaspoons dried marjoram leaves

1 teaspoon salt

¼ teaspoon pepper

1 cup uncooked instant rice

¼ cup chopped fresh basil leaves

Mix all ingredients except rice and basil in 3½- to 6-quart slow cooker.

Cover and cook on low heat setting 6 to 8 hours or until vegetables are tender.

Stir in rice. Cover and cook on low heat setting about 15 minutes or until rice is tender. Stir in basil.

1 Serving: Calories 120 (Calories from Fat 10); Fat 1g (Saturated 0g); Cholesterol 0mg; Sodium 1040mg; Carbohydrate 28g (Dietary Fiber 4g); Protein 4g

Creamy Leek and Potato Soup

8 servings

SLOW-COOKER SIZE:
3½- to 6-quart

PREP:
20 min

COOK:
Low 8 to 10 hours; High 4 to 5 hours

FINISHING COOK TIME:
Low 20 to 30 min

Betty's Success Tip

Leeks grow best in sandy soil. The easiest way to remove the sand is to cut the leek lengthwise, almost to the root end, then hold it under cool running water while fanning the leaves, so the water can wash out the sand.

Ingredient Substitution

Leeks are very tasty but take a few more minutes to clean. To save time, use a chopped large onion instead.

Serving Suggestion

This is really an all-season soup. Serve it warm on a chilly evening, and sprinkle each serving with crumbled cooked bacon to added a hearty smoke flavor. Or in the summer, chill it in the refrigerator, and you'll have a delicious, refreshing cold soup ready to enjoy on the deck.

6 medium leeks (2 pounds), thinly sliced

4 medium potatoes (1½ pounds), cut into ½-inch cubes

2 cans (14½ ounces each) ready-to-serve chicken or vegetable broth

¼ cup margarine or butter

½ teaspoon salt

¼ teaspoon pepper

1 cup half-and-half

Chopped fresh chives, if desired

Mix all ingredients except half and half and chives in 3½- to 6-quart slow cooker.

Cover and cook on low heat setting 8 to 10 hours (or high heat setting 4 to 5 hours) or until vegetables are tender.

Pour vegetable mixture by batches into blender or food processor. Cover and blend on high speed until smooth; return to cooker. Stir in half-and-half.

Cover and cook on low heat setting 20 to 30 minutes or until hot. Sprinkle with chives.

1 Serving: Calories 190 (Calories from Fat 90); Fat 10g (Saturated 3g); Cholesterol 10mg; Sodium 720mg; Carbohydrate 22g (Dietary Fiber 3g); Protein 6g

Butternut Squash Soup

6 servings

SLOW-COOKER SIZE:
3½- to 4-quart

PREP:
15 min

COOK:
Low 6 to 8 hours

FINISHING COOK TIME:
Low 30 min

Betty's Success Tip

Use a wire whisk to stir the soup after you add the cream cheese so the soup has a smooth consistency.

Serving Suggestion

Stir in a 1-pound bag of frozen mixed vegetables (thawed and drained) with the cream cheese for a vegetable soup that's totally different but sure to be delicious!

2 tablespoons margarine or butter

1 medium onion, chopped (½ cup)

1 butternut squash (2 pounds), peeled, seeded and cubed

2 cups water

½ teaspoon dried marjoram leaves

¼ teaspoon ground black pepper

⅛ teaspoon ground red pepper (cayenne)

4 chicken bouillon cubes

1 package (8 ounces) cream cheese, cubed

Melt margarine in 10-inch skillet over medium heat. Cook onion in margarine, stirring occasionally, until crisp-tender.

Mix onion and remaining ingredients except cream cheese in 3½- to 4-quart slow cooker. Cover and cook on low heat setting 6 to 8 hours or until squash is tender.

Place one-third to one-half of the mixture at a time in blender or food processor. Cover and blend on high speed until smooth. Return mixture to slow cooker; stir in cream cheese. Cover and cook on low heat setting about 30 minutes or until cheese is melted, stirring with wire whisk until smooth.

1 Serving: Calories 235 (Calories from Fat 155); Fat 17g (Saturated 9g); Cholesterol 40mg; Sodium 940mg; Carbohydrate 17g (Dietary Fiber 2g); Protein 5g

Creamy Split Pea Soup

8 servings

SLOW-COOKER SIZE:
3½- to 4-quart

PREP:
20 min

COOK:
Low 10 to 11 hours

FINISHING COOK TIME:
Low 30 min

Betty's Success Tip

This meatless pea soup is a twist on the traditional soup made with a ham bone. If you prefer your soup with a bit of smoky flavor, just add 1 cup diced fully cooked smoked ham with the peas and reduce the salt to 1 teaspoon.

Ingredient Substitution

If you have it on hand, you can use a 48-ounce can of chicken broth and 2 cups water instead of the 6 cups water. You can also substitute 2 cups peeled and cubed butternut squash for the sweet potato.

2 cups dried green split peas, sorted and rinsed

6 cups water

½ cup dry sherry or apple juice

1 large dark-orange sweet potato, peeled and cubed (2 cups)

1 large onion, chopped (1 cup)

4 cloves garlic, finely chopped

2 teaspoons salt

3 cups firmly packed chopped fresh spinach leaves

1 cup whipping (heavy) cream

2 tablespoons chopped fresh dill weed

Freshly ground pepper to taste

Mix split peas, water, sherry, sweet potato, onion, garlic and salt in 3½- to 4-quart slow cooker.

Cover and cook on low heat setting 10 to 11 hours or until peas and vegetables are tender.

Stir in spinach, whipping cream and dill weed. Cover and cook on low heat setting about 30 minutes or until spinach is wilted. Season with pepper.

1 Serving: Calories 235 (Calories from Fat 90); Fat 10g (Saturated 6g); Cholesterol 35mg; Sodium 910mg; Carbohydrate 35g (Dietary Fiber 11g); Protein 12g

Barley-Vegetable Soup
10 servings

SLOW-COOKER SIZE:
5- to 6-quart

PREP:
25 min

COOK:
Low 6 to 8 hours

FINISHING COOK TIME:
Low 10 min

Betty's Success Tip

Stirring in the tomatoes at the end of the cooking time helps them maintain their texture and adds a fresher tomato flavor.

Finishing Touch

Instead of serving bread or rolls, top this warming vegetable soup with a handful of herb-flavored croutons and a little shredded Parmesan cheese. Finish the meal with a selection of fresh fruit.

1 cup uncooked barley

1 dried bay leaf

½ teaspoon fennel seed

1½ cups baby-cut carrots, cut crosswise in half

2 medium stalks celery, sliced (1 cup)

1 medium onion, chopped (½ cup)

1 small green bell pepper, chopped (½ cup)

2 cloves garlic, finely chopped

1 large dark-orange sweet potato, peeled and cubed (2 cups)

1½ cups frozen whole kernel corn (from 1-pound bag)

1½ cups frozen cut green beans (from 1-pound bag)

1¼ teaspoons salt

¼ teaspoon pepper

2 cans (14 ounces each) vegetable broth

6 cups water

1 can (14½ ounces) diced tomatoes with herbs, undrained

Layer all ingredients except broth, water and tomatoes in order listed in 5- to 6-quart slow cooker. Pour broth and water over ingredients; do not stir.

Cover and cook on low heat setting 6 to 8 hours or until barley is tender.

About 10 minutes before serving, stir tomatoes into soup. Cover and cook on low heat setting about 10 minutes or until thoroughly heated. Remove bay leaf.

1 Serving: Calories 135 (Calories from Fat 10); Fat 1g (Saturated 0g); Cholesterol 0mg; Sodium 730mg; Carbohydrate 32g (Dietary Fiber 6g); Protein 4g

French Onion Soup

8 servings

SLOW-COOKER SIZE:
3½- to 6-quart

PREP:
50 min

STARTING COOK TIME:
High 30 to 50 min

COOK:
Low 7 to 9 hours; High 3 to 4 hours

Betty's Success Tip

Here's some "broth math" to help you if don't have any ready-to-serve beef broth on hand. You can use three 10½-ounce cans of condensed beef broth with 2½ soup cans of water, or 7 cups of your homemade beef broth. Or add 7 cups of water with 7 beef bouillon cubes or 2 heaping tablespoons of beef bouillon granules.

Ingredient Substitution

Vegetarians in your family? Use 4 cans of ready-to-serve vegetable broth instead of the beef broth. The color will not be a rich, deep brown, though, so Golden French Onion Soup may be a more appropriate name!

3 large onions, sliced (3 cups)

3 tablespoons margarine or butter, melted

3 tablespoons all-purpose flour

1 tablespoon Worcestershire sauce

1 teaspoon sugar

¼ teaspoon pepper

4 cans (14½ ounces each) ready-to-serve beef broth

Cheesy Broiled French Bread (below)

Mix onions and margarine in 3½- to 6-quart slow cooker.

Cover and cook on high heat setting 30 to 35 minutes or until onions begin to slightly brown around edges.

Mix flour, Worcestershire sauce, sugar and pepper. Stir flour mixture and broth into onions. Cover and cook on low heat setting 7 to 9 hours (or high heat setting 3 to 4 hours) or until onions are very tender.

Prepare Cheesy Broiled French Bread. Place 1 slice bread on top of each bowl of soup. Serve immediately.

Cheesy Broiled French Bread

8 slices French bread, 1 inch thick

¾ cup shredded mozzarella cheese (3 ounces)

2 tablespoons grated or shredded Parmesan cheese

Set oven control to broil. Place bread slices on rack in broiler pan. Sprinkle with cheeses. Broil with tops 5 to 6 inches from heat about 3 minutes or until cheese is melted.

1 Serving: Calories 185 (Calories from Fat 70); Fat 8g (Saturated 3g); Cholesterol 5mg; Sodium 1240mg; Carbohydrate 21g (Dietary Fiber 2g); Protein 9g

Borscht

6 servings

SLOW-COOKER SIZE:
3½- to 6-quart

PREP:
25 min

COOK:
Low 6 to 8 hours; High 3 to 4 hours

Betty's Success Tip

Shredding cabbage is easy when you use a long, sharp knife. Cut the cabbage into fourths, and remove the core. Thinly slice the fourths by cutting across the leaves to make long, thin strips.

Ingredient Substitution

Instead of shredding cabbage, you can use cabbage slaw mix found in the produce section of the supermarket. If other vegetables, such as shredded carrots, are in the mix, they will just add to the flavor of the soup.

Serving Suggestion

This streamlined version of the colorful eastern European favorite can be served hot or chilled. Serve it hot tonight for dinner. Any leftover soup will be ready in the refrigerator for a quick, no-fuss lunch.

2 cans (16 ounces each) diced beets, undrained

2 cans (10½ ounces each) condensed beef broth

1 small onion, finely chopped (¼ cup)

2 cups shredded cabbage

1 tablespoon sugar

1 tablespoon lemon juice

¾ cup sour cream, if desired

Chopped fresh dill weed, if desired

Mix all ingredients except sour cream and dill weed in 3½- to 6-quart slow cooker.

Cover and cook on low heat setting 6 to 8 hours (or high heat setting 3 to 4 hours) or until cabbage is tender.

Top each serving with sour cream and dill weed.

1 Serving: Calories 70 (Calories from Fat 10); Fat 1g (Saturated 0g); Cholesterol 0mg; Sodium 720mg; Carbohydrate 15g (Dietary Fiber 3g); Protein 3g

Low-Fat Beef Stew

8 servings

SLOW-COOKER SIZE:
3½- to 6-quart

PREP:
15 min

COOK:
Low 8 to 9 hours

1 medium onion, chopped (½ cup)

1 package (8 ounces) baby-cut carrots (about 30)

1 can (14½ ounces) diced tomatoes, undrained

1 can (10½ ounces) condensed beef broth

½ cup all-purpose flour

1 tablespoon Worcestershire sauce

1 teaspoon salt

1 teaspoon sugar

1 teaspoon dried marjoram leaves

¼ teaspoon pepper

12 new potatoes (1½ pounds), cut into fourths

2 cups sliced mushrooms (about 5 ounces) or 1 package (3.4 ounces) fresh shiitake mushrooms, sliced

1 pound beef stew meat, cut into ½-inch pieces

Mix all ingredients except beef in 3½- to 6-quart slow cooker. Add beef (do not stir). Cover and cook on low heat setting 8 to 9 hours or until vegetables are tender.

Stir well.

1 Serving: Calories 220 (Calories from Fat 55); Fat 6g (Saturated 2g); Cholesterol 30mg; Sodium 770mg; Carbohydrate 31g (Dietary Fiber 4g); Protein 14g

Provençal Beef with Zinfandel

12 servings

SLOW-COOKER SIZE:
5- to 6-quart

COOK:
Low 7 to 8 hours

FINISHING COOK TIME:
20 to 30 min

Ingredient Substitution

Choose a hearty red Zinfandel or your favorite red wine for cooking this stew. If you prefer, you can use beef broth instead of the wine. To save time, you may want to use beef stew meat instead of cutting the beef roast into pieces.

Serving Suggestion

This flavorful, hearty stew tastes wonderful with egg noodles, but you might want to try something different. For a change, serve with hot cooked barley, wild rice, brown rice or couscous.

6 slices bacon, cut into ½-inch pieces

3-pound beef boneless chuck roast, trimmed of fat and cut into 1-inch pieces

1 large onion, cut into ½-inch wedges

3 cups baby-cut carrots

1 cup red Zinfandel wine

¾ cup beef broth

3 tablespoons all-purpose flour

1 teaspoon dried basil leaves

½ teaspoon dried thyme leaves

½ teaspoon salt

¼ teaspoon pepper

1 can (14½ ounces) diced tomatoes, undrained

1 package (8 ounces) sliced mushrooms

½ cup julienne-cut sun-dried tomatoes (not oil-packed)

Hot cooked egg noodles, if desired

Chopped fresh parsley or basil leaves, if desired

Cook bacon in 12-inch nonstick skillet over medium-high heat, stirring occasionally, until crisp. Place bacon in 5- to 6-quart slow cooker. Discard all but 1 tablespoon drippings in skillet. Cook beef in drippings in skillet 2 to 3 minutes, stirring occasionally, until brown. Stir onion into beef. Cook 1 minute, stirring occasionally. Spoon into cooker.

Stir remaining ingredients except mushrooms, sun-dried tomatoes, noodles and parsley into mixture in cooker.

Cover and cook on low heat setting 7 to 8 hours or until beef is tender.

Stir in mushrooms and sun-dried tomatoes. Cover and cook on low heat setting 20 to 30 minutes or until tender. Serve beef mixture over noodles; sprinkle with parsley.

1 Serving: Calories 280 (Calories from Fat 135); Fat 15g (Saturated 6g); Cholesterol 70mg; Sodium 380mg; Carbohydrate 10g (Dietary Fiber 2g); Protein 26g

Provençal Beef with Zinfandel

Vegetable Beef Stew

4 servings

SLOW-COOKER SIZE:
3½- to 4-quart

PREP:
10 min

COOK:
Low 8 to 10 hours

Betty's Success Tip

It saves time to use stew beef, but take a few minutes to trim any extra fat off the beef before adding it to the bag with the stew seasoning. This will help reduce the amount of fat in the finished dish.

Finishing Touch

Ladle the stew into bowls, and sprinkle each serving with crumbled crisply cooked bacon and chopped fresh parsley. Serve with chunks of warm crusty bread to soak up all the flavorful gravy.

1½ cups baby-cut carrots

2 medium potatoes, peeled and cut into 1-inch pieces

1 medium stalk celery, cut into 1-inch pieces

1 envelope (1½ ounces) beef stew seasoning

1 pound beef stew meat

1 cup water

1 cup frozen whole kernel corn (from 1-pound bag)

1 cup frozen cut green beans (from 1-pound bag)

Layer carrots, potatoes and celery in 3½- to 4-quart slow cooker. Place stew seasoning in resealable plastic food-storage bag. Add beef to bag; toss to coat. Add beef to cooker; sprinkle with any remaining seasoning. Add water. Layer frozen corn and green beans on top.

Cover and cook on low heat setting 8 to 10 hours, until beef is tender. Stir stew before serving.

1 Serving: Calories 330 (Calories from Fat 115); Fat 13g (Saturated 5g); Cholesterol 70mg; Sodium 680mg; Carbohydrate 28g (Dietary Fiber 5g); Protein 26g

Top Beef Dishes and Stews with . . .

- Crushed herb-flavored seasoned croutons
- Canned French-fried onions
- Chopped tomatoes and avocados
- Pine nuts or coarsely chopped walnuts
- Crumbled crispy, cooked bacon or bacon bits
- Chunky salsa

Mexican Beef Stew

6 servings

SLOW-COOKER SIZE:
3½- to 4-quart

PREP:
5 min

COOK:
Low 9 to 11 hours

FINISHING COOK TIME:
High 15 to 30 min

Ingredient Substitution

Frozen small whole onions, also called pearl onions, are loaded with flavor and are so convenient to use. If you don't have them on hand, you can substitute ½ cup chopped onion.

Finishing Touch

Mexican-inspired dishes are fun to serve because everyone can personalize their serving. Pass shredded Mexican cheese blend, chopped avocado, sliced olives, sour cream and chopped fresh cilantro leaves for an extra-special touch.

2 pounds beef stew meat

1 can (28 ounces) whole tomatoes, undrained

1 cup frozen small whole onions (from 1-pound bag)

1 teaspoon chili powder

1 envelope (1¼ ounces) taco seasoning mix

1 can (15 ounces) black beans, rinsed and drained

1 can (11 ounces) whole kernel corn with red and green peppers, drained

Mix beef, tomatoes, frozen onions and chili powder in 3½- to 4-quart slow cooker.

Cover and cook on low heat setting 9 to 11 hours or until beef is tender.

Stir in taco seasoning mix, using wire whisk. Stir in beans and corn. Cover and cook on high heat setting 15 to 30 minutes or until thickened.

1 Serving: Calories 440 (Calories from Fat 160); Fat 18g (Saturated 7g); Cholesterol 95mg; Sodium 850mg; Carbohydrate 38g (Dietary Fiber 8g); Protein 40g

Colombian Beef and Sweet Potato Stew

6 servings

SLOW-COOKER SIZE:
4- to 5-quart

PREP:
15 min

COOK:
Low 8 hours

FINISHING COOK TIME:
Low 15 min

Betty's Success Tip

Your family will love the sweet and savory flavor of this Colombian-inspired stew. To save time, purchase already cut-up beef stew meat instead of the beef boneless chuck.

Serving Suggestion

A great way to enjoy this chunky stew is over fluffy cooked couscous.

1 pound beef boneless chuck

½ teaspoon salt

¼ teaspoon pepper

1½ teaspoons olive or vegetable oil

3 cups 1-inch cubes peeled sweet potatoes

2 teaspoons finely chopped garlic

2 whole cloves

1 dried bay leaf

1 stick cinnamon

1 large onion, cut into eighths

1 can (28 ounces) Italian-style pear-shaped tomatoes, undrained

8 dried apricots, cut in half

Chopped fresh parsley

Remove excess fat from beef. Cut beef into 1-inch pieces. Sprinkle beef with salt and pepper. Heat oil in 10-inch skillet over medium-high heat. Cook beef in oil about 5 minutes, stirring occasionally, until brown.

Mix beef and remaining ingredients except apricots and parsley in 4- to 5-quart slow cooker. Cover and cook on low heat setting about 8 hours or until beef is tender. Stir in apricots.

Cover and cook on low heat setting about 15 minutes or until apricots are softened. Discard cloves, bay leaf and cinnamon stick. Sprinkle stew with parsley.

1 Serving: Calories 280 (Calories from Fat 90); Fat 10g (Saturated 3g); Cholesterol 45mg; Sodium 440mg; Carbohydrate 35g (Dietary Fiber 6g); Protein 19g

Colombian Beef and Sweet Potato Stew

Burgundy Stew with Herb Dumplings

8 servings

SLOW-COOKER SIZE:
3½- to 6-quart

PREP:
25 min

COOK:
Low 8 to 10 hours; High 4 to 5 hours

FINISHING COOK TIME:
High 25 to 35 min

Betty's Success Tip

To make fluffy dumplings, drop the dumpling dough onto the stew pieces rather than directly into the liquid. The dumplings will steam rather than settle into the liquid and become soggy. Also, be sure the stew is piping hot, so the dumplings will start to cook from the steam right away.

Ingredient Substitution

Save time cleaning and slicing carrots, and use 2 cups of baby-cut carrots instead.

Serving Suggestion

Want to save some time by not making the dumplings? Instead, just serve the stew in bowls with big chunks of crusty Italian bread for dipping into the stew and soaking up all the delicious wine-flavored broth.

2 pounds beef boneless bottom or top round, cut into 1-inch pieces

4 medium carrots, cut into ¼-inch slices (2 cups)

2 medium stalks celery, sliced (1 cup)

2 medium onions, sliced

1 can (14½ ounces) diced tomatoes, undrained

1 can (8 ounces) sliced mushrooms, drained

¾ cup dry red wine or beef broth

1½ teaspoons salt

1 teaspoon dried thyme leaves

1 teaspoon ground mustard (dry)

¼ teaspoon pepper

¼ cup water

3 tablespoons all-purpose flour

Herb Dumplings (below)

Mix all ingredients except water, flour and Herb Dumplings in 3½- to 6-quart slow cooker.

Cover and cook on low heat setting 8 to 10 hours (or high heat setting 4 to 5 hours) or until vegetables and beef are tender. Mix water and flour; gradually stir into beef mixture.

Prepare Herb Dumplings. Drop dough by spoonfuls onto hot beef mixture. Cover and cook on high heat setting 25 to 35 minutes or until toothpick inserted in center of dumplings comes out clean.

Herb Dumplings

Mix 1½ cups Bisquick® Original baking mix, ½ teaspoon dried thyme leaves and ¼ teaspoon dried sage leaves, crumbled. Stir in ½ cup milk just until baking mix is moistened.

1 Serving: Calories 255 (Calories from Fat 65); Fat 7g (Saturated 2g); Cholesterol 55mg; Sodium 1030mg; Carbohydrate 26g (Dietary Fiber 3g); Protein 25g

Beef Stew with Shiitake Mushrooms

8 servings

SLOW-COOKER SIZE:
3½- to 4-quart

PREP:
20 min

COOK:
Low 8 to 9 hours

Betty's Success Tip

To make sure everything is done at the same time, cut the meat and vegetables into the sizes specified in the recipe.

Ingredient Substitution

Shiitake mushrooms add a wonderful, rich flavor to this easy beef stew, but if they aren't available, you can use 2 cups sliced regular white mushrooms.

12 new potatoes (1½ pounds), cut into fourths

1 medium onion, chopped (½ cup)

1 bag (8 ounces) baby-cut carrots

1 package (3.4 ounces) fresh shiitake mushrooms, sliced

1 can (14½ ounces) diced tomatoes, undrained

1 can (10½ ounces) condensed beef broth

⅓ cup all-purpose flour

1 tablespoon Worcestershire sauce

1 teaspoon salt

1 teaspoon sugar

1 teaspoon dried marjoram leaves

¼ teaspoon pepper

1 pound beef stew meat, cut into ½-inch pieces

Mix all ingredients except beef in 3½- to 4-quart slow cooker. Add beef.

Cover and cook on low heat setting 8 to 9 hours or until vegetables and beef are tender. Stir well before serving.

1 Serving: Calories 230 (Calories from Fat 65); Fat 7g (Saturated 3g); Cholesterol 35mg; Sodium 640mg; Carbohydrate 29g (Dietary Fiber 3g); Protein 16g

Scottish Lamb Stew

6 servings

SLOW-COOKER SIZE:
3½- to 4-quart

PREP:
20 min

COOK:
Low 9 to 10 hours

FINISHING COOK TIME:
Low 15 min

Ingredient Substitution

Beef stew meat can be used instead of the lamb. For a heartier taste with a subtle nutty flavor, use 1 cup of ale or dark beer in place of 1 cup of the chicken broth.

Serving Suggestion

Quick-cooking barley cooks up fast and can be made when the peas are stirred into the stew. Common in Scottish cooking, barley complements this lamb stew nicely.

⅓ cup all-purpose flour

½ teaspoon ground mustard

½ teaspoon seasoned salt

2 pounds lamb boneless shoulder or stew meat, cut into 1½-inch pieces

1 tablespoon vegetable oil

3 medium potatoes, cut into 1-inch pieces

2 medium carrots, cut into ½-inch pieces

1 cup frozen small whole onions (from 1-pound bag)

1 teaspoon seasoned salt

2¼ cups chicken broth

1½ cups frozen green peas (from 1-pound bag)

Hot cooked barley or rice, if desired

Apple mint jelly, if desired

Place flour, mustard and the ½ teaspoon seasoned salt in resealable plastic food-storage bag. Add lamb to bag; toss to coat. Heat oil in 12-inch skillet over medium-high heat. Cook lamb in oil, stirring occasionally, until brown.

Place potatoes, carrots and onions in 3½- to 4-quart slow cooker. Sprinkle with the 1 teaspoon seasoned salt. Place lamb on vegetables. Pour broth over lamb.

Cover and cook on low heat setting 9 to 10 hours or until lamb is tender.

Stir in peas. Cover and cook on low heat setting 15 minutes. Serve stew with barley and jelly.

1 Serving: Calories 385 (Calories from Fat 125); Fat 14g (Saturated 4g); Cholesterol 110mg; Sodium 850mg; Carbohydrate 26g (Dietary Fiber 4g); Protein 39g

Scottish Lamb Stew

Irish Stew

8 servings

SLOW-COOKER SIZE:
3½- to 6-quart

PREP:
15 min

COOK:
Low 8 to 10 hours; High 3 to 5 hours

Ingredient Substitution

This stew also can be made with 2 pounds of lean beef stew meat instead of the lamb. It is so easy, you will want to make it an everyday favorite.

Serving Suggestion

Plan to serve this stew on a Saturday or Sunday evening. Take the time to bake a loaf of Irish soda bread, using your favorite recipe. Complete the meal with tall glasses of full-bodied stout beer. This meal is so good, it will put you in the mood to dance a jig!

Finishing Touch

Like green peas in your Irish stew? Thaw a cup of frozen green peas, or rinse them under cold running water until separated and thawed. Stir them into the stew after you have skimmed off the fat, and let the heat of the stew warm the peas.

2 pounds lean lamb stew meat

6 medium potatoes (2 pounds), cut into ½-inch slices

3 medium onions, sliced

1 teaspoon salt

¼ teaspoon pepper

1 teaspoon dried thyme leaves

1 can (14½ ounces) ready-to-serve beef broth

Chopped fresh parsley, if desired

Layer half each of the lamb, potatoes and onions in 3½- to 6-quart slow cooker. Sprinkle with half each of the salt, pepper and thyme. Repeat layers and sprinkle with remaining seasonings. Pour broth over top.

Cover and cook on low heat setting 8 to 10 hours (or high heat setting 3 to 5 hours) or until lamb and vegetables are tender.

Skim fat from stew. Sprinkle parsley over stew.

1 Serving: Calories 250 (Calories from Fat 65); Fat 7g (Saturated 2g); Cholesterol 60mg; Sodium 590mg; Carbohydrate 27g (Dietary Fiber 3g); Protein 23g

Green Chile and Pork Stew

6 servings

SLOW-COOKER SIZE:
3½- to 4-quart

PREP:
20 min

COOK:
Low 6 to 7 hours

Betty's Success Tip

An easy way to skim the fat from stews and soups is to place a slice of bread on top of the mixture for a few minutes to absorb the fat. Or use a spoon to carefully remove any excess fat.

1½ pound pork boneless loin, cut into cubes

2 cans (4 ounces each) whole green chile peppers, drained and cut into strips

1 jar (20 ounces) thick-and-chunky salsa

1 can (15¼ ounces) whole kernel corn, drained

1 can (15 ounces) garbanzo beans, rinsed and drained

1 medium onion, chopped (½ cup)

1 cup chicken broth

3 teaspoons chili powder

3 teaspoons dried cilantro leaves, if desired

2 teaspoons sugar

Mix all ingredients in 3½- to 4-quart slow cooker.

Cover and cook on low heat setting at least 6 to 7 hours or until pork is tender.

1 Serving: Calories 390 (Calories from Fat 110); Fat 12g (Saturated 4g); Cholesterol 70mg; Sodium 1040mg; Carbohydrate 44g (Dietary Fiber 10g); Protein 36g

Storing and Reheating Stews and Soups

In most cases, the flavors in stews and soups mellow and meld with time. So make them ahead, cover and refrigerate for up to 3 days. (But store those made with fish or shellfish no longer than 1 day.)

Stews thickened with flour or cornstarch may separate after freezing. If you plan to freeze one of these stews, save the thickening step until you reheat it.

Soups freeze well, so it's easy to double the recipe and freeze half of it so you'll always have a meal on hand when you need it. Just pour the soup into freezer containers, leaving ¼- to ½-inch headspace (it expands as it freezes). Freeze broth in freezer containers or in ice-cube trays. Once the broth is frozen, transfer the "broth cubes" to a heavy plastic freezer bag. Soups and broths can be kept frozen for 2 to 3 months.

Freezing may affect the flavor and texture of some soups:

- The flavor of green bell pepper intensifies, and onion gradually loses its flavor. So you may need to adjust the seasoning to taste during reheating.

- Freezing makes potatoes soft and grainy. So wait to add the cooked potatoes until it's time to reheat.

- Thick soups tend to become thicker during storage. Add a little broth, milk or half-and-half while reheating, until the soup reaches the desired consistency.

Thaw soups in the refrigerator; once they've thawed, use them right away. Heat broth-based soups over medium heat, stirring occasionally, until hot. You can also reheat these soups in the microwave oven. Reheat thick purees or soups containing milk, cream, eggs or cheese over low heat, stirring frequently. Don't let them boil, or the ingredients may separate.

Curried Pork Stew

6 servings

SLOW-COOKER SIZE:
3½- to 4-quart

PREP:
20 min

COOK:
Low 8 to 9 hours

FINISHING COOK TIME:
Low 1 hour

Betty's Success Tip

Curry powder is a blend that can be made with up to 20 different spices. Therefore, it can vary in taste from blend to blend. To get the best flavor, use your favorite curry powder.

Serving Suggestion

Serve this stew over basmati rice along with yogurt, mango chutney, cilantro and pita folds or Indian naan bread.

3 tablespoons all-purpose flour

2 tablespoons curry powder

½ teaspoon salt

1 pound pork boneless center cut loin, cut into 1-inch pieces

1 tablespoon olive or vegetable oil

1 medium onion, chopped (½ cup)

1 pound small red potatoes, cut into fourths (3 cups)

1 can (14½ ounces) whole tomatoes, undrained

½ cup apple juice

2½ cups cauliflowerets

Mix flour, 1 tablespoon of the curry powder and the salt in resealable plastic food-storage bag. Add pork to bag; toss to coat. Heat oil in 10-inch skillet over medium-high heat. Cook pork in oil, stirring occasionally, until brown.

Place onion and potatoes in 3½- to 4-quart slow cooker. Top with pork and tomatoes. Mix apple juice and remaining 1 tablespoon curry powder; pour over pork.

Cover and cook on low heat setting 8 to 9 hours or until pork and potatoes are tender.

Stir in cauliflowerets. Cover and cook on low heat setting about 1 hour or until cauliflower is tender.

1 Serving: Calories 360 (Calories from Fat 110); Fat 12g (Saturated 4g); Cholesterol 70mg; Sodium 420mg; Carbohydrate 38g (Dietary Fiber 5g); Protein 30g

Curried Pork Stew

Hearty Pork Stew

6 servings

SLOW-COOKER SIZE:
3½- to 6-quart

PREP:
25 min

COOK:
Low 6 to 7 hours; High 3 to 4 hours

FINISHING COOK TIME:
High 30 to 45 min

Serving Suggestion

Serve stew over biscuits to make 8 servings out of 6! Heat oven to 450°. Mix 2¼ cups Bisquick mix with ⅔ cup milk until soft dough forms. Drop 8 spoonfuls of dough onto ungreased cookie sheet. Bake about 10 minutes or until golden brown. Split a biscuit in half, and place both halves in bowl. Spoon stew over the top.

Ingredient Substitution

Parsnips, that root vegetable that looks like a creamy white carrot, have a slightly sweet flavor that goes nicely with pork. However, instead of the parsnips, two more sliced carrots can be used and the stew will be just as colorful and tasty.

1½ pounds pork boneless loin, cut into 1-inch cubes

3 medium carrots, cut into ¼-inch slices (1½ cups)

1 medium onion, chopped (½ cup)

1 box (32 ounces) ready-to-serve chicken broth

2 cups ½-inch diced peeled parsnips

1½ cups 1-inch cubes peeled butternut squash

½ teaspoon salt

½ teaspoon pepper

3 tablespoons all-purpose flour

3 tablespoons margarine or butter, softened

Mix all ingredients except flour and margarine in 3½- to 6-quart slow cooker.

Cover and cook on low heat setting 6 to 7 hours (or high heat setting 3 to 4 hours) or until pork is no longer pink and vegetables are tender.

Mix flour and margarine. Gently stir flour mixture, 1 spoonful at a time, into pork mixture until blended.

Cover and cook on high heat setting 30 to 45 minutes, stirring occasionally, until thickened.

1 Serving: Calories 275 (Calories from Fat 115); Fat 13g (Saturated 4g); Cholesterol 50mg; Sodium 1010mg; Carbohydrate 21g (Dietary Fiber 4g); Protein 23g

Hearty Pork Stew

Jambalaya

8 servings

SLOW-COOKER SIZE:
3½- to 6-quart

PREP:
20 min

COOK:
Low 7 to 8 hours; High 3 to 4 hours

FINISHING COOK TIME:
Low 1 hour

Ingredient Substitution

Spicy, heavily smoked andouille sausage is traditional for jambalaya. Any sausage will taste good, however, and smoked turkey sausage will add flavor with less fat.

Serving Suggestion

Here's a fun way of serving rice. Spray the inside of a ½-cup measuring cup with cooking spray. For each serving, press the hot rice into the cup. Place the cup upside down in the bottom of a soup bowl and un-mold. Spoon the jambalaya around the mound of rice.

Finishing Touch

If you prefer more "heat," sprinkle additional red pepper sauce just before serving. If you want to use fresh parsley and thyme, add them with the shrimp so the flavor isn't lost during the long cooking.

1 large onion, chopped (1 cup)

1 medium green bell pepper, chopped (1 cup)

2 medium stalks celery, chopped (1 cup)

3 cloves garlic, finely chopped

1 can (28 ounces) diced tomatoes, undrained

2 cups chopped fully cooked smoked sausage

1 tablespoon parsley flakes

½ teaspoon dried thyme leaves

½ teaspoon salt

¼ teaspoon pepper

¼ teaspoon red pepper sauce

¾ pound uncooked peeled deveined medium shrimp, thawed if frozen

4 cups hot cooked rice, for serving

Mix all ingredients except shrimp and rice in 3½- to 6-quart slow cooker.

Cover and cook on low heat setting 7 to 8 hours (or high heat setting 3 to 4 hours) or until vegetables are tender.

Stir in shrimp. Cover and cook on low heat setting about 1 hour or until shrimp are pink and firm.

Serve jambalaya with rice.

1 Serving: Calories 255 (Calories from Fat 90); Fat 10g (Saturated 4g); Cholesterol 60mg; Sodium 710mg; Carbohydrate 31g (Dietary Fiber 2g); Protein 12g

Jambalaya

Ham and Lentil Stew

10 servings

SLOW-COOKER SIZE:
5- to 6-quart

PREP:
15 min

COOK:
Low 8 to 10 hours

Betty's Success Tip

When it comes to slow cooking, lentils are a nice alternative to dried beans. Unlike beans, lentils don't require soaking before cooking—saving you even more time!

Finishing Touch

For extra crunch, top this homey lentil stew with canned shoestring potatoes. Pass a bottle of red pepper sauce or ground red pepper for those who like their stew a little hotter.

1 pound fully cooked smoked ham, cut into ½-inch cubes (3 cups)

4 medium stalks celery, chopped (2 cups)

4 medium carrots, chopped (2 cups)

1 large onion, chopped (1 cup)

2 cans (10½ ounces each) condensed chicken broth

2 cups dried lentils (1 pound), sorted and rinsed

4 cups water

Mix all ingredients in 5- to 6-quart slow cooker.

Cover and cook on low heat setting 8 to 10 hours or until lentils are tender.

1 Serving: Calories 195 (Calories from Fat 45); Fat 5g (Saturated 2g); Cholesterol 25mg; Sodium 1080mg; Carbohydrate 26g (Dietary Fiber 10g); Protein 23g

Smoky Ham and Navy Bean Stew

4 servings

SLOW-COOKER SIZE:
3½- to 4-quart

PREP:
15 min

COOK:
Low 10 to 12 hours

Betty's Success Tip

Liquid smoke is a liquid seasoning used to flavor meat, poultry and seafood. It is made by burning hickory chips and condensing the smoke into liquid form. A few drops go a long way, so use sparingly. Look for it in the barbecue and steak sauce section of your supermarket.

Serving Suggestion

A basket of warm baking powder biscuits served with spiced apple butter turns this stew into a simple, hearty meal. Fruit crisp topped with whipped cream provides the perfect ending to a nearly effortless dinner.

1 pound fully cooked smoked ham, cut into ½-inch cubes (3 cups)

1 cup dried navy beans, sorted and rinsed

2 medium stalks celery, sliced (1 cup)

1 small onion, chopped (¼ cup)

2 medium carrots, sliced (1 cup)

2 cups water

¼ teaspoon dried thyme leaves

¼ teaspoon liquid smoke

¼ cup chopped fresh parsley

Mix all ingredients except parsley in 3½- to 4-quart slow cooker.

Cover and cook on low heat setting 10 to 12 hours or until beans are tender. Stir in parsley before serving.

1 Serving. Calories 360 (Calories from Fat 100); Fat 11g (Saturated 4g); Cholesterol 65mg; Sodium 1730mg; Carbohydrate 37g (Dietary Fiber 9g); Protein 37g

Chicken and Vegetable Tortellini Stew

6 servings

SLOW-COOKER SIZE:
3½- to 4-quart

PREP:
35 min

COOK:
Low 6 to 8 hours

FINISHING COOK TIME:
15 to 20 min

Ingredient Substitution

Save time cleaning and slicing carrots by using 1 cup baby-cut carrots. Keeping a bag of ready-to-eat baby-cut carrots on hand is helpful when it comes to making soups and stews.

Serving Suggestion

Serve with crusty garlic French bread and a salad of crisp Romaine lettuce, cherry tomatoes and thin slices of red onion tossed with your favorite Caesar or ranch dressing.

2 medium carrots, sliced (1 cup)

2 cloves garlic, finely chopped

1 pound boneless, skinless chicken thighs (5 thighs), cut into ¾-inch pieces

1 medium fennel bulb, chopped

1 can (19 ounces) cannellini beans, rinsed and drained

½ teaspoon salt

¼ teaspoon pepper

1 can (14 ounces) chicken broth

2 cups water

1 package (9 ounces) refrigerated cheese-filled tortellini

1 cup firmly packed fresh baby spinach leaves

2 medium green onions, sliced (2 tablespoons)

1 teaspoon dried basil leaves

2 tablespoons shredded fresh Parmesan cheese

Layer carrots, garlic, chicken, fennel and beans in 3½- to 4-quart slow cooker. Sprinkle with salt and pepper. Pour broth and water over ingredients.

Cover and cook on low heat setting 6 to 8 hours or until chicken is no longer pink in center.

About 20 minutes before serving, stir tortellini, spinach, onions and basil into chicken mixture. Cover and cook on high heat setting 15 to 20 minutes or until tortellini are tender. Sprinkle individual servings with Parmesan cheese.

1 Serving: Calories 325 (Calories from Fat 100); Fat 11g (Saturated 4g); Cholesterol 85mg; Sodium 640mg; Carbohydrate 34g (Dietary Fiber 8g); Protein 31g

Chicken and Vegetable Tortellini Stew

Chicken Stew

6 servings

SLOW-COOKER SIZE:
3½- to 4-quart

PREP:
12 min

COOK:
Low 8 to 10 hours

Betty's Success Tip

A variety of fresh mushrooms work well in this satisfying stew. Try crimini, shiitake or white or brown button mushrooms. Use one kind, or mix two or three different types of mushrooms together.

Serving Suggestion

Serve the stew in individual pasta bowls with chunks of crusty bread to soak up every last drop of sauce left over in the dish. If you like peas in your stew, heat 1 cup of frozen green peas in the microwave oven and stir into the stew before serving.

3 medium potatoes (about 1 pound), cut into 1½-inch cubes

2 cups baby-cut carrots

1 package (8 ounces) fresh whole mushrooms, cut in half

12 boneless, skinless chicken thighs (about 2½ pounds)

½ teaspoon salt

1 teaspoon instant chopped onion

¼ teaspoon garlic powder

1 tablespoon tomato paste

1 jar (15 ounces) roasted chicken gravy

½ cup dry white wine or water

Toss potatoes, carrots and mushrooms in 3½- to 4-quart slow cooker. Arrange chicken on top. Sprinkle salt, onion and garlic powder over chicken. Stir tomato paste into jar of gravy. Pour gravy mixture and wine over all.

Cover and cook on low heat setting 8 to 10 hours or until vegetables are tender.

1 Serving: Calories 365 (Calories from Fat 135); Fat 15g (Saturated 5g); Cholesterol 85mg; Sodium 740mg; Carbohydrate 25g (Dietary Fiber 3g); Protein 35g

Brunswick Stew

10 servings

SLOW-COOKER SIZE:
3½- to 6-quart

PREP:
20 min

COOK:
Low 8 to 10 hours; High 3 to 4 hours

Betty's Success Tip

Traditionally, Brunswick Stew is made with whole kernel corn, but we like the creaminess that the cream-style corn gives this Southern favorite. Be sure to cut the potatoes into ½-inch pieces, so they will be tender when the stew is done cooking.

Ingredient Substitution

Lima is the popular bean for this stew, but a drained 16-ounce can of butter beans gives the same great results.

Serving Suggestion

Brunswick Stew is a popular classic from Virginia's Brunswick County, hence its name. This hearty stew originally was made of squirrel and onion, but today chicken is the more popular meat of choice. Warm baking powder biscuits slathered with butter, another Southern favorite, will be all you need for a satisfying meal.

1½ pounds skinless, boneless chicken breasts, cut into 1-inch pieces

3 medium potatoes, cut into ½-inch pieces

1 medium onion, chopped (½ cup)

1 can (28 ounces) crushed tomatoes, undrained

1 can (15 to 16 ounces) lima beans, rinsed and drained

1 can (14¾ ounces) cream-style corn

1 tablespoon Worcestershire sauce

¾ teaspoon salt

½ teaspoon dried marjoram leaves

8 slices bacon, cooked and crumbled

¼ teaspoon red pepper sauce

Mix all ingredients except bacon and pepper sauce in 3½- to 6-quart slow cooker.

Cover and cook on low heat setting 8 to 10 hours (or high heat setting 3 to 4 hours) or until potatoes are tender.

Stir in bacon and pepper sauce.

1 Serving: Calories 250 (Calories from Fat 55); Fat 6g (Saturated 2g); Cholesterol 50mg; Sodium 630mg; Carbohydrate 31g (Dietary Fiber 6g); Protein 24g

Top Chicken Dishes and Stews with . . .

- Chutney
- Pesto
- Plain yogurt mixed with finely chopped cucumber
- Chunky salsa
- Chopped fresh chives
- Chopped fresh rosemary leaves

Fisherman's Wharf Seafood Stew

6 servings

SLOW-COOKER SIZE:
3½- to 4-quart

PREP:
35 min

COOK:
Low 8 to 9 hours

FINISHING COOK TIME:
High 15 to 20 min

Betty's Success Tip

The easiest way to remove sand from a leek is to first cut the leek lengthwise, almost to the root end. Then, hold the leek under cool running water while fanning the leaves, so the water can wash out the sand.

Finishing Touch

For those who prefer fish stew with a little more spice, pass a bottle or two of your favorite hot green or red pepper sauce at the table.

2 tablespoons olive or vegetable oil

1 cup sliced leek (white and light green portion)

2 cloves garlic, finely chopped

1 cup sliced baby-cut carrots (¼ inch thick)

3 cups sliced, quartered roma (plum) tomatoes (6 large)

½ cup chopped green bell pepper

½ teaspoon fennel seed

1 dried bay leaf

1 cup dry white wine or water

1 bottle (8 ounces) clam juice

1 pound cod (1 inch thick), cut into 1-inch pieces

½ pound uncooked peeled deveined medium shrimp

1 teaspoon sugar

1 teaspoon dried basil leaves

½ teaspoon salt

¼ teaspoon red pepper sauce

2 tablespoons chopped fresh parsley

Mix oil, leek and garlic in 3½- to 4-quart slow cooker. Add carrots, tomatoes, bell pepper, fennel seed, bay leaf, wine and clam juice; stir.

Cover and cook on low heat setting 8 to 9 hours or until vegetables are tender.

About 20 minutes before serving, gently stir in cod, shrimp, sugar, basil, salt and pepper sauce. Cover and cook on high heat setting 15 to 20 minutes or until fish flakes easily with fork. Remove bay leaf. Stir in parsley.

1 Serving: Calories 180 (Calories from Fat 55); Fat 6g (Saturated 1g); Cholesterol 95mg; Sodium 430mg; Carbohydrate 10g (Dietary Fiber 2g); Protein 22g

Fisherman's Wharf Seafood Stew

Curried Sweet Potato and Lentil Stew

6 servings

SLOW-COOKER SIZE:
3½- to 6-quart

PREP:
10 min

COOK:
Low 5 to 6 hours

FINISHING COOK TIME:
High 15 min

Betty's Success Tip

Try cooking the spices together before they are added to the other ingredients. This technique gives this curry its wonderful flavor.

3 cups 1-inch cubes peeled sweet potatoes

1½ cups baby-cut carrots

1 small onion, finely chopped (¼ cup)

¾ cup dried lentils, sorted and rinsed

2 teaspoons olive or vegetable oil

1 tablespoon curry powder

1 teaspoon ground cumin

½ teaspoon salt

¼ teaspoon pepper

1 teaspoon finely chopped gingerroot

1 clove garlic, finely chopped

1 can (14½ ounces) vegetable or chicken broth

1 package (10 ounces) frozen green beans, thawed

½ cup plain fat-free yogurt

Mix sweet potatoes, carrots, onion and lentils in 3½- to 6-quart slow cooker.

Heat oil in 8-inch skillet over medium heat. Add curry powder, cumin, salt, pepper, gingerroot and garlic. Cook 1 minute, stirring constantly. Stir in broth. Pour mixture into slow cooker; stir.

Cover and cook on low heat setting 5 to 6 hours or until vegetables and lentils are tender.

Turn heat setting to high; add green beans. Cover and cook about 15 minutes or until green beans are crisp-tender. Serve topped with yogurt.

1 Serving: Calories 200 (Calories from Fat 20); Fat 2g (Saturated 0g); Cholesterol 0mg; Sodium 540mg; Carbohydrate 45g (Dietary Fiber 10g); Protein 10g

Curried Sweet Potato and Lentil Stew

Winter Vegetable Stew

8 servings

SLOW-COOKER SIZE:
4- to 5-quart

PREP:
20 min

COOK:
Low 8 to 10 hours

FINISHING COOK TIME:
High 20 min

Ingredient Substitution

Parsnips, root vegetables that look like creamy white carrots, have a slightly sweet flavor. If you don't have any on hand, you can use carrots instead.

Serving Suggestion

Sprinkle the stew with chopped fresh chives or thyme leaves or shredded Parmesan cheese. Enjoy this meatless meal with a loaf of crusty Italian bread.

1 can (28 ounces) plum tomatoes

4 medium red potatoes, cut into ½-inch pieces

4 medium stalks celery, cut into ½-inch pieces (2 cups)

3 medium carrots, cut into ½-inch pieces (1½ cups)

2 medium parsnips, peeled and cut into ½-inch pieces

2 medium leeks, cut into ½-inch pieces

1 can (14½ ounces) chicken broth

½ teaspoon dried thyme leaves

½ teaspoon dried rosemary leaves

½ teaspoon salt

3 tablespoons cornstarch

3 tablespoons cold water

Drain tomatoes, reserving liquid. Cut up tomatoes. Mix tomatoes, reserved liquid and remaining ingredients except cornstarch and water in 4- to 5-quart slow cooker.

Cover and cook on low heat setting 8 to 10 hours or until vegetables are tender.

Mix cornstarch and water; gradually stir into slow cooker until blended. Cover and cook on high heat setting about 20 minutes, stirring occasionally, until thickened.

1 Serving: Calories 120 (Calories from Fat 0); Fat 0g (Saturated 0g); Cholesterol 0mg; Sodium 570mg; Carbohydrate 31g (Dietary Fiber 5g); Protein 4g

Family Favorite Chili

8 servings

SLOW-COOKER SIZE:
3½- to 6-quart

PREP:
20 min

COOK:
Low 6 to 8 hours; High 3 to 4 hours

FINISHING COOK TIME:
High 15 to 20 min

Betty's Success Tip

Starting with hot cooked ground beef is safer because getting cold, uncooked ground beef to a safe temperature in a slow cooker takes too long. Also, using cooked and drained ground beef helps eliminate that extra fat and liquid that would accumulate during cooking.

Ingredient Substitution

Like a hot and spicy chili? Use a pound of ground beef and a pound of hot and spicy pork or Italian bulk sausage instead of all beef. Cook and drain the two together before adding to the cooker.

2 pounds ground beef

1 large onion, chopped (1 cup)

2 cloves garlic, finely chopped

1 can (28 ounces) diced tomatoes, undrained

1 can (15 ounces) tomato sauce

2 tablespoons chili powder

1½ teaspoons ground cumin

½ teaspoon salt

½ teaspoon pepper

1 can (15 or 16 ounces) kidney or pinto beans, rinsed and drained

Cook beef in 12-inch skillet over medium heat, stirring occasionally, until brown; drain.

Mix beef and remaining ingredients except beans in 3½- to 6-quart slow cooker.

Cover and cook on low heat setting 6 to 8 hours (or high heat setting 3 to 4 hours) or until onion is tender.

Stir in beans. Cover and cook on high heat setting 15 to 20 minutes or until slightly thickened.

1 Serving: Calories 335 (Calories from Fat 155); Fat 17g (Saturated 7g); Cholesterol 65mg; Sodium 820mg; Carbohydrate 24g (Dietary Fiber 6g); Protein 28g

Hearty Steak Chili

8 servings

SLOW-COOKER SIZE:
3½- to 4-quart

PREP:
15 min

COOK:
Low 6 to 7 hours

FINISHING COOK TIME:
High 15 min

Ingredient Substitution

You can also use 1 can (28 ounces) whole tomatoes instead of the diced tomatoes. Use a spoon to break up the whole tomatoes in the slow cooker.

Finishing Touch

Add some zip to your serving bowls by brushing the edges of the bowls with shortening or margarine. Then sprinkle with chili powder.

1 pound beef boneless round steak, cut into ½-inch pieces

1 large onion, chopped (1 cup)

2 medium stalks celery, cut into ½-inch pieces (1 cup)

2 cans (14½ ounces each) diced tomatoes, undrained

1 can (15 ounces) tomato sauce

3 teaspoons chili powder

2 teaspoons ground cumin

¼ teaspoon dried oregano leaves

¼ teaspoon ground cinnamon

1 medium bell pepper, cut into 1-inch pieces (1 cup)

1 can (15 to 16 ounces) kidney beans, rinsed and drained

Shredded Cheddar cheese, if desired

Mix all ingredients except bell pepper, beans and cheese in 3½- to 4-quart slow cooker.

Cover and cook on low heat setting 6 to 7 hours or until beef and vegetables are tender.

Stir in bell pepper and beans. Uncover and cook on high setting about 15 minutes or until slightly thickened. Serve with cheese.

1 Serving: Calories 170 (Calories from Fat 25); Fat 3g (Saturated 1g); Cholesterol 30mg; Sodium 640mg; Carbohydrate 24g (Dietary Fiber 6g); Protein 18g

Mexican Beef Chili

6 servings

SLOW-COOKER SIZE:
3½- to 4-quart

PREP:
15 min

COOK:
Low 8 to 10 hours

Betty's Success Tip

Cinnamon sticks and baking cocoa may seem like odd ingredients for a chili recipe, but the two ingredients are based on the spicy Mexican mole sauce that includes Mexican or bitter chocolate. Baking cocoa makes the sauce taste richer without adding sweetness.

Finishing Touch

This chili is flavorful and delicious on its own. But a dollop of sour cream, a sprinkle of sliced green onions and shredded Cheddar cheese make it extra special.

2 pounds beef boneless chuck, cut into 1-inch cubes

2 tablespoons chili powder

½ teaspoon salt

1 teaspoon ground cumin

2 tablespoons instant chopped onion

½ teaspoon garlic powder

1 can (15½ ounces) dark red kidney beans, drained

2 cans (14½ ounces each) diced tomatoes with basil, garlic and oregano, undrained

1 tablespoon baking cocoa

2 cinnamon sticks

Mix all ingredients in 3½- to 4-quart slow cooker.

Cover and cook on low heat setting 8 to 10 hours or until beef is tender. Remove cinnamon sticks before serving.

1 Serving: Calories 395 (Calories from Fat 160); Fat 18g (Saturated 7g); Cholesterol 95mg; Sodium 670mg; Carbohydrate 26g (Dietary Fiber 7g); Protein 39g

Spoon on Chilies . . .

- Guacamole
- Sour cream mixed with lime juice
- Shredded Cheddar or Monterey Jack cheese
- Crushed corn or tortilla chips, plain or flavored
- Thick-and-chunky salsa
- Chopped fresh cilantro
- Chopped fresh vegetables such as tomatoes, green onions, avocados, onions and jicama

Chunky Pork and Beef Sausage Chili

6 servings

SLOW-COOKER SIZE:
3½- to 6-quart

COOK:
Low 8 to 10 hours; High 3 to 5 hours

Ingredient Substitution

For a "white" chili, leave out the sausage and use 2 pounds of pork. Add a can of great Northern or pinto beans instead of the black beans.

Serving Suggestion

Decided at the last minute to invite some friends over for chili? Stir in an extra can or two of your favorite beans. Each can will increase the number of servings by two.

Finishing Touch

Let everyone add his or her own special touch by passing bowls of shredded Cheddar cheese, chopped avocado, sliced jalapeño chilies, chopped onion, sliced ripe olives, chopped fresh cilantro and sour cream.

1 pound lean boneless pork, cut into ¾-inch pieces

½ pound fully cooked smoked beef sausage, cut into ½-inch slices

1 large onion, chopped (1 cup)

2 medium stalks celery, sliced (1 cup)

2 cloves garlic, finely chopped

1 can (15 ounces) black beans, rinsed and drained

1 can (15 ounces) chunky tomato sauce

1 can (10 ounces) diced tomatoes and green chilies

1 cup water

1½ teaspoons chili powder

½ teaspoon ground cumin

½ teaspoon salt

¼ teaspoon pepper

Mix all ingredients in 3½- to 6-quart slow cooker.

Cover and cook on low heat setting 8 to 10 hours (or high heat setting 3 to 5 hours) or until pork is tender.

1 Serving: Calories 380 (Calories from Fat 160); Fat 18g (Saturated 7g); Cholesterol 70mg; Sodium 1420mg; Carbohydrate 31g (Dietary Fiber 7g); Protein 30g

Turkey and Brown Rice Chili

6 servings

SLOW-COOKER SIZE:
3½- to 6-quart

PREP:
15 min

COOK:
Low 8 to 10 hours; High 4 to 5 hours

FINISHING COOK TIME:
High 15 min

Betty's Success Tip

This is a lower-fat chili because it is made with ground turkey breast. Make sure that you are buying ground turkey breast and not regular ground turkey, which includes both light and dark meat and will be higher in fat.

Ingredient Substitution

Have ground beef in the freezer? Use it instead of the turkey and you won't need the oil to cook it in. Stir in either brown or white rice to finish the chili.

Finishing Touch

Enjoy this chili topped with your favorite salsa and corn chips. Like cilantro? Stir a couple of tablespoons of chopped fresh cilantro into the chili before serving.

1 tablespoon vegetable oil

¾ pound ground turkey breast

1 large onion, chopped (1 cup)

2 cans (14½ ounces each) diced tomatoes, undrained

1 can (15 or 16 ounces) chili beans in sauce, undrained

1 can (4 ounces) chopped green chile peppers, drained

½ cup water

1 tablespoon sugar

2 teaspoons chili powder

1 teaspoon ground cumin

½ teaspoon salt

2 cups cooked brown rice

Heat oil in 12-inch skillet over medium heat. Cook turkey and onion in oil, stirring frequently, until turkey is no longer pink; drain.

Mix turkey mixture and remaining ingredients except rice in 3½- to 6-quart slow cooker.

Cover and cook on low heat setting 8 to 10 hours (or **high heat setting 4 to 5 hours**).

Stir in rice.

Cover and cook on high heat setting about 15 minutes or **until rice is hot**.

1 Serving: Calories 235 (Calories from Fat 30); Fat 4g (Saturated 1g); Cholesterol 40mg; **Sodium** 980mg; Carbohydrate 37g (Dietary Fiber 6g); Protein 20g

Turkey Chili

10 servings

SLOW-COOKER SIZE:
5- to 6-quart

PREP:
20 min

COOK:
Low 7 to 8 hours

HOLD TIME:
Low up to 4 hours

Betty's Success Tip

There's a surprise ingredient in this recipe—cornmeal. It's a delicious addition that thickens the chili with Tex-Mex pizzazz.

Ingredient Substitution

Mix and match the flavors of this chili by using black beans instead of pinto beans or ground beef instead of the ground turkey.

2½ pounds ground turkey

2 large onions, chopped (2 cups)

1 large green bell pepper, chopped (1½ cups)

1 can (28 ounces) diced tomatoes, undrained

2 cans (15½ ounces each) pinto beans, undrained

1 can (14 ounces) seasoned chicken broth with roasted garlic

2 cans (4½ ounces each) diced green chile peppers, undrained

⅓ cup cornmeal

1 tablespoon chili powder

1 tablespoon dried oregano leaves

2 teaspoons ground cumin

1 teaspoon salt

Cook turkey in 12-inch skillet over medium-high heat 5 to 8 minutes, stirring frequently, until no longer pink; drain.

Mix turkey, onions, bell pepper, tomatoes, pinto beans, broth and chile peppers in 5- to 6-quart slow cooker. Mix remaining ingredients in small bowl; stir into turkey mixture.

Cover and cook on low heat setting 7 to 8 hours or until chili is thickened and bubbling. Chili will hold on low heat setting up to 4 hours. If chili becomes too thick while holding, stir in up to ½ cup hot water to thin.

1 Serving: Calories 345 (Calories from Fat 70); Fat 8g (Saturated 2g); Cholesterol 5mg; Sodium 660mg; Carbohydrate 35g (Dietary Fiber 10g); Protein 35g

Turkey Chili

White Chili with Chicken

6 servings

SLOW-COOKER SIZE:
3½- to 4-quart

PREP:
15 min

COOK:
Low 8 to 10 hours

Betty's Success Tip

White chili—usually made with white beans, chicken and chile peppers instead of red beans, beef and tomatoes—is still packed with plenty of spicy chili flavor. You can add more kick by increasing the amount of red pepper sauce.

Ingredient Substitution

Keep a package of frozen diced cooked chicken in the freezer. It's a lifesaver when you're in a big hurry and don't have time to cut chicken into strips.

1 pound boneless, skinless chicken thighs (5 thighs), cut into thin strips

1 cup dried great Northern beans, sorted and rinsed

1 medium onion, chopped (½ cup)

1 clove garlic, finely chopped

2 teaspoons dried oregano leaves

½ teaspoon salt

1 can (10¾ ounces) condensed cream of chicken soup

5 cups water

1 teaspoon ground cumin

¼ teaspoon red pepper sauce

1 can (4½ ounces) chopped green chile peppers, undrained

Mix chicken, beans, onion, garlic, oregano, salt, soup and water in 3½- to 4-quart slow cooker.

Cover and cook on low heat setting 8 to 10 hours or until beans are tender and chicken is no longer pink in center.

Just before serving, stir in cumin, pepper sauce and chile peppers. Serve with additional red pepper sauce if desired.

1 Serving: Calories 260 (Calories from Fat 80); Fat 9g (Saturated 3g); Cholesterol 50mg; Sodium 700mg; Carbohydrate 23g (Dietary Fiber 6g); Protein 21g

Chunky Chicken Chili with Hominy

6 servings

SLOW-COOKER SIZE:
3½- to 4-quart

PREP:
5 min

COOK:
Low 7 to 9 hours

FINISHING COOK TIME:
Low 15 min

Betty's Success Tip

Go ahead and make the chili ahead of time and refrigerate or freeze. Chili is often better the next day because the flavors have a chance to blend. Thaw frozen chili in the refrigerator, and reheat in a saucepan over medium-low heat, stirring occasionally, until hot.

Ingredient Substitution

For extra spice, use hot chili seasoning instead of the mild, and add a small can of chopped green chile peppers with the tomatoes. You can also vary the taste by using black beans or chili beans instead of the hominy.

2 pounds boneless, skinless chicken thighs (10 thighs)

2 cans (14½ ounces each) diced tomatoes with green chile peppers, undrained

1 can (15 ounces) tomato sauce

1 envelope (1¼ ounces) mild chili seasoning mix

2 cans (15½ ounces each) hominy or posole, drained

Sour cream, if desired

Cilantro, if desired

Place chicken in 3½- to 4-quart slow cooker. Mix tomatoes, tomato sauce and chili seasoning; pour over chicken.

Cover and cook on low heat setting 7 to 9 hours or until chicken is no longer pink in center.

Stir to break up chicken. Stir in hominy. Cover and cook on low heat setting about 15 minutes, until heated through. Serve chili with sour cream and cilantro.

1 Serving: Calories 365 (Calories from Fat 125); Fat 14g (Saturated 4g); Cholesterol 95mg; Sodium 1640mg; Carbohydrate 31g (Dietary Fiber 7g); Protein 36g

Spicy Black Bean Barbecue Chili

6 servings

SLOW-COOKER SIZE:
3½- to 4-quart

PREP:
15 min

STAND:
1 hour

COOK:
Low 10 to 12 hours

FINISHING COOK TIME:
High 30 min

Betty's Success Tip

Get a jump start on making this spicy chili by soaking the beans in cold water overnight rather than using the quick-soak method.

Finishing Touch

Black beans and rice are a natural pair. Serve this hearty vegetarian chili over a mound of cooked rice and top with chopped bell pepper and fresh cilantro for added color and flavor.

2 cups dried black beans, sorted and rinsed

10 cups water

1 tablespoon olive or vegetable oil

1 large onion, chopped (1 cup)

6 cloves garlic, finely chopped

4 cups water

1 can (14½ ounces) diced tomatoes with green chile peppers, undrained

1 cup hickory barbecue sauce

1 chipotle chile pepper in adobo sauce, finely chopped, plus 1 teaspoon adobo sauce (from 7-ounce can)

2 cups frozen veggie crumbles

Heat beans and the 10 cups water to boiling in 4-quart Dutch oven; reduce heat. Simmer uncovered 10 minutes; remove from heat. Cover and let stand 1 hour.

Heat oil in 10-inch skillet over medium-high heat. Cook onion and garlic in oil about 8 minutes, stirring occasionally, until onion is tender and light golden brown.

Drain beans. Place beans in 3½- to 4-quart slow cooker. Add the 4 cups water and onion mixture.

Cover and cook on low heat setting 10 to 12 hours or until beans are tender.

Stir in tomatoes, barbecue sauce, chile pepper, adobo sauce and frozen veggie crumbles. Cover and cook on high heat setting 30 minutes.

1 Serving: Calories 350 (Calories from Fat 35); Fat 4g (Saturated 1g); Cholesterol 0mg; Sodium 840mg; Carbohydrate 66g (Dietary Fiber 11g); Protein 22g

Spicy Black Bean Barbecue Chili

Vegetarian Chili with Baked Tortilla Strips

6 servings

SLOW-COOKER SIZE:
3½- to 6-quart

PREP:
5 min

COOK:
Low 5 to 6 hours

FINISHING COOK TIME:
Low 15 min

Ingredient Substitution

Use any canned beans that you have on hand for the pinto or kidney beans. For variety, try great Northern, black, garbanzo or lima beans, as well as black-eyed peas.

Serving Suggestion

This bean-packed chili is great served over hot cooked brown or white rice to make a heartier meatless meal. You decide if you want the tortilla strips on top.

Finishing Touch

For a cool zing, mix a tablespoon or two of fresh lime juice into 1 cup of sour cream to spoon on top of the chili. Sprinkle with chopped fresh cilantro or sliced green onions.

Baked Tortilla Strips (below)

1 can (15 or 16 ounces) spicy chili beans in sauce, undrained

1 can (15 to 16 ounces) pinto beans, undrained

1 can (15 to 16 ounces) dark red kidney beans, drained

1 can (14½ ounces) chili-style chunky tomatoes, undrained

1 large onion, chopped (1 cup)

2 to 3 teaspoons chili powder

⅛ teaspoon ground red pepper (cayenne)

Prepare Baked Tortilla Strips.

Mix remaining ingredients in 3½- to 6-quart slow cooker.

Cover and cook on low heat setting 5 to 6 hours or until flavors have blended.

Stir well before serving. Spoon chili over tortilla strips, or sprinkle tortilla strips on top.

Baked Tortilla Strips

Heat oven to 400°. Cut 2 flour tortillas (8 inches in diameter) in half; cut each half crosswise into ½-inch strips. Place in single layer on ungreased cookie sheet. Bake 10 to 12 minutes or until strips are crisp and edges are light brown.

1 Serving: Calories 220 (Calories from Fat 20); Fat 2g (Saturated 0g); Cholesterol 0mg; Sodium 880mg; Carbohydrate 48g (Dietary Fiber 12g); Protein 14g

Vegetarian Chili with Baked Tortilla Strips

Hearty Main Dishes

Beef Carbonnade with Potatoes

8 servings

SLOW-COOKER SIZE:
3½- to 4-quart

PREP:
12 min

COOK:
Low 8 to 10 hours

Betty's Success Tip

Carbonnade is a French term that describes any meat cooked over hot coals or directly over flames. We simplified the process by converting the dish into a slow-cooker recipe.

Ingredient Substitution

If you prefer to skip the beer, use the same quantity of nonalcoholic beer, apple cider or beef broth instead. And if you can't find tomato beef oxtail soup mix at your supermarket, use a 10¾-ounce can of condensed tomato soup with 1 teaspoon beef bouillon granules instead.

1 medium onion, sliced

8 small red potatoes, cut into fourths

2½-pound beef round steak, cut into 8 serving pieces

1 tablespoon packed brown sugar

½ teaspoon ground nutmeg

½ teaspoon salt

¼ teaspoon pepper

1 package (1.8 ounces) tomato beef flavor (oxtail) soup mix

1 can (12 ounces) beer

Place onion and potatoes in 3½- to 4-quart slow cooker. Arrange beef on top. Sprinkle beef with brown sugar, nutmeg, salt, pepper and soup mix (dry). Pour beer over all.

Cover and cook on low heat setting 8 to 10 hours or until beef is tender.

Spoon pan juices over beef before serving.

1 Serving: Calories 310 (Calories from Fat 45); Fat 5g (Saturated 2g); Cholesterol 75mg; Sodium 600mg; Carbohydrate 35g (Dietary Fiber 3g); Protein 31g

Beef Pot Roast with Vegetables

6 servings

SLOW-COOKER SIZE:
3½- to 4-quart

PREP:
12 min

COOK:
Low 9 to 10 hours

Betty's Success Tip

Because the grain in a pot roast changes direction, it isn't always easy to get tender slices. To slice pot roast, place the roast on a carving board or platter. Hold the meat in place with a meat fork, and cut between the muscles. Remove one section of the meat at a time. Turn the section so that the grain of the meat runs parallel to the carving board, and cut meat across the grain into ¼-inch slices.

Ingredient Substitution

If you've used the last of your chili sauce, not to worry; ketchup will do in a pinch.

3-pound beef boneless chuck pot roast

2 dried bay leaves

2 medium stalks celery, cut into 3-inch pieces

6 small red potatoes, cut into fourths

1 cup baby-cut carrots

1 jar (4.5 ounces) whole mushrooms, drained

1 can (10¾ ounces) condensed cream of mushroom soup

2 tablespoons chili sauce

½ package (2.2-ounce size) beefy onion soup mix (1 envelope)

Place beef in 3½- to 4-quart slow cooker. Arrange bay leaves on top of beef; arrange celery, potatoes, carrots and mushrooms around beef. Top beef with condensed mushroom soup, chili sauce and beefy onion soup mix (dry).

Cover and cook on low heat setting 9 to 10 hours or until beef is tender. Discard bay leaves.

1 Serving: Calories 595 (Calories from Fat 260); Fat 29g (Saturated 11g); Cholesterol 140mg; Sodium 1100mg; Carbohydrate 34g (Dietary Fiber 4g); Protein 50g

Pot Roast–Style Beef Steak

4 servings

SLOW-COOKER SIZE:
3½- to 4-quart

PREP:
25 min

COOK:
Low 8 to 10 hours

FINISHING COOK TME:
5 min

Betty's Success Tip

Get a head start on preparing this dish by cutting up the carrots and onion the night before. Wrap in plastic wrap or put into covered plastic containers and refrigerate. Potatoes will turn brown, so peel and cut them just before adding to the slow cooker.

Serving Suggestion

Pair this beef steak and vegetable dish with a hearty cracked wheat bread, perfect for dipping into the rich, flavorful gravy.

1½-pound beef boneless top round steak (½ inch thick)

1 tablespoon all-purpose flour

½ teaspoon salt

⅛ teaspoon pepper

4 medium potatoes, peeled and each cut into 6 pieces

4 large carrots, cut into 1-inch pieces

1 medium onion, thinly sliced

1 dried bay leaf

1 can (14 ounces) beef broth

1 teaspoon Worcestershire sauce

2 tablespoons cornstarch

Cut beef into 4 equal pieces. Mix flour, salt and pepper in shallow bowl. Add beef pieces; turn to coat both sides.

Spray 12-inch nonstick skillet with cooking spray; heat over medium-high heat. Cook beef in skillet 4 to 6 minutes, turning once, until brown.

Mix potatoes, carrots and onion in 3½- to 4-quart slow cooker. Add bay leaf. Place beef on vegetables. Mix 1½ cups of the beef broth (reserve remaining broth) and Worcestershire sauce; pour over beef.

Cover and cook on low heat setting 8 to 10 hours or until beef is tender.

About 5 minutes before serving, remove beef and vegetables from cooker, using slotted spoon; place on serving platter. Cover to keep warm.

Pour liquid from cooker into 1½-quart saucepan; remove bay leaf. Mix reserved beef broth and the cornstarch in small bowl until smooth. Stir into liquid in saucepan. Heat to boiling over medium-high heat, stirring constantly. Boil and stir 1 minute. Serve sauce with beef and vegetables.

1 Serving: Calories 370 (Calories from Fat 55); Fat 6g (Saturated 2g); Cholesterol 90mg; Sodium 860mg; Carbohydrate 40g (Dietary Fiber 4g); Protein 39g

Pot Roast–Style Beef Steak

Beef Roast with Shiitake Mushroom Sauce

5 servings, with leftovers

SLOW-COOKER SIZE:
3½- to 4-quart

PREP:
20 min

COOK:
Low 8 to 10 hours

MICROWAVE:
3 min

Betty's Success Tip

To clean mushrooms, brush them with a soft vegetable brush and then wipe clean with a damp cloth. Don't run mushrooms under water or their texture will become mushy.

Ingredient Substitution

Fresh shiitake mushrooms add a wonderful, rich flavor to this beef roast, but if they aren't available, you can use 2 cups sliced regular white mushrooms instead.

Leftovers . . . What a Great Idea

Use the leftovers from this meal for Beef and Asparagus over Noodles (page 150) and for Chinese Beef and Broccoli (page 151).

3½ ounces fresh shiitake mushrooms, sliced

4-pound beef boneless rump or tip roast, trimmed of fat

¼ cup hoisin sauce

2 cloves garlic, finely chopped

½ teaspoon salt

¼ cup water

2 tablespoons cornstarch

2 medium green onions, sliced (2 tablespoons)

Place mushrooms in 3½- to 4-quart slow cooker. Top with beef. Spread hoisin sauce over beef; sprinkle with garlic and salt.

Cover and cook on low heat setting 8 to 10 hours or until beef is tender.

About 10 minutes before serving, remove beef from cooker; place on serving platter, and cover to keep warm. Mix water and cornstarch in 4-cup glass measuring cup or medium microwavable bowl until smooth. Pour juices from cooker into cornstarch mixture; mix well. Microwave uncovered on High 2 to 3 minutes, stirring once halfway through cooking, until mixture boils and thickens slightly.

Cut roast in half; set one half aside. Cut remaining half into slices; place on serving platter. Remove 1½ cups sauce and set aside. Spoon some of the remaining sauce over beef slices. Sprinkle with onions. Serve with any remaining sauce.

Divide reserved roast into 2 portions. Slice each; cut slices into 2 × ¼-inch strips. Divide strips evenly into 2 plastic storage containers with lids. Add 1 cup sauce to 1 container; cover and label for Beef and Asparagus over Noodles (page 150). Add ½ cup sauce to other container; cover and label for Chinese Beef and Broccoli (page 151). Refrigerate both containers up to 3 days or freeze up to 2 months for later use. If frozen, thaw in refrigerator before using.

1 Serving: Calories 225 (Calories from Fat 55); Fat 6g (Saturated 6g); Cholesterol 95mg; Sodium 340mg; Carbohydrate 9g (Dietary Fiber 1g); Protein 37g

Beef Roast with Shiitake Mushroom Sauce

Swiss Steak

6 servings

SLOW-COOKER SIZE:
3½- to 6-quart

PREP:
15 min

COOK:
Low 7 to 9 hours

1½-pound beef boneless round, tip or chuck steak, about ¾ inch thick

3 tablespoons all-purpose flour

1 teaspoon ground mustard

½ teaspoon salt

2 tablespoons vegetable oil

1 large onion, sliced

1 large green bell pepper, sliced

1 can (14½ ounces) whole tomatoes, undrained

2 cloves garlic, finely chopped

Cut beef into 6 serving pieces. Mix flour, mustard and salt; coat beef (do not pound in).

Heat oil in 10-inch skillet over medium heat. Cook beef in oil until brown on both sides. Place beef in 3½- to 6-quart slow cooker. Top with onion and bell pepper. Mix tomatoes and garlic; pour over beef and vegetables. Cover and cook on low heat setting 7 to 9 hours or until beef is tender.

1 Serving: Calories 205 (Calories from Fat 70); Fat 8g (Saturated 2g); Cholesterol 60mg; Sodium 360mg; Carbohydrate 11g (Dietary Fiber 2g); Protein 24g

www.bettycrocker.com

New England Pot Roast

8 servings

SLOW-COOKER SIZE:
4- to 6-quart

PREP:
30 min

COOK:
Low 8 to 10 hours

Betty's Success Tip

Place roast on carving board or platter. With meat fork in meat to hold meat in place, cut between muscles and around bones. Remove one section of meat at a time. Turn section so meat grain runs parallel to carving board. Cut meat across grain into ¼-inch slices.

Ingredient Substitution

A 3-pound beef bottom round, rolled rump, tip or chuck eye roast can be substituted; decrease salt to ¾ teaspoon.

4-pound beef arm, blade or cross rib pot roast

8 small potatoes, cut in half

8 medium carrots, cut into fourths

8 small onions

1 jar (8 ounces) prepared horseradish

1 to 2 teaspoons salt

1 teaspoon pepper

1 cup water

Pot Roast Gravy (below)

Cook beef in 12-inch skillet over medium heat until brown on all sides.

Place potatoes, carrots and onions in 4- to 6-quart slow cooker. Place beef on vegetables. Mix horseradish, salt and pepper; spread evenly over beef. Pour water into slow cooker. Cover and cook on low heat setting 8 to 10 hours or until beef and vegetables are tender.

Pot Roast Gravy

½ cup cold water

¼ cup all-purpose flour

Skim excess fat from broth (above) in Dutch oven. Add enough water to broth to measure 2 cups. Shake ½ cup cold water and the flour in tightly covered container; gradually stir into broth. Heat to boiling, stirring constantly. Boil and stir 1 minute.

1 Serving: Calories 385 (Calories from Fat 100); Fat 11g (Saturated 4g); Cholesterol 85mg; Sodium 690mg; Carbohydrate 40g (Dietary Fiber 6g); Protein 37g

Asian BBQ Beef Brisket

8 servings

SLOW-COOKER SIZE:
3½- to 4-quart

PREP:
20 min

COOK:
Low 9 to 11 hours

Betty's Success Tip

Be sure to use fresh beef brisket instead of a "corned" beef brisket. Corned beef brisket has been cured in seasoned brine, which may be too strong a flavor for this dish.

Ingredient Substitution

If you can't find fresh beef brisket, cooking the same cut of meat you use for a pot roast, such as beef boneless bottom roast or chuck roast, will also work.

1 tablespoon vegetable oil

3-pound fresh beef brisket (not corned beef)

¾ cup barbecue sauce

¾ cup teriyaki baste and glaze (from 12-ounce bottle)

1 small onion, chopped (¼ cup)

1 to 2 chipotle chile peppers in adobo sauce (from 7-ounce can), finely chopped

Heat oil in 12-inch skillet over medium-high heat. Cook beef in oil until brown on both sides. Place beef in 3½- to 4-quart slow cooker. Mix remaining ingredients; pour over beef.

Cover and cook on low heat setting 9 to 11 hours, until beef is tender.

Remove beef from cooker; place on cutting board. Cut beef across grain into thin slices. Skim fat from sauce in cooker. Serve sauce with beef.

1 Serving: Calories 345 (Calories from Fat 125); Fat 14g (Saturated 5g); Cholesterol 95mg; Sodium 1400mg; Carbohydrate 14g (Dietary Fiber 0g); Protein 38g

Zesty Italian Beef Tips

6 servings

SLOW-COOKER SIZE:
3½- to 4-quart

PREP:
10 min

COOK:
Low 8 to 10 hours

Betty's Success Tip

Cut up the stew meat so all pieces are the same size. This ensures even cooking so every bite will be tender.

Ingredient Substitution

Kalamata or Greek olives add a pleasant, tangy flavor, but large ripe olives can be substituted.

2 pounds beef stew meat

1 cup frozen small whole onions (from 1-pound bag)

1 jar (6 ounces) pitted Kalamata or Greek olives, drained

⅓ cup sun-dried tomatoes in oil, drained and chopped

1 jar (28 ounces) marinara sauce

6 cups hot cooked pasta

Place beef and frozen onions in 3½- to 4-quart slow cooker. Top with olives and tomatoes. Pour marinara sauce over top.

Cover and cook on low heat setting 8 to 10 hours or until beef is tender. Serve over pasta.

1 Serving: Calories 660 (Calories from Fat 245); Fat 27g (Saturated 8g); Cholesterol 95mg; Sodium 990mg; Carbohydrate 69g (Dietary Fiber 5g); Protein 40g

Thawing Meats in the Microwave

Place wrapped meat in a microwavable dish. After half of the microwave defrosting time indicated in the chart below, remove from wrapper, separate pieces, and arrange thickest parts to outside edges of dish. For bacon, hot dogs and sausages, pierce packages with a fork. Defrost as directed below until few ice crystals remain in center. Let stand 5 to 10 minutes to complete thawing.

Meat Type	Amount	Defrosting Time (Defrost setting)
Steak, ½-inch thick	1 pound	7 to 9 minutes, turning over after 4 minutes
1 inch thick	1 pound	8 to 11 minutes, turning over after 4 minutes
Chops, ½-inch thick	1 pound (about 4 chops)	6 to 9 minutes, rearranging after 4 minutes
Ribs, back	1 pound	7 to 9 minutes, rearranging after 4 minutes
Ground	1 pound	8 to 10 minutes, turning over after 4 minutes
Meatballs, cooked	1 pound (24 balls)	7 to 9 minutes, separating after 3 minutes
Patties, ¾-inch thick	1 pound (4 patties)	8 to 10 minutes, turning over after 4 minutes
Bacon, sliced	1 pound	5 to 6 minutes
Hot Dogs	1 pound (about 10)	5 to 7 minutes, turning over after 3 minutes
	½ pound	2 to 4 minutes, turning over after 3 minutes
Sausages, cooked or uncooked (bratwurst, Italian, Polish)	1 pound (about 6)	6 to 8 minutes, turning over after 3 minutes

Corned Beef and Cabbage Dinner

8 servings

SLOW-COOKER SIZE:
5- to 6½-quart

PREP:
15 min

COOK:
Low 10 to 12 hours

FINISHING COOK TIME:
High 30 to 35 min

Betty's Success Tip

To keep cabbage wedges whole, don't remove the core from the cabbage; just cut through it so a bit of the core holds each wedge together.

Serving Suggestion

Pile leftover corned beef and cabbage on slices of toasted rye bread, and spread with apple mustard. Top the sandwich filling with a slice of Swiss cheese, and heat it under the broiler until the cheese melts and bubbles.

2 pounds small red potatoes

1½ cups baby-cut carrots

1 medium onion, cut into 8 wedges

2- to 2½-pound well-trimmed corned beef brisket with seasoning packet

2 cups apple juice

Water

8 thin wedges cabbage

Horseradish Sauce (below)

Place potatoes, carrots and onion in 5- to 6½-quart slow cooker. Thoroughly rinse beef; place on top of vegetables. Sprinkle beef with contents of seasoning packet. Add apple juice and just enough water to cover beef.

Cover and cook on low heat setting 10 to 12 hours, until beef is tender.

Remove beef from cooker; place on serving platter and cover to keep warm. Add cabbage wedges to vegetables and broth in cooker. Cover and cook on high heat setting 30 to 35 minutes or until cabbage is crisp-tender.

Make Horseradish Sauce. Cut beef across grain into thin slices. Remove vegetables from slow cooker, using slotted spoon. Serve beef and vegetables with sauce.

Horseradish Sauce

½ cup sour cream

¼ cup mayonnaise or salad dressing

2 tablespoons prepared horseradish

2 teaspoons Dijon mustard

Mix all ingredients.

1 Serving: Calories 430 (Calories from Fat 215); Fat 24g (Saturated 8g); Cholesterol 90mg; Sodium 1040mg; Carbohydrate 41g (Dietary Fiber 6g); Protein 19g

Corned Beef and Cabbage Dinner

Cabbage Roll Casserole

6 servings

SLOW-COOKER SIZE:
3½- to 6-quart

PREP:
15 min

COOK:
Low 4 to 6 hours

Betty's Success Tip

It is important to cook the ground beef before adding it to the cooker. Because the beef is ground, there is a greater risk that bacteria may start to grow before the temperature inside the cooker gets high enough.

Ingredient Substitution

No coleslaw mix on hand? Substitute 4½ cups shredded cabbage and one shredded carrot. If you own a food processor with a shredding attachment, this is a great time to use it.

Finishing Touch

Place squares of processed American cheese over the top of the finished casserole, or sprinkle with shredded Cheddar cheese. Cover and let it stand a few minutes so the cheese melts. Kids will love it!

1 pound ground beef

1 medium onion, chopped (½ cup)

5 cups coleslaw mix

½ cup uncooked instant rice

¼ cup water

2 teaspoons paprika

½ teaspoon salt

¼ teaspoon pepper

1 can (15 ounces) chunky Italian-style tomato sauce

Cook beef and onion in 10-inch skillet over medium heat, stirring occasionally, until beef is brown; drain.

Mix beef mixture and remaining ingredients in 3½- to 6-quart slow cooker. (Cooker will be very full, but cabbage will cook down.)

Cover and cook on low heat setting 4 to 6 hours or until cabbage is tender.

1 Serving: Calories 300 (Calories from Fat 125); Fat 14g (Saturated 5g); Cholesterol 45mg; Sodium 600mg; Carbohydrate 27g (Dietary Fiber 3g); Protein 17g

Corned Beef Brisket with Horseradish Sour Cream

8 servings

SLOW-COOKER SIZE:
5- to 6-quart

PREP:
10 min

COOK:
Low 8 to 9 hours

Betty's Success Tip

Corned beef was originally "corned," or preserved with granular salt, because there was no refrigeration. Today, the beef is cured in brine and spices are added for a distinctive tangy flavor. Because we use crushed red pepper flakes in this recipe, there's no need to use the additional seasonings found in the seasoning packet.

Serving Suggestion

Boiled potatoes and cabbage complement the spicy flavor of corned beef. Serve this corned beef brisket with boiled small red potatoes and steamed green cabbage wedges and add slices of hearty rye bread to round out the meal.

1 large sweet onion (Bermuda, Maui, Spanish, Walla Walla), sliced

3- to 3½- pound well-trimmed corned beef brisket

¾ teaspoon crushed red pepper flakes

1 cup reduced-sodium chicken broth

1 tablespoon Worcestershire sauce

Horseradish Sour Cream (below)

Place onion in 5- to 6-quart slow cooker. Thoroughly rinse beef; discard seasoning packet. Place beef on onion; sprinkle with red pepper. Mix broth and Worcestershire sauce; pour over beef.

Cover and cook on low heat setting 8 to 9 hours or until beef is tender.

Remove beef from cooker; place on cutting board. Remove onion with slotted spoon; place with beef; cover with aluminum foil to keep warm. Cut beef against grain into slices. Serve with onion and Horseradish Sour Cream.

Horseradish Sour Cream

½ cup sour cream

1 tablespoon cream-style horseradish

2 tablespoons chopped fresh parsley

Mix all ingredients.

1 Serving: Calories 340 (Calories from Fat 235); Fat 26g (Saturated 9g); Cholesterol 130mg; Sodium 1460mg; Carbohydrate 3g (Dietary Fiber 0g); Protein 23g

Hungarian Goulash

8 servings

SLOW-COOKER SIZE:
3½- to 6-quart

PREP:
20 min

COOK:
Low 8 to 10 hours; High 4 to 5 hours

FINISHING COOK TIME:
High 30 min

Ingredient Substitution

Just discovered you are all out of fresh garlic? Use ¼ teaspoon garlic powder instead.

Finishing Touch

For a special touch, top each serving of goulash with a dollop of sour cream, or toss the hot noodles with a tablespoon or two of poppy seeds.

2 tablespoons vegetable oil

2 pounds beef stew meat, cut into 1-inch pieces

1 large onion, sliced

1 can (14½ ounces) ready-to-serve beef broth

1 can (6 ounces) tomato paste

2 cloves garlic, finely chopped

1 tablespoon Worcestershire sauce

1 tablespoon paprika

1 teaspoon salt

¼ teaspoon caraway seeds, if desired

¼ teaspoon pepper

¼ cup cold water

3 tablespoons all-purpose flour

1 medium bell pepper, cut into strips

8 cups hot cooked noodles, for serving

Heat oil in 10-inch skillet over medium-high heat. Cook beef in oil about 10 minutes, stirring occasionally, until brown; drain. Place beef and onion in 3½- to 6-quart slow cooker.

Mix broth, tomato paste, garlic, Worcestershire sauce, paprika, salt, caraway seed and pepper; stir into beef mixture.

Cover and cook on low heat setting 8 to 10 hours, or high heat setting 4 to 5 hours, until beef is tender.

Mix water and flour; gradually stir into beef mixture. Stir in bell pepper. Cover and cook on high heat setting 30 minutes.

Serve goulash over noodles.

1 Serving: Calories 435 (Calories from Fat 135); Fat 15g (Saturated 5g); Cholesterol 110mg; Sodium 770mg; Carbohydrate 50g (Dietary Fiber 4g); Protein 29g

Hungarian Goulash

Savory Beef Short Rib Dinner

4 servings

SLOW-COOKER SIZE:
4- to 6-quart

PREP:
35 min

COOK:
Low 8 to 10 hours

MICROWAVE:
4 min

Betty's Success Tip

This recipe calls for dry sun-dried tomatoes, which absorb juices and become tender during cooking. Don't confuse them with oil-packed sun-dried tomatoes. Look for dry sun-dried tomatoes in the produce department near the other dried foods.

Ingredient Substitution

To cut down on prep time, use 16 baby-cut carrots instead of the whole carrots.

2 pounds beef short ribs

½ large onion, cut into 4 wedges

2 sun-dried tomato halves (not oil-packed), cut into thin strips

4 medium carrots, cut lengthwise in half, then cut crosswise in half

8 small red potatoes (1 pound)

1 clove garlic, finely chopped

½ teaspoon salt

½ teaspoon dried thyme leaves

½ teaspoon dried basil leaves

¼ teaspoon pepper

½ cup dry red wine or water

1 cup water

1 teaspoon beef bouillon granules

2 tablespoons all-purpose flour

Cook ribs in 12-inch nonstick skillet over medium-high heat, turning frequently, until brown on all sides. While ribs are browning, layer onion, tomatoes, carrots, potatoes and garlic in 4- to 6-quart slow cooker.

Place ribs on vegetables in cooker. Sprinkle ribs with salt, thyme, basil and pepper. Drain off any fat from skillet; add wine, ½ cup of the water and the bouillon to skillet. Heat to boiling over medium heat, stirring occasionally. Pour hot wine mixture over ribs.

Cover and cook on low heat setting 8 to 10 hours or until ribs are tender.

About 15 minutes before serving, remove ribs and vegetables, using slotted spoon; place in serving bowl. Skim fat from juices in cooker.

Mix remaining ½ cup water and the flour in 4-cup glass measuring cup or medium microwavable bowl until smooth. Pour juices from cooker into flour mixture; mix well. Microwave uncovered on High 3 to 4 minutes, stirring once halfway through cooking, until mixture boils. Pour sauce over ribs and vegetables.

1 Serving: Calories 425 (Calories from Fat 115); Fat 13g (Saturated 5g); Cholesterol 50mg; Sodium 710mg; Carbohydrate 55g (Dietary Fiber 6g); Protein 22g

Slow-Simmered Spaghetti Meat Sauce

8 servings

SLOW-COOKER SIZE:
3½- to 4-quart

PREP:
20 min

COOK:
Low 8 to 10 hours

Ingredient Substitution

A half-pound of pork sausage can be used instead of the Italian sausage if it's more readily available. No fresh garlic? Use ¼ teaspoon garlic powder or ½ teaspoon instant minced garlic instead.

Serving Suggestion

For a meal in a snap, serve with purchased garlic bread and a buy-in-the-bag Caesar salad mix. A slice of store-bought cheesecake is the perfect dessert.

1 pound lean ground beef

½ pound bulk Italian pork sausage

2 medium carrots, finely chopped (1 cup)

1 medium green bell pepper, chopped (1 cup)

1 medium onion, chopped (½ cup)

2 cloves garlic, finely chopped

1 can (28 ounces) crushed tomatoes, undrained

1 can (8 ounces) tomato sauce

1 can (6 ounces) tomato paste

1 tablespoon packed brown sugar

1 tablespoon dried Italian seasoning

½ teaspoon salt

¼ teaspoon pepper

16 ounces uncooked spaghetti

Shredded fresh Parmesan cheese, if desired

Cook beef and sausage in 10-inch skillet over medium heat, stirring frequently, until beef is brown and sausage is no longer pink, about 8 minutes; drain.

Mix beef mixture and remaining ingredients except spaghetti and Parmesan cheese in 3½- to 4-quart slow cooker.

Cover and cook on low heat setting 8 to 10 hours.

About 20 minutes before serving, cook and drain spaghetti as directed on package. Serve sauce with hot cooked spaghetti and Parmesan cheese.

1 Serving: Calories 440 (Calories from Fat 125); Fat 14g (Saturated 5g); Cholesterol 45mg; Sodium 850mg; Carbohydrate 62g (Dietary Fiber 5g); Protein 23g

Italian Meatballs with Marinara Sauce

6 servings (4 meatballs each)

SLOW-COOKER SIZE:
3½- to 4-quart

PREP:
15 min

BAKE:
35 min

COOK:
Low 6 to 7 hours

Ingredient Substitution

Substitute any flavor of marinara or spaghetti sauce, such as herbed, sun-dried tomato or garlic and onion, to vary the flavor in this recipe.

Serving Suggestion

These meatballs make a great filling for sandwiches. Cut 8 small rustic sourdough or Italian rolls horizontally in half. Place 3 meatballs in each roll; top each sandwich with a 1-ounce slice of provolone cheese, and drizzle with marinara sauce.

¾ **pound ground beef**

¾ **pound ground pork**

1 **small onion, chopped (¼ cup)**

2 **cloves garlic, finely chopped**

2 **teaspoons Italian seasoning**

¼ **cup Italian-style dry bread crumbs**

1 **egg, slightly beaten**

1 **jar (28 ounces) marinara sauce**

Heat oven to 375°. Line jelly roll pan, 15½ × 10½ × 1 inch, with aluminum foil; spray with cooking spray. Mix beef, pork, onion, garlic, Italian seasoning, bread crumbs and egg. Shape mixture into twenty-four 1½-inch balls. Place in pan. Bake 30 to 35 minutes or until no longer pink in center.

Place meatballs in 3½- to 4-quart slow cooker. Pour marinara sauce over meatballs.

Cover and cook on low heat setting 6 to 7 hours to blend and develop flavors.

1 Serving: Calories 410 (Calories from Fat 200); Fat 22g (Saturated 7g); Cholesterol 105mg; Sodium 950mg; Carbohydrate 29g (Dietary Fiber 2g); Protein 24g

Sloppy Joes
24 sandwiches

SLOW-COOKER SIZE:
3½- to 6-quart

PREP:
15 min

COOK:
Low 7 to 9 hours; High 3 to 4 hours

Betty's Success Tip

Next time you're asked to bring something to one of your kid's events, bring Sloppy Joes. Kids love them. And you can keep the sandwich filling warm in the cooker for a couple of hours. Just be sure to stir it occasionally so that it doesn't start to get too brown around the edges.

Ingredient Substitution

Stir 1 cup drained sauerkraut into the mixture before serving. It will add a nice flavor twist, and no one will guess the "secret ingredient."

Serving Suggestion

You can serve this tasty beef mixture over hot cooked rice or pasta rather than using as a sandwich filling. Or spoon it over tortilla chips and top each serving with shredded lettuce and shredded cheese.

3 pounds ground beef

1 large onion, coarsely chopped (1 cup)

¾ cup chopped celery

1 cup barbecue sauce

1 can (26½ ounces) sloppy joe sauce

24 hamburger buns

Cook beef and onion in Dutch oven over medium heat, stirring occasionally, until beef is brown; drain.

Mix beef mixture and remaining ingredients except buns in 3½- to 6-quart slow cooker.

Cover and cook on low heat setting 7 to 9 hours (or high heat setting 3 to 4 hours) or until vegetables are tender.

Uncover and cook on high heat setting until desired consistency. Stir well before serving. Fill buns with beef mixture.

1 Sandwich: Calories 155 (Calories from Fat 80); Fat 9g (Saturated 3g); Cholesterol 30mg; Sodium 270mg; Carbohydrate 8g (Dietary Fiber 1g); Protein 11g

Swedish Meatballs

12 servings (5 meatballs each)

SLOW-COOKER SIZE:
5- to 6-quart

PREP:
1 hour 15 min

COOK:
Low 3 to 4 hours

HOLD TIME:
Low up to 2 hours

Ingredient Substitution

Used up the last of your dry bread crumbs? Finely crushed cracker crumbs or corn flakes, or quick-cooking or old-fashioned oats will work in place of dry bread crumbs.

Serving Suggestion

Leftover meatballs? Make a box of flavored mashed potatoes, heat the meatballs in their sauce and spoon over the potatoes. Serve this quick and easy meal with buttered sliced beets.

1½ cups milk

4 eggs

1½ cups plain dry bread crumbs

¼ cup instant minced onion

2 teaspoons ground mustard

2 teaspoons celery salt

1 teaspoon ground nutmeg

1 teaspoon salt

1 teaspoon pepper

4 pounds lean ground beef

3 cans (10¾ ounces each) condensed cream of mushroom soup

1½ cups water

1 teaspoon dried dill weed, if desired

Heat oven to 375°. Spray 2 rectangular pans, 15½ × 10½ × 1 inch, with cooking spray.

Beat milk and eggs in large bowl with wire whisk until blended. Stir in bread crumbs, onion, mustard, celery salt, nutmeg, salt and pepper. Mix in beef until well blended. Shape mixture into 60 meatballs, about 2 inches in diameter; place in pans. Bake uncovered about 30 minutes or until no longer pink in center and juice is clear.

Spray 5- to 6-quart slow cooker with cooking spray. Transfer meatballs to cooker. Mix soup, water and dill weed in large bowl; pour over meatballs. Stir to coat meatballs with sauce.

Cover and cook on low heat setting 3 to 4 hours or until meatballs are very tender and sauce is bubbling. Meatballs will hold on low heat setting up to 2 hours. If sauce becomes too thick while holding, stir in up to ½ cup hot water. Stir well before serving.

1 Serving: Calories 465 (Calories from Fat 260); Fat 29g (Saturated 11g); Cholesterol 160mg; Sodium 1200mg; Carbohydrate 17g (Dietary Fiber 1g); Protein 34g

Picadillo

12 servings

SLOW-COOKER SIZE:
3½- to 6-quart

PREP:
20 min

COOK:
Low 3 to 4 hours

Betty's Success Tip

This Mexican version of hash is a combination of ingredients that might surprise you—ground beef, apples, raisins and almonds. The flavors and textures add a distinctive flair to these recipes.

2 pounds ground beef

1 large onion, chopped (1 cup)

1 cup raisins

2 teaspoons chili powder

1 teaspoon salt

¾ teaspoon ground cinnamon

½ teaspoon ground cumin

½ teaspoon pepper

2 cloves garlic, finely chopped

2 medium apples, peeled and chopped

2 cans (10 ounces each) diced tomatoes and green chile peppers, undrained

⅓ cup slivered almonds, toasted

Cook beef and onion in 12-inch skillet over medium heat, stirring occasionally, until beef is brown; drain.

Mix beef mixture and remaining ingredients except almonds in 3½- to 6-quart slow cooker.

Cover and cook on low heat setting 3 to 4 hours or until most of the liquid is absorbed. Stir in almonds.

1 Serving: Calories 245 (Calories from Fat 115); Fat 13g (Saturated 5g); Cholesterol 45mg; Sodium 310mg; Carbohydrate 18g (Dietary Fiber 2g); Protein 16g

Mini Cheeseburger Bites

8 servings (3 bites each)

SLOW-COOKER SIZE:
3½- to 4-quart

PREP:
15 min

COOK:
Low 3 to 4 hours

HOLD TIME:
Low up to 3 hours

Betty's Success Tips

These bites will become a favorite as appetizers as well as quick suppers.

Ingredient Substitution

To add a little zip to these mini burgers, use Monterey Jack cheese with jalapeño peppers instead of American cheese.

Serving Suggestion

For a kid's birthday party, spoon the meat mixture on small round bun halves. Let kids decorate their own open-face sandwiches with ketchup and mustard in squeeze containers. Set out bowls of shredded cheese, sliced pickles, cherry tomato halves and sliced olives so they can make silly faces.

1 Serving: Calories 495 (Calories from Fat 210); Fat 24g (Saturated 9g); Cholesterol 60mg; Sodium 620mg; Carbohydrate 45g (Dietary Fiber 3g); Protein 24g

1 pound lean ground beef

2 tablespoons ketchup

2 teaspoons instant minced onion

1 teaspoon yellow mustard

8 ounces American cheese, cut into 2-inch cubes (2 cups)

24 miniature sandwich buns, split

Cook beef in 10-inch skillet over medium-high heat about 8 minutes, stirring frequently, until brown; drain. Stir in ketchup, onion and mustard.

Spray 3½- to 4-quart slow cooker with cooking spray. Spoon beef mixture into cooker. Top with cheese.

Cover and cook on low heat setting 3 to 4 hours or until mixture is hot and cheese is melted.

Serve beef mixture with buns. Beef mixture will hold on low heat setting up to 3 hours.

Cheesy Italian Tortellini

4 to 6 servings

SLOW-COOKER SIZE:
3½- to 6-quart

PREP:
15 min

COOK:
Low 7 to 8 hours

FINISHING COOK TIME:
Low 15 min

Ingredient Substitution

A can of plain diced tomatoes and ½ teaspoon dried Italian seasoning can be used instead of the diced tomatoes with Italian seasoning.

½ pound ground beef

½ pound Italian sausage

1 container (15 ounces) refrigerated marinara sauce

1 cup sliced fresh mushrooms

1 can (14½ ounces) diced tomatoes with Italian seasonings, undrained

1 package (9 ounces) refrigerated cheese tortellini

1 cup shredded mozzarella or pizza-style cheese (4 ounces)

Break beef and sausage into large pieces in 10-inch skillet. Cook over medium heat about 10 minutes, stirring occasionally, or until brown.

Mix beef mixture, marinara sauce, mushrooms and tomatoes in 3½- to 6-quart slow cooker.

Cover and cook on low heat setting 7 to 8 hours. Stir in tortellini; sprinkle with cheese. Cover and cook on low heat setting about 15 minutes longer or until tortellini is tender.

1 Serving: Calories 550 (Calories from Fat 280); Fat 31g (Saturated 12g); Cholesterol 135mg; Sodium 1260mg; Carbohydrate 37g (Dietary Fiber 3g); Protein 34g

Three-Bean Casserole

8 servings

SLOW-COOKER SIZE:
3½ - to 6-quart

PREP:
20 min

COOK:
High 2 to 2½ hours

1 pound bulk pork sausage

2 medium stalks celery, sliced (1 cup)

1 medium onion, chopped (½ cup)

1 large clove garlic, finely chopped

2 cans (21 ounces each) baked beans in tomato sauce

1 can (15 to 16 ounces) lima or butter beans, drained

1 can (15 to 16 ounces) kidney beans, drained

½ cup ketchup

1 tablespoon ground mustard

1 tablespoon honey or packed brown sugar

1 tablespoon white or cider vinegar

¼ teaspoon red pepper sauce

Cook sausage, celery, onion and garlic in 10-inch skillet over medium heat about 10 minutes, stirring occasionally, until sausage is no longer pink; drain.

Mix sausage mixture and remaining ingredients in 3½- to 6-quart slow cooker. Cover and cook on high heat setting 2 hours to 2 hours 30 minutes to blend flavors.

1 Serving: Calories 255 (Calories from Fat 45); Fat 5g (Saturated 2g); Cholesterol 20mg; Sodium 1290mg; Carbohydrate 51g (Dietary Fiber 12g); Protein 14g

Sprinkle Casseroles and Soups with . . .

- Toasted nuts
- Toasted sesame seeds
- Crushed unsweetened cereal mixed with dried herbs
- Crushed tortilla or corn chips mixed with grated Parmesan cheese and parsley
- Toasted pumpkin seeds or sunflower nuts
- Cheese-flavored fish-shaped crackers

Mexican Pork Roast with Chili Sauce

6 servings, with leftovers

SLOW-COOKER SIZE:
4- to 6-quart

PREP:
15 min

COOK:
Low 8 to 10 hours

FINISHING COOK TIME:
Microwave 3 min

Betty's Success Tip

Chipotle chile peppers are actually dried, smoked jalapeños. In addition to being canned, they are sold dried and pickled. Adobo sauce consists of ground chiles, herbs and vinegar. Look for chipotle chiles in adobo sauce in the Mexican-foods section of your supermarket.

Serving Suggestion

For a more casual meal, wrap the pork in a flour tortilla and top with the chili sauce.

Leftovers . . . What a Great Idea

The leftovers from this dish are used in Cheesy Pork Quesadillas (page 152).

1 medium onion, chopped (½ cup)

1 medium green bell pepper, chopped (1 cup)

4-pound pork boneless butt or shoulder roast, trimmed of fat

1 tablespoon packed brown sugar

2 tablespoons finely chopped chipotle chile peppers in adobo sauce (from 7 ounce can)

2 tablespoons ketchup

¾ teaspoon salt

1 clove garlic, finely chopped

½ cup water

¼ cup all-purpose flour

Place onion and bell pepper in 4- to 6-quart slow cooker. Top with pork roast. Mix brown sugar, chile peppers, ketchup, salt and garlic; spread over pork.

Cover and cook on low heat setting 8 to 10 hours or until pork is tender.

About 10 minutes before serving, remove pork from cooker; place on cutting board, and cover to keep warm. Mix water and flour in 4-cup glass measuring cup or medium microwavable bowl until smooth. Pour juices from cooker into flour mixture; mix well. Microwave uncovered on high heat setting 2 to 3 minutes, stirring once halfway through cooking, until mixture boils and thickens slightly.

Cut pork in half; reserve one half of pork and 1 cup of the sauce. Cut remaining half of pork into slices; place on serving platter. Serve with remaining sauce.

Shred the reserved pork with 2 forks; place in plastic storage container with lid. Add 1 cup reserved sauce; cover and label for Cheesy Pork Quesadillas (page 152). Refrigerate up to 3 days or freeze up to 2 months. If frozen, thaw in refrigerator before using.

1 Serving: Calories 330 (Calories from Fat 160); Fat 18g (Saturated 6g); Cholesterol 95mg; Sodium 370mg; Carbohydrate 9g (Dietary Fiber 0g); Protein 33g

Apricot-Glazed Pork Roast and Stuffing

6 servings

SLOW-COOKER SIZE:
3½- to 4-quart

PREP:
10 min

COOK:
Low 7 to 8 hours

Betty's Success Tip

To give this tasty roast more color, brown all sides in a tablespoon of vegetable oil in a 12-inch skillet over medium-high heat before brushing with the jam.

Ingredient Substitution

If you don't have any balsamic vinegar, use 1 tablespoon cider or white vinegar. Also, peach jam will work if apricot jam isn't readily available on your pantry shelf.

1 Serving: Calories 515 (Calories from Fat 125); Fat 14g (Saturated 5g); Cholesterol 95mg; Sodium 950mg; Carbohydrate 61g (Dietary Fiber 4g); Protein 40g

4 cups herb-seasoned stuffing cubes

¾ cup chicken broth

½ cup dried apricots, chopped

⅓ cup frozen chopped onions (from 12-ounce bag)

2- to 2½-pound pork boneless loin roast

⅓ cup apricot jam

1 tablespoon balsamic vinegar

Spray 3½- to 4-quart slow cooker with cooking spray. Mix stuffing, broth, apricots and onions in cooker. Place pork on stuffing mixture. Mix jam and vinegar; brush over pork.

Cover and cook on low heat setting 7 to 8 hours or until pork is tender.

Remove pork from cooker; place on cutting board. Stir stuffing before serving. Cut pork into slices; serve with stuffing.

Hunter's-Style Pork Roast

8 servings

SLOW-COOKER SIZE:
3½- to 4-quart

PREP:
10 min

COOK:
Low 9 to 11 hours

FINISHING COOK TIME:
High 15 to 30 min

Betty's Success Tip

Cacciatore, a popular Italian dish also referred to as hunter's-style, usually contains thickened tomato gravy with mushrooms, tomatoes and other vegetables. Chicken Cacciatore is the most popular example, but pork makes a delicious change.

Ingredient Substitution

Hunter's gravy mix is a packaged gravy mix flavored with mushrooms and wine, but an envelope of any pork or beef gravy mix can be used instead.

2½- to 3-pound pork boneless sirloin or loin roast

1 cup baby-cut carrots

2 cans (14½ ounces each) diced tomatoes with roasted garlic, undrained

1 envelope (1¼ ounces) hunter's gravy mix

2 tablespoons all-purpose flour

2 tablespoons water

1 jar (4½ ounces) sliced mushrooms, drained

1 package (8 or 9 ounces) frozen cut green beans, thawed and drained

Place pork in 3½- to 4-quart slow cooker; top with carrots. Mix tomatoes and gravy mix (dry); pour over pork and carrots.

Cover and cook on low heat setting 9 to 11 hours or until pork is tender.

Remove pork and carrots to serving platter, using slotted spoon; cover with aluminum foil. Mix flour and water. Gradually stir flour mixture, mushrooms and green beans into liquid in cooker. Cover and cook on high heat setting 15 to 30 minutes or until slightly thickened. Serve sauce with pork and carrots.

1 Serving: Calories 265 (Calories from Fat 100); Fat 11g (Saturated 4g); Cholesterol 85mg; Sodium 450mg; Carbohydrate 12g (Dietary Fiber 3g); Protein 33g

Pork Roast with Creamy Mustard Sauce

8 servings

SLOW-COOKER SIZE:
3½- to 6-quart

PREP:
15 min

COOK:
Low 7 to 9 hours

FINISHING COOK TIME:
High 15 min

Ingredient Substitution

White wine blends nicely with the flavor of mustard. If you don't have wine on hand, you can use chicken broth.

Serving Suggestion

Want to serve potatoes but tired of the same old boiled or baked potato? For a change, serve potato dumplings, German spaetzle or Italian gnocchi. The kids will think they're fun to eat. You will find them in the frozen section at the supermarket. Or look for a box of gnocchi in the dried pasta section of the store. Toss the cooked dumplings with melted butter, and add a sprinkle of chopped fresh parsley or dill weed for a touch of color and flavor.

2½- to 3-pound pork boneless sirloin roast

1 tablespoon vegetable oil

¾ cup dry white wine

2 tablespoons all-purpose flour

1 teaspoon salt

½ teaspoon pepper

2 medium carrots, finely chopped or shredded

1 medium onion, finely chopped (½ cup)

1 small shallot, finely chopped (2 tablespoons)

¼ cup half-and-half

2 to 3 tablespoons country-style Dijon mustard

Trim excess fat from pork. Heat oil in 10-inch skillet over medium-high heat. Cook pork in oil about 10 minutes, turning occasionally, until brown on all sides.

Place pork in 3½- to 6-quart slow cooker. Mix remaining ingredients except half-and-half and mustard; pour over pork.

Cover and cook on low heat setting 7 to 9 hours or until pork is tender.

Remove pork from cooker; cover and keep warm. Skim fat from pork juices in cooker if desired. Stir half-and-half and mustard into juices.

Cover and cook on high heat setting about 15 minutes or until slightly thickened. Serve sauce with pork.

1 Serving: Calories 175 (Calories from Fat 80); Fat 9g (Saturated 3g); Cholesterol 55mg; Sodium 390mg; Carbohydrate 5g (Dietary Fiber 1g); Protein 20g

Pork Chop and Potato Skillet

6 servings

SLOW-COOKER SIZE:
3½- to 6-quart

PREP:
15 min

COOK:
Low 6 to 7 hours

FINISHING COOK TIME:
Low 15 min

6 medium new potatoes (about 1½ pounds), cut into eighths

1 can (10¾ ounces) condensed cream of mushroom soup

1 can (4 ounces) mushroom pieces and stems, drained

2 tablespoons dry white wine or apple juice

¾ teaspoon chopped fresh or ¼ teaspoon dried thyme leaves

½ teaspoon garlic powder

½ teaspoon Worcestershire sauce

3 tablespoons all-purpose flour

6 pork loin or rib chops, ½-inch thick (about 1½ pounds)

1 tablespoon diced pimiento

1 package (10 ounces) frozen green peas, rinsed and drained

Place potatoes in 3½- to 6-quart slow cooker. Mix soup, mushrooms, wine, thyme, garlic powder, Worcestershire sauce and flour; spoon half of soup mixture over potatoes. Place pork on potatoes; cover with remaining soup mixture. Cover and cook on low heat setting 6 to 7 hours or until pork is tender.

Remove pork; keep warm. Stir pimiento and green peas into slow cooker. Cover and cook on low heat setting 15 minutes.

1 Serving: Calories 275 (Calories from Fat 100); Fat 11g (Saturated 4g); Cholesterol 65mg; Sodium 520mg; Carbohydrate 21g (Dietary Fiber 4g); Protein 27g

Asian Hoisin Ribs

4 servings

SLOW-COOKER SIZE:
3½- to 4-quart

PREP:
10 min

COOK:
Low 8 to 10 hours

Ingredient Substitution

The sesame oil adds a nice subtle sesame flavor to the ribs. However, if you don't have sesame oil, sprinkle the ribs with toasted sesame seed before serving.

Serving Suggestion

Serve these ribs with bowls of steaming rice and Chinese-style coleslaw. Finish the meal with fresh pineapple chunks sprinkled with chopped fresh mint.

3 pounds pork bone-in country-style ribs

1 medium onion, sliced

½ cup hoisin sauce

⅓ cup seasoned rice vinegar

¼ cup soy sauce

1 tablespoon grated gingerroot or 1 teaspoon ground ginger

2 teaspoons sesame oil, if desired

Fresh cilantro leaves, if desired

Place ribs in 3½- to 4-quart slow cooker. Cover with onion slices. Mix remaining ingredients except cilantro; pour over ribs and onion.

Cover and cook on low heat setting 8 to 10 hours or until ribs are tender.

Remove ribs to serving platter; keep warm. Skim fat from surface of juices in cooker. Serve ribs with sauce; sprinkle with cilantro.

1 Serving: Calories 450 (Calories from Fat 215); Fat 24g (Saturated 8g); Cholesterol 115mg; Sodium 1500 mg; Carbohydrate 18g (Dietary Fiber 2g); Protein 43g

Hot and Spicy Riblets

6 servings

SLOW-COOKER SIZE:
3½- to 4-quart

PREP:
10 min

COOK:
Low 6 to 7 hours

FINISHING COOK TIME:
High 25 to 30 min

HOLD TIME:
Low up to 2 hours

Betty's Success Tip

For these smaller, party-sized pieces, be sure to ask your butcher to cut the ribs lengthwise across the bones, then crosswise into one-rib pieces.

Ingredient Substitution

Out of fresh garlic? Check your spice rack. One medium clove of garlic is equal to ⅛ teaspoon garlic powder or ¼ teaspoon instant minced garlic.

1 rack (3 pounds) pork back ribs, cut lengthwise across bones in half, then cut into 1-rib pieces

3 cloves garlic, finely chopped

1 cup ketchup

¼ cup packed brown sugar

¼ cup chopped chipotle chile peppers in adobo sauce (from 7-ounce can)

1 tablespoon cider vinegar

1 tablespoon Worcestershire sauce

1 teaspoon salt

Spray 3½- to 4-quart slow cooker with cooking spray. Place riblets in cooker. Sprinkle with garlic.

Cover and cook on low heat setting 6 to 7 hours or until ribs are tender.

About 35 minutes before serving, mix remaining ingredients in 2-cup glass measuring cup or small bowl. Drain and discard juices from cooker. Pour or spoon sauce over riblets, stirring gently to coat evenly. Increase heat setting to high; cover and cook 25 to 30 minutes or until riblets are glazed.

Turn to low heat setting to serve. Riblets will hold on low heat setting up to 2 hours.

1 Serving: Calories 630 (Calories from Fat 390); Fat 42g (Saturated 12g); Cholesterol 125mg; Sodium 1320mg; Carbohydrate 24g (Dietary Fiber 0g); Protein 42g

Sweet-Savory Ribs

6 servings

SLOW-COOKER SIZE:
5- to 6-quart

COOK:
Low 8 to 9 hours

FINISHING COOK TIME:
1 hour

3½ pounds pork loin back ribs, pork spareribs or beef short ribs or 3 pounds pork country-style ribs, cut into 2- to 3-rib portions

½ teaspoon salt

¼ teaspoon pepper

½ cup water

Sweet-Savory Sauce (below)

Cut ribs into 2- or 3-rib portions. Place ribs in 5- to 6-quart slow cooker. Sprinkle with ½ teaspoon salt and ¼ teaspoon pepper. Pour ½ cup water into slow cooker. Cover and cook on low heat setting 8 to 9 hours or until tender.

Remove ribs. Drain and discard liquid from slow cooker. Make Sweet-Savory Sauce; pour into bowl. Dip ribs into sauce to coat. Place ribs in slow cooker. Pour any remaining sauce over ribs. Cover and cook on low heat setting 1 hour.

Sweet-Savory Sauce

1 cup chili sauce

¾ cup grape jelly

1 tablespoon plus 1½ teaspoons dry red wine or beef broth

1 teaspoon Dijon mustard

Heat all ingredients in 1-quart saucepan over medium heat, stirring occasionally, until jelly is melted.

1 Serving: Calories 735 (Calories from Fat 540); Fat 60g (Saturated 25g); Cholesterol 225mg; Sodium 220mg; Carbohydrate 1g (Dietary Fiber 0g); Protein 48g

Country-Style Ribs and Sauerkraut

5 servings

SLOW-COOKER SIZE:
3½- to 4-quart

PREP:
10 min

COOK:
Low 8 to 10 hours

Betty's Success Tip

Sauerkraut sometimes can be quite salty. Do a quick taste test before adding it to the slow cooker. If you find it too salty, rinse it in a strainer under cold water, then drain well.

Serving Suggestion

Serve this German-inspired entrée with plenty of rye bread and butter. Offer mugs of cold beer to the adults and apple cider to the kids.

2 pounds pork boneless country-style ribs

1 medium cooking apple, sliced

1 small onion, sliced

1 can (16 ounces) sauerkraut, rinsed and drained

3 tablespoons packed brown sugar

1 teaspoon caraway seed

¼ cup dry white wine or apple juice

Place ribs, apple and onion in 3½- to 4-quart slow cooker. Top with sauerkraut, brown sugar and caraway seed; mix lightly. Pour wine over top.

Cover and cook on low heat setting 8 to 10 hours, until ribs are tender.

1 Serving: Calories 415 (Calories from Fat 190); Fat 21g (Saturated 7g); Cholesterol 10mg; Sodium 670mg; Carbohydrate 17g (Dietary Fiber 3g); Protein 38g

Honey-Dijon Ham

6 servings, with leftovers

SLOW-COOKER SIZE:
4- to 6-quart

PREP:
15 min

COOK:
Low 6 to 8 hours

Ingredient Substitution

Many types of mustard are delicious with ham. If you prefer the taste of country-style mustard, a coarsely ground mustard, or all-American yellow mustard, go ahead and use it— but then you may want to alter the name of the recipe as well!

Serving Suggestion

Baked potatoes and warm dinner rolls complete this family-friendly meal. Provide sour cream, chopped green onions, bacon bits and shredded cheese, and let everyone top their potatoes as they choose.

Leftovers . . . What a Great Idea

Use the leftovers from this meal for Ham and Asparagus Chowder (page 118) and for Supper Ham Frittata (page 153).

5-pound bone-in fully cooked smoked ham

⅓ cup apple juice

¼ cup packed brown sugar

1 tablespoon honey

1 tablespoon Dijon mustard

Place ham in 4- to 6-quart slow cooker. Add apple juice. Mix brown sugar, honey and mustard; spread over ham.

Cover and cook on low heat setting 6 to 8 hours or until ham is hot and glazed.

Remove ham from cooker; place on cutting board. Cut ham in half; reserve one half. Cut remaining half of ham into slices; place on serving platter to serve.

Cut reserved ham into ½-inch cubes. Place 1½ cups cubes in each of 2 resealable plastic food-storage bags. Seal and label bags for Ham and Asparagus Chowder (page 118) and Supper Ham Frittata (page 153). Refrigerate both bags up to 3 days or freeze up to 1 month for later use. If frozen, thaw in refrigerator before using.

1 Serving: Calories 155 (Calories from Fat 45); Fat 5g (Saturated 2g); Cholesterol 50mg; Sodium 1130mg; Carbohydrate 8g (Dietary Fiber 0g); Protein 19g

Honey-Dijon Ham

Ham with Fruit Chutney

8 servings

SLOW-COOKER SIZE:
3½- to 4-quart

PREP:
5 min

COOK:
Low 6 to 8 hours

Serving Suggestion

Serve this easy-to-make ham and fruit chutney with steamed small red potatoes, cooked asparagus spears and crusty sourdough dinner rolls with butter.

Finishing Touch

Spoon fruit chutney into a clear glass bowl and place in the center of a decorative glass platter. Arrange ham slices around the chutney. A jar of colorful spiced crab apples and sprigs of Italian parsley tucked around the ham make a pretty garnish.

3-pound fully cooked smoked boneless ham

¼ teaspoon pepper

2 jars (6 ounces each) fruit chutney (1½ cups)

1 cup dried fruit and raisin mixture (from 6-ounce bag), chopped

1 cup frozen small whole onions (from 1-pound bag)

1 tablespoon balsamic vinegar

Place ham in 3½- to 4-quart slow cooker. Sprinkle with pepper. Mix remaining ingredients; pour over ham.

Cover and cook on low heat setting 6 to 8 hours or until ham is hot.

Remove ham from cooker; place on cutting board. Stir fruit chutney before serving. Cut ham into slices; serve with fruit chutney.

1 Serving: Calories 395 (Calories from Fat 145); Fat 16g (Saturated 5g); Cholesterol 100mg; Sodium 2580mg; Carbohydrate 26g (Dietary Fiber 2g); Protein 39g

Ham with Cheesy Potatoes

8 servings

SLOW-COOKER SIZE:
5- to 6-quart

PREP:
5 min

COOK:
Low 5 to 6 hours

Ingredient Substitution

Omit the ham and this makes a great side dish for roasted chicken, pork chops or loin roast.

1 bag (28 ounces) frozen diced potatoes with onions and peppers, thawed

2 cups shredded Cheddar and Monterey Jack cheese blend (8 ounces)

1 can (10¾ ounces) condensed cream of celery soup

1 container (8 ounces) sour cream

3-pound fully cooked smoked boneless ham

Spray 5- to 6-quart slow cooker with cooking spray. Mix frozen potatoes, cheese, soup and sour cream in cooker. Cut ham lengthwise in half; place ham on potato mixture.

Cover and cook on low heat setting 5 to 6 hours or until potatoes are tender.

Remove ham from cooker; place on cutting board. Gently stir potatoes well before serving. Cut ham into slices; serve with potatoes.

1 Serving: Calories 665 (Calories from Fat 370); Fat 41g (Saturated 17g); Cholesterol 150mg; Sodium 3320mg; Carbohydrate 28g (Dietary Fiber 3g); Protein 49g

Ham and Asparagus Chowder

4 servings

PREP:
5 min

COOK:
15 min

Ingredient Substitution

Fresh green asparagus mixed with pink ham makes this an elegant chowder to serve in springtime, when asparagus is at its peak. However, you can make this chowder with 1½ cups of canned or thawed frozen whole kernel corn and enjoy it all year around.

Serving Suggestion

Mix up a package of corn muffin mix and pop them in the oven before preparing the chowder. Serve with honey to drizzle over the warm muffins.

Leftovers . . . What a Great Idea

This dish uses leftovers from Honey-Dijon Ham (page 114).

1½ cups cubed unpeeled red potatoes

½ cup water

1½ cups 1½-inch pieces fresh asparagus

1 bag (1½ cups) cubed cooked Honey-Dijon Ham (page 114), thawed if frozen

1 can (10¾ ounces) condensed cream of mushroom soup

1 cup milk

Freshly ground black pepper, if desired

Heat potatoes and water to boiling in 2-quart saucepan. Reduce heat to medium; cover and cook 5 minutes or until potatoes are crisp-tender.

Add asparagus and ham; cover and cook 3 to 5 minutes or until thoroughly heated. Stir in soup and milk. Heat over high heat, stirring occasionally, 3 to 5 minutes or until hot. Sprinkle with pepper before serving.

1 Serving: Calories 260 (Calories from Fat 90); Fat 10g (Saturated 3g); Cholesterol 30mg; Sodium 1240mg; Carbohydrate 28g (Dietary Fiber 2g); Protein 15g

Layered Turkey and Sweet Potato Casserole

4 servings

PREP:
10 min

BAKE:
30 min

**Leftovers . . .
What a Great Idea**

This dish uses leftovers from Turkey Breast Stuffed with Wild Rice and Cranberries (page 125).

1 can (18 ounces) vacuum-pack sweet potatoes

1 container (2 cups) Turkey Breast Stuffed with Wild Rice and Cranberries (page 125), thawed if frozen

1 can (10¾ ounces) condensed cream of chicken soup

⅓ cup milk

¼ cup slivered almonds, if desired

Heat oven to 350°. Grease 2-quart casserole.

Mash sweet potatoes with fork; spread in casserole. Spread turkey mixture over sweet potatoes.

Mix soup and milk; spoon over turkey mixture. Sprinkle with almonds.

Bake uncovered about 30 minutes or until hot in center.

1 Serving: Calories 385 (Calories from Fat 90); Fat 10g (Saturated 2g); Cholesterol 60mg; Sodium 650mg; Carbohydrate 53g (Dietary Fiber 6g); Protein 27

Turkey Verde

6 servings

SLOW-COOKER SIZE:
3½- to 4-quart

PREP:
15 min

COOK:
Low 8 to 10 hours

Betty's Success Tip

To warm tortillas before serving, wrap them in aluminum foil and heat in a 325° oven for about 15 minutes. Or place on a microwavable paper towel and microwave on High for 30 seconds.

Ingredient Substitution

Verde means "green" in Spanish, so Turkey Verde simply means turkey in green sauce. Green sauce also complements pork, so try this with a 2½-pound pork boneless loin roast in place of the turkey breast.

2½-pound boneless turkey breast half, thawed if frozen and skin removed

1 jar (16 ounces) mild green salsa

1 medium onion, chopped (½ cup)

1 medium potato, chopped (¾ cup)

4 cloves garlic, finely chopped

½ cup chicken broth

1 teaspoon ground cumin

6 flour tortillas (8 to 10 inches in diameter), warmed

Place turkey in 3½- to 4-quart slow cooker. Mix salsa, onion, potato, garlic, broth and cumin; pour over turkey.

Cover and cook on low heat setting 8 to 10 hours or until turkey is no longer pink when center is cut.

Remove turkey from cooker; place on cutting board. Cut turkey into slices; serve with sauce and tortillas.

1 Serving: Calories 375 (Calories from Fat 45); Fat 5g (Saturated 1g); Cholesterol 125mg; Sodium 700mg; Carbohydrate 35g (Dietary Fiber 3g); Protein 50g

Maple-Glazed Turkey Breast

4 servings

SLOW-COOKER SIZE:
3½- to 6-quart

PREP:
5 min

COOK:
Low 4 to 5 hours

1 package (6 ounces) seasoned long-grain and wild rice

1¼ cups water

1 boneless turkey breast (about 1 pound)

¼ cup maple-flavored syrup

½ cup chopped walnuts

½ teaspoon ground cinnamon

Mix uncooked rice, seasoning packet from rice and water in 3½- to 6-quart slow cooker. Place turkey breast, skin side up, on rice mixture. Drizzle with maple syrup. Sprinkle with walnuts and cinnamon.

Cover and cook on low heat setting 4 to 5 hours or until juice of turkey is no longer pink when center is cut.

1 Serving: Calories 305 (Calories from Fat 90); Fat 10g (Saturated 1g); Cholesterol 75mg; Sodium 170mg; Carbohydrate 25g (Dietary Fiber 1g); Protein 30g

Bacon and Corn Bread–Stuffed Turkey Breast

8 servings

SLOW-COOKER SIZE:
5- to 6-quart

PREP:
25 min

COOK:
Low 7 to 8 hours

STAND:
10 min

Betty's Success Tip

Although you normally remove the netting on a turkey before cooking, in this case leaving it on makes sense because it helps hold the turkey and stuffing together as they cook. Of course, you'll want to remove the netting before serving!

Serving Suggestion

Cooking your Thanksgiving turkey in a slow cooker allows you to spend more time with family and friends instead of being stuck in the kitchen for most of the day. For a traditional holiday meal, serve with cranberry sauce and sweet potatoes.

4 slices bacon, cut into ½-inch pieces

1 cup chopped red and green bell peppers

1 medium onion, chopped (½ cup)

½ cup frozen whole kernel corn

4 cups corn bread stuffing mix

1 teaspoon dried marjoram leaves

½ teaspoon seasoned salt

¼ teaspoon pepper

1½ cups water

3- to 4-pound frozen boneless whole turkey breast, thawed

Cook bacon in 12-inch skillet over medium heat, stirring occasionally, until brown. Stir in bell peppers, onion and corn. Cook 4 to 5 minutes, stirring occasionally, until vegetables are tender. Stir in stuffing mix, marjoram, seasoned salt, pepper and water until moistened.

Leave netting on turkey breast. Cut turkey breast (and netting) lengthwise in half from side without cutting completely through other side. Spoon and spread about 1 cup stuffing mixture onto turkey; fold turkey over filling. Tie 3 or 4 times with string (over netting) to hold together. Spray 5- to 6-quart slow cooker with cooking spray. Place stuffed turkey breast in cooker. Spoon remaining stuffing mixture around turkey.

Cover and cook on low heat setting 7 to 8 hours or until juice of turkey is no longer pink when center is cut. Remove turkey breast from cooker to serving platter; cover with foil. Let stand at room temperature 10 minutes before slicing. Remove string and netting before serving.

1 Serving: Calories 390 (Calories from Fat 110); Fat 12g (Saturated 4g); Cholesterol 100mg; Sodium 810mg; Carbohydrate 30g (Dietary Fiber 2g); Protein 40g

Bacon and Corn Bread–Stuffed Turkey Breast

Turkey Breast with Sherried Stuffing

6 servings

SLOW-COOKER SIZE:
3½- to 4-quart

PREP:
20 min

COOK:
Low 6 to 7 hours

STAND:
10 min

Ingredient Substitution

No sherry on hand? Use apple juice, apple cider or chicken broth instead to keep the stuffing moist and flavorful.

Serving Suggestion

Use any leftover turkey to make sandwiches the next day. Place the sliced turkey (cold or reheated) between slices of whole-grain bread. Reheat the leftover stuffing in the microwave and add a big spoonful of stuffing next to each sandwich. Warm a jar of roasted turkey gravy in the microwave and pour over the sandwiches. What could be easier!

¼ cup chopped onion

1 medium stalk celery, sliced (½ cup)

2- to 2½-pound boneless, skinless turkey breast half, thawed if frozen

1 jar (12 ounces) roasted turkey gravy

⅓ cup dry sherry

1 package (6 ounces) turkey-flavor one-step stuffing mix

Spray 3½- to 4-quart slow cooker with cooking spray. Place onion and celery in cooker. Top with turkey breast half. Pour gravy and sherry over top. Top with dry stuffing.

Cover and cook on low heat setting 6 to 7 hours or until turkey is no longer pink when center is cut.

About 15 minutes before serving, remove turkey from cooker; place on cutting board. Stir stuffing and cooking juices until mixed. Cover and let stand 10 minutes. Cut turkey into slices; serve with stuffing.

1 Serving: Calories 320 (Calories from Fat 55); Fat 6g (Saturated 1g); Cholesterol 100mg; Sodium 870mg; Carbohydrate 27g (Dietary Fiber 1g); Protein 40g

Turkey Breast Stuffed with Wild Rice and Cranberries

10 servings

SLOW-COOKER SIZE:
3½- to 6-quart

PREP:
25 min

COOK:
Low 8 to 9 hours

Leftovers . . .
What a Great Idea

Use extra cooked turkey and stuffing in Layered Turkey and Sweet Potato Casserole (page 119).

Remove stuffing from turkey. Chop turkey and mix with stuffing. Divide mixture among freezer or refrigerator containers, placing 2 cups in each. Cover and refrigerate up to 4 days or freeze up to 4 months. To thaw frozen turkey mixture, place container in refrigerator about 8 hours.

4 cups cooked wild rice

¾ cup finely chopped onion

½ cup dried cranberries

⅓ cup slivered almonds

2 medium peeled or unpeeled cooking apples, coarsely chopped (2 cups)

4- to 5-pound boneless whole turkey breast, thawed if frozen

Mix all ingredients except turkey. Cut turkey into slices at 1-inch intervals about three-fourths of the way through, forming deep pockets.

Place turkey in 3½- to 6-quart slow cooker. Stuff pockets with wild rice mixture. Place remaining rice mixture around edge of cooker.

Cover and cook on low heat setting 8 to 9 hours or until turkey is no longer pink in center.

1 Serving: Calories 400 (Calories from Fat 125); Fat 14g (Saturated 3g); Cholesterol 115mg; Sodium 100mg; Carbohydrate 26g (Dietary Fiber 4g); Protein 47g

Simmering Turkey Breast

12 servings

SLOW-COOKER SIZE:
5-quart

PREP:
15 min

COOK:
Low 8 to 9 hours

Serving Suggestion

Broccoli spears and a tossed green salad are great side dishes that always go well with turkey.

6½-pound bone-in turkey breast, thawed if frozen

1 medium onion, chopped (½ cup)

1 medium stalk celery, chopped (½ cup)

1 bay leaf

1 teaspoon salt

½ teaspoon coarsely ground pepper

1 teaspoon chicken bouillon granules

½ cup water

Remove gravy packet or extra parts from turkey breast. Place onion, celery and bay leaf in cavity of turkey. Place turkey in 5-quart slow cooker.

Sprinkle turkey with salt and pepper. Mix bouillon and water until granules are dissolved; pour over turkey.

Cover and cook on low heat setting 8 to 9 hours or until juice of turkey is no longer pink when center is cut. Remove bay leaf.

1 Serving: Calories 310 (Calories from Fat 115); Fat 13g (Saturated 4g); Cholesterol 125mg; Sodium 410mg; Carbohydrate 1g (Dietary Fiber 0g); Protein 47g

Southwestern Turkey

6 servings

SLOW-COOKER SIZE:
2½- to 4-quart

PREP:
15 min

COOK:
Low 4 to 6 hours

Serving Suggestion

Make some boil-in-the-bag rice as a bed for this yummy turkey. It'll take about 15 minutes to cook. Pop some whole kernel corn into the microwave for a pleasing side dish.

Finishing Touch

Cilantro is a popular herb used in many Southwestern recipes. It has a pungent flavor and aroma with a cool, minty overtone. Sprinkle a couple tablespoons of chopped fresh cilantro over the turkey just before serving to add extra flavor to this dish.

1 tablespoon olive or vegetable oil

1¼ pounds turkey breast tenderloins, cut into 1-inch cubes

1 can (14½ ounces) diced tomatoes with Mexican seasoning, undrained

½ medium green bell pepper, thinly sliced

1 tablespoon chili powder

2 tablespoons lime juice

1 teaspoon sugar

½ teaspoon salt

Heat oil in 12-inch skillet over medium-high heat. Cook turkey in oil 4 to 6 minutes, stirring occasionally, until brown. Place turkey in 2½- to 4-quart slow cooker.

Mix remaining ingredients; pour over turkey.

Cover and cook on low heat setting 4 to 6 hours or until turkey is no longer pink in center.

1 Serving: Calories 125 (Calories from Fat 20); Fat 3g (Saturated 0g); Cholesterol 60mg; Sodium 350mg; Carbohydrate 5g (Dietary Fiber 1g); Protein 23g

Turkey Drumsticks with Plum Sauce

4 servings

SLOW-COOKER SIZE:
5- to 6-quart

PREP:
10 min

COOK:
Low 8 to 10 hours

FINISHING COOK TIME:
High 15 to 20 min

Ingredient Substitution

Plum sauce is a sweet-and-sour sauce made from plums, apricots, sugar and seasonings. You can find it in the Asian-foods section of the supermarket or at an Asian grocery store. If plum sauce isn't available, use apricot or cherry preserves and it will still be delicious!

Serving Suggestion

Keep to the Asian theme by serving this plum-good turkey with crisply cooked pea pods. A fresh salad of assorted melon—cantaloupe, honeydew and watermelon—drizzled lightly with your favorite fruit salad dressing makes a light yet satisfying meal.

4 turkey drumsticks (2½ to 3 pounds), skin removed

½ teaspoon salt

¼ teaspoon pepper

⅔ cup plum sauce

⅓ cup sliced green onions

1 tablespoon soy sauce

1 tablespoon cornstarch

1 tablespoon cold water

3 cups hot cooked rice, for serving

Sprinkle turkey with salt and pepper. Place turkey in 5- to 6-quart slow cooker. Mix plum sauce, green onions and soy sauce; pour over turkey.

Cover and cook on low heat setting 8 to 10 hours or until juice of turkey is no longer pink when centers of thickest pieces are cut.

Remove turkey from cooker. Cover with aluminum foil to keep warm.

Remove any fat from sauce. Mix cornstarch and water; stir into sauce.

Cover and cook on high heat setting 15 to 20 minutes or until sauce has thickened. Cut turkey from drumsticks. Serve with sauce and rice.

1 Serving: Calories 510 (Calories from Fat 80); Fat 9g (Saturated 3g); Cholesterol 210mg; Sodium 680mg; Carbohydrate 50g (Dietary Fiber 1g); Protein 58g

Rosemary Turkey and Sweet Potatoes

6 servings

SLOW-COOKER SIZE:
3½- to 6-quart

PREP:
15 min

COOK:
Low 8 to 10 hours

Betty's Success Tip

Potatoes sometimes take longer to cook than other vegetables or meats in a slow cooker. By putting them into the cooker first, they are in liquid during the long cooking time and will be done in the same time as the other ingredients.

Ingredient Substitution

If you're not a sweet potato lover, use 3 medium white potatoes, cut into 2-inch pieces, instead. There's no need to peel the white potatoes because the skins are nutritious and add a nice color contrast to the green beans.

3 medium sweet potatoes, peeled and cut into 2-inch pieces

1 package (10 ounces) frozen cut green beans

3 turkey thighs (about 3 pounds), skin removed

1 jar (12 ounces) home-style turkey gravy

2 tablespoons all-purpose flour

1 teaspoon parsley flakes

½ teaspoon dried rosemary leaves, crumbled

⅛ teaspoon pepper

Layer sweet potatoes, green beans and turkey in 3½- to 6-quart slow cooker. Mix remaining ingredients until smooth; pour over mixture in cooker.

Cover and cook on low heat setting 8 to 10 hours or until juice of turkey is no longer pink when centers of thickest pieces are cut.

Remove turkey and vegetables from cooker, using slotted spoon. Stir sauce; serve with turkey and vegetables.

1 Serving: Calories 335 (Calories from Fat 70); Fat 8g (Saturated 3g); Cholesterol 155mg; Sodium 450mg; Carbohydrate 26g (Dietary Fiber 4g); Protein 44g

Turkey Teriyaki

4 servings

SLOW-COOKER SIZE:
3½- to 4-quart

PREP:
15 min

COOK:
Low 9 to 10 hours

MICROWAVE:
2 min

Betty's Success Tip

A "teriyaki" recipe simply means it has a marinade made from a mixture of soy sauce, sake (or sherry), sugar, ginger and seasonings. Beef, chicken and fish are commonly used, but you can add a tasty twist to this Japanese-inspired dish by using turkey.

Ingredient Substitution

Fresh gingerroot tastes best in this dish, but if you're out, use ground ginger instead. You can use ¼ to ½ teaspoon of the dried spice in place of the fresh seasoning.

2 bone-in turkey thighs (about 2 pounds), skin removed

½ cup teriyaki baste and glaze (from 12-ounce bottle)

2 tablespoons orange marmalade

½ teaspoon grated gingerroot

1 clove garlic, finely chopped

1 tablespoon water

2 teaspoons cornstarch

Spray 3½- to 4-quart slow cooker with cooking spray. Place turkey in slow cooker. Mix teriyaki glaze, marmalade, gingerroot and garlic; spoon over turkey. Turn turkey to coat with teriyaki mixture.

Cover and cook on low heat setting 9 to 10 hours or until juice of turkey is no longer pink when centers of thickest pieces are cut.

About 10 minutes before serving, remove turkey from cooker; place on serving platter. Remove and discard bones; cut turkey into serving pieces.

Mix water and cornstarch in 2-cup glass measuring cup or small microwavable bowl until smooth. Pour juices from cooker into cornstarch mixture; mix well. Microwave uncovered on High 1 to 2 minutes, stirring once halfway through cooking, until mixture boils and thickens slightly. Serve sauce with turkey.

1 Serving: Calories 255 (Calories from Fat 45); Fat 5g (Saturated 2g); Cholesterol 140mg; Sodium 1480mg; Carbohydrate 14g (Dietary Fiber 0g); Protein 38g

Turkey Sausage–Bean Bake

4 servings

SLOW-COOKER SIZE:
2- to 3½-quart

PREP:
20 min

COOK:
Low 6 to 8 hours

Betty's Success Tip

Dried leaf herbs are called for in most slow cooker recipes because they tend to hold their flavor better than fresh herbs during long cooking times. However, if you have fresh herbs on hand, stir in 1 tablespoon fresh marjoram and 1 teaspoon fresh thyme leaves at the end of the cooking time.

Ingredient Substitution

It doesn't matter what type of beans you use in this recipe. Butter, kidney and black beans are super alternatives to the great Northern beans.

½-pound fully cooked smoked turkey sausage ring, cut into ½-inch slices

⅔ cup shredded carrot

¼ cup chopped onion

2 cans (15½ ounces each) great Northern beans, drained and ¾ cup liquid reserved

1 teaspoon dried marjoram leaves

¼ teaspoon dried thyme leaves

¼ teaspoon pepper

Mix all ingredients including reserved bean liquid in 2- to 3½-quart slow cooker.

Cover and cook on low heat setting 6 to 8 hours or until hot and bubbly, to blend and develop flavors.

1 Serving: Calories 335 (Calories from Fat 55); Fat 6g (Saturated 2g); Cholesterol 30mg; Sodium 580mg; Carbohydrate 55g (Dietary Fiber 14g); Protein 29g

Turkey Sausage Cassoulet

4 servings

SLOW-COOKER SIZE:
2- to 3½-quart

PREP:
20 min

COOK:
Low 6 to 8 hours

Betty's Success Tip

Turkey sausage is lower in fat than pork sausage but still is high in flavor! Check the label on the sausage you select to be sure it is made with turkey breast, which is lower in fat than turkey sausage made with dark meat.

Ingredient Substitution

A *cassoulet* is a classic French dish of dried white beans and various meats. Traditionally, it is covered and cooked very slowly to blend the flavors, so making it in a slow cooker is ideal. This cassoulet takes a shortcut by using canned beans and turkey sausage. You can use any canned beans you have on hand, such as butter, kidney or black beans, and voilà—you'll still have a wonderful cassoulet.

½-pound fully cooked smoked turkey sausage ring, cut into ½-inch slices

1 medium carrot, shredded (⅔ cup)

1 small onion chopped (¼ cup)

2 cans (15 or 16 ounces each) great Northern beans, drained and ¾ cup liquid reserved

1 teaspoon dried marjoram leaves

¼ teaspoon dried thyme leaves

¼ teaspoon pepper

Mix all ingredients including reserved bean liquid in 2- to 3½-quart slow cooker.

Cover and cook on low heat setting 6 to 8 hours or until vegetables are tender.

1 Serving: Calories 340 (Calories from Fat 55); Fat 6g (Saturated 2g); Cholesterol 30mg; Sodium 580mg; Carbohydrate 57g (Dietary Fiber 14g); Protein 29g

Harvest Sausage-Vegetable Casserole

4 servings

SLOW-COOKER SIZE:
3½- to 4-quart

PREP:
20 min

COOK:
Low 7 to 8 hours

Ingredient Substitution

Diced tomatoes come in a variety of flavors such as roasted garlic, crushed red pepper and basil and olive oil, garlic and spices. Feel free to use your favorite in this tasty casserole.

Serving Suggestion

Freshly baked baking powder biscuits are a nice addition to this full-flavored dish. Pass the Dijon mustard for those who want to add a dollop to their stew.

3 tablespoons zesty Italian dressing

1 tablespoon Dijon mustard

2 medium unpeeled potatoes, cut into ½-inch slices (2 cups)

2 medium onions, sliced (1½ cups)

2 medium carrots, cut into ½-inch slices (1 cup)

2 cups chopped green cabbage

1 ring (1 pound) fully cooked smoked turkey or chicken sausage, cut into ½-inch slices

1 can (14½ ounces) diced tomatoes with green pepper, celery and onion, undrained

Mix dressing and mustard. Arrange potato slices in even layer in 3½- to 4-quart slow cooker; drizzle with one-third of the dressing mixture. Arrange onion slices on potatoes; drizzle with one-third of the dressing mixture. Top with carrots and cabbage, drizzle with remaining dressing mixture.

Arrange sausage slices on vegetables. Pour tomatoes in even layer over sausage.

Cover and cook on low heat setting 7 to 8 hours or until vegetables are tender.

1 Serving: Calories 335 (Calories from Fat 135); Fat 15g (Saturated 3g); Cholesterol 60mg; Sodium 1630mg; Carbohydrate 34g (Dietary Fiber 5g); Protein 21g

Brazilian Saffron Chicken and Rice

6 servings

SLOW-COOKER SIZE:
3½- to 4-quart

PREP:
20 min

COOK:
Low 5 to 6 hours

FINISHING COOK TIME:
High 1 hour

Betty's Success Tip

Sometimes bone-in chicken pieces become so tender during cooking that the meat separates and falls from the bone. If this happens, just pick out the bones before serving.

Ingredient Substitution

If you're having a hard time finding yellow rice mix at your grocery store, use an 8-ounce package of chicken-flavored rice mix and ¼ teaspoon ground turmeric instead.

3- to 3½-pound cut-up broiler-fryer chicken

¾ teaspoon garlic salt

1 tablespoon olive or vegetable oil

½ cup chopped fully cooked smoked ham (3 ounces)

1 medium onion, chopped (½ cup)

1 medium red bell pepper, chopped (1 cup)

1 can (14 ounces) chicken broth

1 package (8 ounces) yellow rice mix

⅓ cup sliced pimiento-stuffed olives

Sprinkle chicken with garlic salt. Heat oil in 12-inch skillet over medium-high heat. Cook chicken in oil until brown on all sides; drain. Place chicken in 3½- to 4-quart slow cooker. Top with ham, onion and bell pepper. Add broth.

Cover and cook on low heat setting 5 to 6 hours or until juice of chicken is no longer pink when centers of thickest pieces are cut.

Remove chicken from cooker. Stir rice mix (dry) into mixture in cooker; return chicken to cooker. Cover and cook on high heat setting about 1 hour or until rice is tender. Serve chicken and rice with olives.

1 Serving: Calories 430 (Calories from Fat 145); Fat 16g (Saturated 5g); Cholesterol 95mg; Sodium 930mg; Carbohydrate 36g (Dietary Fiber 1g); Protein 35g

Brazilian Saffron Chicken and Rice

Chicken Cacciatore

6 servings

SLOW-COOKER SIZE:
3½- to 6-quart

PREP:
20 min

COOK:
Low 4 to 6 hours

3- to 3½-pound cut-up broiler-fryer chicken, skin removed

⅓ cup all-purpose flour

1 medium green bell pepper, cut crosswise in half; cut each half into fourths

2 medium onions, cut crosswise in half; cut each half into fourths

1 can (14½ ounces) diced tomatoes, undrained

1 can (4 ounces) sliced mushrooms, drained

1½ teaspoons chopped fresh or ½ teaspoon dried oregano leaves

1 teaspoon chopped fresh or ¼ teaspoon dried basil leaves

½ teaspoon salt

2 cloves garlic, finely chopped

Grated Parmesan cheese, if desired

Place half of the chicken in 3½- to 6-quart slow cooker. Mix bell pepper, onions and remaining ingredients except cheese; spoon half of mixture over chicken. Add remaining chicken; top with remaining vegetable mixture. Cover and cook on low heat setting 4 to 6 hours or until juice of chicken is no longer pink when centers of thickest pieces are cut.

Serve with cheese.

1 Serving: Calories 365 (Calories from Fat 180); Fat 20g (Saturated 5g); Cholesterol 85mg; Sodium 620mg; Carbohydrate 19g (Dietary Fiber 3g); Protein 30g

Coq au Vin

6 servings

SLOW-COOKER SIZE:
3½- to 6-quart

PREP:
10 min

COOK:
Low 4 to 6 hours

FINISHING COOK TIME
High 30 min

Betty's Success Tip

To make a bouquet garni, tie ½ teaspoon dried thyme leaves, 2 large sprigs fresh parsley and 1 bay leaf in cheesecloth bag or place in tea ball. This classic trio of herbs hails from France and is used frequently in many types of recipes.

⅓ cup all-purpose flour

1 teaspoon salt

¼ teaspoon pepper

8 slices bacon

3- to 3½-pound cut-up broiler-fryer chicken, skin removed

¾ cup frozen small whole onions (from 16-ounce bag)

3 cups sliced mushrooms (8 ounces)

1 cup chicken broth

1 cup dry red wine or non-alcoholic red wine

½ teaspoon salt

4 medium carrots, cut into ½-inch slices

1 clove garlic, finely chopped

Bouquet garni

Mix flour, 1 teaspoon salt and the pepper. Coat chicken with flour mixture.

Cook bacon in 12-inch skillet over medium heat until crisp. Remove bacon with slotted spoon and drain on paper towels. Crumble and refrigerate. Cook chicken in bacon fat over medium heat about 15 minutes or until brown on all sides.

Place carrots in 3½- to 6-quart slow cooker. Top with chicken. Mix remaining ingredients except mushrooms and bacon; pour over chicken.

Cover and cook on low heat setting 4 to 6 hours or until juice of chicken is no longer pink when centers of thickest pieces are cut.

Stir in mushrooms and bacon. Cover and cook on high heat setting 30 minutes. Remove bouquet garni; skim off excess fat.

1 Serving: Calories 380 (Calories from Fat 160); Fat 18g (Saturated 5g); Cholesterol 90mg; Sodium 960mg; Carbohydrate 23g (Dietary Fiber 3g); Protein 34g

Chicken Stroganoff Pot Pie

4 servings

SLOW-COOKER SIZE:
3½- to 6-quart

PREP:
20 min

COOK:
Low 4 hours

FINISHING COOK TIME:
High 1 hour 10 min

Betty's Success Tip

A bag of frozen vegetables for stew—potatoes, carrots, onions and peas—is really handy for this recipe.

Ingredient Substitution

If you like, you can use a 1-ounce envelope of beef stroganoff mix instead of chicken gravy. The sauce will have slightly more sour cream flavor.

Serving Suggestion

What's so great about a pot pie is that it is a complete meal—chicken, vegetables and bread—all in one. Add a little crispness and color to the meal by serving a leafy green salad. Toss a bag of romaine salad greens with a drained can of mandarin orange segments and your favorite poppy seed dressing. Sprinkle each serving with some toasted sliced almonds.

1 envelope (0.87 to 1.2 ounces) chicken gravy mix

1 can (10½ ounces) condensed chicken broth

1 pound skinless, boneless chicken breasts, cut into 1-inch pieces

1 bag (16 ounces) frozen stew vegetables, thawed and drained

1 jar (4 ounces) sliced mushrooms, drained

½ cup sour cream

1 tablespoon all-purpose flour

1½ cups Bisquick Original or Reduced Fat baking mix

4 medium green onions, chopped (¼ cup)

½ cup milk

1 cup frozen green peas, thawed

Mix gravy mix and broth in 3½- to 6-quart slow cooker until smooth. Stir in chicken, stew vegetables and mushrooms.

Cover and cook on low heat setting about 4 hours or until chicken is tender.

Mix sour cream and flour. Stir sour cream mixture into chicken mixture. Cover and cook on high heat setting 20 minutes.

Mix baking mix and onions; stir in milk just until moistened. Stir in peas. Drop dough by rounded tablespoonfuls onto chicken-vegetable mixture.

Cover and cook on high heat setting 45 to 50 minutes or until toothpick inserted in center of topping comes out clean. Serve immediately.

1 Serving: Calories 535 (Calories from Fat 155); Fat 17g (Saturated 7g); Cholesterol 95mg; Sodium 2100mg; Carbohydrate 56g (Dietary Fiber 5g); Protein 45g

Chicken Stroganoff Pot Pie

Creamy Chicken Pot Pie

4 servings

SLOW-COOKER SIZE:
3½- to 6-quart

PREP:
20 min

COOK:
Low 4 hours

FINISHING COOK TIME:
High 1 hour 10 min

Betty's Success Tip

A bag of frozen vegetables for stew—potatoes, carrots, onions and peas—is really handy for this recipe. The size the vegetables are cut varies from brand to brand. The good news is that both the small and medium size pieces of vegetables all were done by the end of the cooking time.

Serving Suggestion

What's so great about a pot pie is that it is a complete meal—chicken, vegetables and bread—all in one. Add a little crispness and color to the meal by serving a leafy green salad. Toss a bag of romaine salad greens with a drained can of mandarin orange segments and your favorite poppy seed dressing. Sprinkle each serving with some toasted sliced almonds.

1 envelope (0.87 to 1.2-ounces) chicken gravy mix

1 can (10½ ounces) condensed chicken broth

1 pound skinless, boneless chicken breasts, cut into 1-inch pieces

1 bag (16 ounces) frozen stew vegetables, thawed and drained

1 jar (4 ounces) sliced mushrooms, drained

½ cup sour cream

1 tablespoon all-purpose flour

1½ cups Bisquick Original or Reduced Fat baking mix

4 medium green onions, chopped (¼ cup)

½ cup milk

1 cup frozen green peas, thawed

Mix gravy mix and broth in 3½- to 6-quart slow cooker until smooth. Stir in chicken, stew vegetables and mushrooms.

Cover and cook on low heat setting about 4 hours or until chicken is tender.

Mix sour cream and flour. Stir sour cream mixture into chicken mixture. Cover and cook on high heat setting 20 minutes.

Mix baking mix and onions; stir in milk just until moistened. Stir in peas. Drop dough by rounded tablespoonfuls onto chicken-vegetable mixture.

Cover and cook on high heat setting 45 to 50 minutes or until toothpick inserted in center of topping comes out clean. Serve immediately.

1 Serving: Calories 535 (Calories from Fat 155); Fat 17g (Saturated 7g); Cholesterol 95mg; Sodium 2100mg; Carbohydrate 56g (Dietary Fiber 5g); Protein 45g

Teriyaki Barbecued Chicken Sandwiches

10 Servings

SLOW-COOKER SIZE:
3½- to 4-quart

PREP:
10 min

COOK:
Low 6 to 7 hours

HOLD TIME:
Low up to 2 hours

Betty's Success Tip

Stir-fry sauces are available in many varieties, from salty to sweet and mild to hot and spicy. Look for them in the Asian-foods section of your supermarket. The sauces are usually made from soy sauce, sesame oil, garlic and various spices.

Ingredient Substitution

Up the flavor factor by replacing the regular ketchup with one of the new hot and spicy or mesquite-flavored ketchups currently available.

2 packages (20 ounces each) boneless, skinless chicken thighs (about 24 thighs)

1 envelope (1 ounce) stir-fry seasoning mix

½ cup ketchup

¼ cup stir-fry sauce

2½ cups coleslaw mix

10 kaiser rolls

Place chicken in 3½- to 4-quart slow cooker. Mix seasoning mix (dry), ketchup and stir-fry sauce; pour over chicken.

Cover and cook on low heat setting 6 to 7 hours or until juice of chicken is no longer pink when centers of thickest pieces are cut and chicken is tender.

Pull chicken into shreds, using 2 forks. Stir well to mix chicken with sauce. To serve, place ¼ cup coleslaw mix on roll and top with chicken. Chicken mixture will hold on low heat setting up to 2 hours.

1 Sandwich: Calories 365 (Calories from Fat 110); Fat 12g (Saturated 3g); Cholesterol 70mg; Sodium 760mg; Carbohydrate 34g (Dietary Fiber 3g); Protein 30g

Garlic Chicken with Italian Beans

4 servings

SLOW-COOKER SIZE:
3½- to 4-quart

PREP:
20 min

COOK:
Low 7 to 8 hours

FINISHING COOK TIME:
Low 15 minutes

Ingredient Substitution

If you find your pantry bare when you go to look for diced tomatoes with balsamic vinegar, basil and olive oil, use diced tomatoes with Italian herbs instead.

Serving Suggestion

Serve this Italian-inspired dish with chunks of crusty Italian bread, and provide small bowls of olive oil for dipping. Add steamed broccoli spears for a tasty and colorful meal.

8 large chicken thighs and drumsticks (about 2 pounds)

½ teaspoon salt

¼ teaspoon pepper

1 tablespoon olive or vegetable oil

1 medium bulb garlic, separated into cloves and peeled (about 15 cloves)

1 can (14½ ounces) diced tomatoes with balsamic vinegar, basil and olive oil, undrained

½ cup chicken broth

2 cans (15½ ounces each) great northern beans, rinsed and drained

Basil pesto, if desired

Sprinkle chicken with salt and pepper. Heat oil in 12-inch skillet over medium-high heat. Cook chicken in oil over medium-high heat until brown on all sides; drain.

Place chicken and garlic in 3½- to 4-quart slow cooker. Pour tomatoes and broth over chicken.

Cover and cook on low heat setting 7 to 8 hours or until chicken is no longer pink when centers of thickest pieces are cut.

Remove chicken from cooker; keep warm. Skim fat from surface of juices in cooker. Stir in beans; cover and cook on low heat setting about 15 minutes or until heated through. Serve chicken with beans and pesto.

1 Serving: Calories 700 (Calories from Fat 260); Fat 29g (Saturated 7g); Cholesterol 130mg; Sodium 690mg; Carbohydrate 61g (Dietary Fiber 15g); Protein 64g

Garlic Chicken with Italian Beans

Chicken–Wild Rice Casserole with Dried Cherries

8 servings

SLOW-COOKER SIZE:
6-quart

PREP:
18 min

COOK:
Low 4 to 6 hours

Betty's Success Tip

It's worth taking a few extra minutes to remove the skin from the drumsticks and thighs. The skin doesn't brown during cooking, so it won't enhance the appearance of the dish.

Finishing Touch

This casserole is a great recipe to make for the holidays. The chunky applesauce and dried cherries or cranberries add a sweet and tart flavor. Parmesan cheese and toasted almonds are a natural with wild rice and chicken. Sprinkle a bit of both over the top of this comfort-food casserole.

1½ cups uncooked wild rice

⅓ cup dried cherries or cranberries

1 tablespoon instant chopped onion

1 cup baby-cut carrots

2 medium stalks celery, cut into 2-inch pieces (1 cup)

1 cup chunky applesauce

½ teaspoon salt

8 chicken drumsticks (about 2 pounds), skin removed

8 chicken thighs (about 2 pounds), skin removed

1 can (10¾ ounces) condensed beefy mushroom soup

1 can (14 ounces) chicken broth

2 teaspoons dried thyme leaves

Mix wild rice, cherries, onion, carrots, celery, applesauce and salt in 6-quart slow cooker. Arrange chicken drumsticks and thighs over rice mixture. Pour soup over chicken; pour broth over all. Sprinkle thyme on chicken.

Cover and cook on high heat setting 4 to 6 hours or until wild rice is tender.

1 Serving: Calories 390 (Calories from Fat 80); Fat 9g (Saturated 3g); Cholesterol 95mg; Sodium 710mg; Carbohydrate 42g (Dietary Fiber 4g); Protein 35g

Chicken Legs with Herbed Onion Sauce

5 servings

SLOW-COOKER SIZE:
3½- to 6-quart

PREP:
15 min

COOK:
Low 4 to 5 hours

Ingredient Substitution

Those fresh little pearl onions can be time-consuming to peel, so using the frozen thawed ones saves you a lot of time. If you don't have pearl onions in the freezer, you can slice and use a large yellow or white onion.

Finishing Touch

Serve all that wonderfully flavored sauce spooned over the chicken legs. Tuck a perky sprig of fresh tarragon or rosemary next to the chicken, or sprinkle a little chopped fresh parsley over the top for that special touch.

10 chicken drumsticks (about 2 pounds), skin removed

2 cups frozen (thawed) pearl onions

¼ cup dry white wine or chicken broth

¼ cup canned evaporated milk

2 tablespoons chopped fresh parsley or 2 teaspoons parsley flakes

1 teaspoon dried tarragon leaves

¼ teaspoon salt

¼ teaspoon dried rosemary leaves, crumbled

1 can (10¾ ounces) condensed cream of chicken soup

Place chicken in 3½- to 6-quart slow cooker. Mix remaining ingredients; pour over chicken.

Cover and cook on low heat setting 4 to 5 hours or until juice of chicken is no longer pink when centers of thickest pieces are cut.

1 Serving: Calories 230 (Calories from Fat 70); Fat 8g (Saturated 3g); Cholesterol 105mg; Sodium 640mg; Carbohydrate 11g (Dietary Fiber 1g); Protein 29g

Thai Chicken

4 servings

SLOW-COOKER SIZE:
3½- to 6-quart

PREP:
15 min

COOK:
Low 8 to 9 hours

Betty's Success Tip

The flavors of peanut butter, tomato and hot chile peppers are a popular Thai combination. We took a shortcut and used hot salsa for the tomatoes and chile peppers. For a little less kick, use a milder salsa.

Ingredient Substitution

Had that bottle of fish sauce on your shelf since the last time you cooked Thai? You can replace the soy sauce in this recipe with fish sauce for a more authentic Thai flavor.

8 chicken thighs (about 2 pounds), skin removed

¾ cup hot salsa

¼ cup peanut butter

2 tablespoons lime juice

1 tablespoon soy sauce

1 teaspoon grated fresh gingerroot

¼ cup chopped peanuts

2 tablespoons chopped fresh cilantro

Place chicken in 3½- to 6-quart slow cooker. Mix remaining ingredients except peanuts and cilantro; pour over chicken.

Cover and cook on low heat setting 8 to 9 hours or until juice of chicken is no longer pink when centers of thickest pieces are cut. Remove chicken from cooker, using slotted spoon; place on serving platter.

Remove fat from sauce. Pour sauce over chicken. Sprinkle with peanuts and cilantro.

1 Serving: Calories 380 (Calories from Fat 215); Fat 24g (Saturated 6g); Cholesterol 85mg; Sodium 550mg; Carbohydrate 8g (Dietary Fiber 3g); Protein 36g

Thai Chicken

Sweet-and-Sour Chicken

6 servings

SLOW-COOKER SIZE:
3½- to 4-quart

PREP:
10 min

COOK:
Low 6 to 7 hours

FINISHING COOK TIME:
High 45 to 60 min

Betty's Success Tip

Sweet-and-sour sauces come in a variety of colors, ranging from pink to golden. The golden-colored variety will give this dish the most attractive look. Some sweet-and-sour sauces turn chicken an unsightly bright pink!

Serving Suggestion

There are several types of rice available. You may want to serve this sweet-and-sour dish over brown rice or jasmine rice for a change of pace. For dessert, serve orange sherbet drizzled with chocolate sauce along with coconut cookies.

1½ cups baby-cut carrots

6 large boneless, skinless chicken thighs (about 2 pounds)

½ teaspoon crushed red pepper flakes

1⅓ cups sweet-and-sour sauce

1 can (20 ounces) pineapple chunks in juice, drained

1 bag (1 pound) frozen stir-fry bell peppers and onions, thawed and drained

6 cups hot cooked rice

Place carrots in 3½- to 4-quart slow cooker. Top with chicken; sprinkle with red pepper.

Cover and cook on low heat setting 6 to 7 hours or until juice of chicken is no longer pink when center of thickest pieces are cut.

Remove chicken from cooker; drain and discard liquid from cooker. Return chicken to cooker. Pour sweet-and-sour sauce over chicken; top with pineapple and stir-fry vegetables. Cover and cook on high heat setting 45 to 60 minutes or until carrots are tender. Serve with rice.

1 Serving: Calories 510 (Calories from Fat 80); Fat 9g (Saturated 3g); Cholesterol 55mg; Sodium 270mg; Carbohydrate 82g (Dietary Fiber 4g); Protein 25g

Spicy Chicken in Peanut Sauce

4 servings

SLOW-COOKER SIZE:
4- to 5-quart

PREP:
15 min

COOK:
Low 7 to 8 hours

Betty's Success Tip

This dish, with many ingredients reminiscent of North African cooking, has a mellow, warm, spicy flavor and gets a burst of heat from the tomatoes with green chile peppers.

Serving Suggestion

Pass small bowls of roasted peanuts and chopped fresh cilantro to sprinkle over the chicken. Add warm pita bread wedges and baby carrots to round out the meal. For a sweet ending, dish up scoops of frozen yogurt.

1 tablespoon olive or vegetable oil

8 large chicken thighs (about 3 pounds), skin removed

1 large onion, chopped (1 cup)

2 cans (14½ ounces each) diced tomatoes with green chile peppers, undrained

1 can (14½ ounces) crushed tomatoes, undrained

2 tablespoons honey

1½ teaspoons ground cumin

1 teaspoon ground cinnamon

⅓ cup creamy peanut butter

2 cups hot cooked couscous

Heat oil in 12-inch nonstick skillet over medium-high heat. Cook chicken in oil about 4 minutes, turning once, until brown.

Mix onion, diced and crushed tomatoes, honey, cumin and cinnamon in 4- to 5-quart slow cooker. Place chicken in slow cooker. Spoon tomato mixture over chicken.

Cover and cook on low heat setting 7 to 8 hours or until juice of chicken is no longer pink when centers of thickest pieces are cut.

Stir in peanut butter until melted and well blended. Serve chicken and sauce over couscous.

1 Serving: Calories 670 (Calories from Fat 290); Fat 32g (Saturated 8g); Cholesterol 115mg; Sodium 890mg; Carbohydrate 51g (Dietary Fiber 7g); Protein 51g

Beef and Asparagus over Noodles

4 servings

PREP:
15 min

COOK:
12 min

Betty's Success Tip

The peak season for asparagus is February to June. Watch for it at your local farmers' market and supermarkets, and choose stalks that are bright green and firm with tight tips.

Serving Suggestion

Make a package of roasted garlic mashed potatoes instead of cooking noodles to serve with this easy skillet dish.

Leftovers . . . What a Great Idea

This dish uses leftovers from Beef Roast with Shiitake Mushroom Sauce (page 84).

3 cups uncooked medium egg noodles (6 ounces)

2 cups 1½-inch pieces fresh asparagus spears

½ cup water

1 container cooked Beef Roast with Shiitake Mushroom Sauce (page 84), thawed if frozen

1½ teaspoons Worcestershire sauce

⅛ teaspoon pepper

1 container (8 ounces) sour cream (1 cup)

Cook and drain noodles as directed on package.

While noodles are cooking, heat asparagus and water to boiling in 10-inch skillet over high heat; reduce heat to medium. Cover and cook 3 to 4 minutes or until asparagus is crisp-tender. Stir in beef roast strips with sauce, Worcestershire sauce and pepper. Cover and cook 3 to 4 minutes or until thoroughly heated.

Stir sour cream into beef mixture. Cover and cook 3 to 4 minutes, stirring frequently, until thoroughly heated. Serve over noodles.

1 Serving: Calories 425 (Calories from Fat 155); Fat 17g (Saturated 8g); Cholesterol 135mg; Sodium 430mg; Carbohydrate 36g (Dietary Fiber 2g); Protein 32g

Chinese Beef and Broccoli

4 servings

PREP:
5 min

COOK:
6 min

Betty's Success Tip

Soy sauce, a common ingredient in Chinese and Japanese cuisine, is made from soybeans, wheat, yeast and salt. There are a number of varieties of soy sauce, which vary in color, texture and taste. Soy sauce lasts for a long time and it's best to store it in a cool dark place at room temperature.

Serving Suggestion

Here's a fun way to serve rice. Spray the inside of a ½-cup measuring cup with cooking spray. For each serving, press hot rice into the cup. Place the cup upside down in the bottom of a soup bowl, and unmold the rice. Spoon the beef mixture around the mound of rice.

Leftovers . . . What a Great Idea

This dish uses leftovers from Beef Roast with Shiitake Mushroom Sauce (page 84).

2 cups uncooked instant rice

2¼ cups water

1 container cooked Beef Roast with Shiitake Mushroom Sauce (page 84), thawed if frozen

¼ cup soy sauce

¼ teaspoon ground ginger

1 bag (14 ounces) frozen broccoli flowerets

Cook rice in 2 cups of the water as directed on package.

While rice is cooking, mix beef roast strips with sauce, remaining ¼ cup water, the soy sauce and ginger in 10-inch skillet. Heat to boiling over medium-high heat; stir in frozen broccoli. Cover and cook 5 to 6 minutes, stirring once, until broccoli is tender. Serve over rice.

1 Serving: Calories 375 (Calories from Fat 35); Fat 4g (Saturated 1g); Cholesterol 60mg; Sodium 1660mg; Carbohydrate 54g (Dietary Fiber 3g); Protein 31g

Cheesy Pork Quesadillas

8 sandwiches

PREP:
5 min

COOK:
12 min

Ingredient Substitution

Experiment with different kinds of cheese and flavors of salsa. Try Monterey Jack cheese with jalapeño peppers and garlic-flavored salsa, for example.

Serving Suggestion

These cheesy quesadillas make great appetizers. Stack quesadillas on a decorative platter lined with napkins in festive colors. Let guests add their own quesadilla toppings such as guacamole, sour cream, lettuce, onions and tomatoes.

Leftovers . . . What a Great Idea

This dish uses leftovers from Mexican Pork Roast with Chili Sauce (page 105).

1 container cooked Mexican Pork Roast with Chili Sauce (page 105), thawed if frozen

½ cup sour cream

8 flour tortillas (10 to 12 inches in diameter)

1 cup thick-and-chunky salsa

8 slices (1 ounce each) Monterey Jack cheese, cut in half

Cook pork with sauce in 1½-quart saucepan over medium-high heat, stirring occasionally, until heated.

Meanwhile, spread sour cream over half of each tortilla.

Top sour cream side of each tortilla with ½ cup pork mixture, 1 tablespoon salsa and 2 half-slices cheese. Fold tortilla over onto filling.

Spray 12-inch skillet with cooking spray; heat over medium-high heat. Cook 2 quesadillas at a time in skillet about 3 minutes, turning once, until filling is heated and tortillas are golden brown. Cut into wedges. Serve with remaining salsa.

1 Sandwich: Calories 590 (Calories from Fat 270); Fat 30g (Saturated 13g); Cholesterol 110mg; Sodium 760mg; Carbohydrate 42g (Dietary Fiber 2g); Protein 38g

Supper Ham Frittata

4 servings

PREP:
20 min

COOK:
18 min

Betty's Success Tip

Don't let the word *frittata* throw you. A frittata is the Italian version of the American omelet. In a frittata, the ingredients are mixed in with the eggs instead of folded inside. Unlike omelets, frittatas are firm and round, because they're cooked slowly over low heat and not folded.

Serving Suggestion

This Italian-inspired egg dish makes a great weekend brunch. Serve with steamed fresh asparagus or broccoli spears, toasted English muffins and freshly squeezed orange juice.

Leftovers . . . What a Great Idea

This dish uses leftovers from Honey-Dijon Ham (page 114).

1½ cups frozen Southern-style cubed hash brown potatoes (from 32-ounce bag)

1 medium zucchini, cut into fourths, then sliced (1 cup)

1 bag (1½ cups) cubed cooked Honey-Dijon Ham (page 114), thawed if frozen

4 eggs

¼ cup milk

¼ teaspoon salt

1 cup shredded Cheddar cheese (4 ounces)

Spray 10-inch nonstick skillet with cooking spray; heat over medium-high heat. Cook potatoes, zucchini and ham in skillet 5 to 8 minutes, stirring frequently, until zucchini is crisp-tender and potatoes are thoroughly cooked.

Meanwhile, beat eggs in medium bowl. Add milk and salt; beat well.

Pour egg mixture over mixture in skillet; reduce heat to medium-low. Cover and cook 5 to 7 minutes, lifting edges occasionally to allow uncooked egg mixture to flow to bottom of skillet, until center is set.

Sprinkle cheese over frittata. Cover and cook 2 to 3 minutes or until cheese is melted. Cut into wedges.

1 Serving: Calories 330 (Calories from Fat 155); Fat 17g (Saturated 8g); Cholesterol 260mg; Sodium 830mg; Carbohydrate 21g (Dietary Fiber 1g); Protein 23g

Meatless Main Dishes

Cheesy Ravioli Casserole

10 servings

SLOW-COOKER SIZE:
5- to 6-quart

PREP:
15 min

COOK:
Low 5½ to 6½ hours

HOLD TIME:
Low up to 30 min

Serving Suggestion

Take a loaf of crusty garlic bread to serve with this family-pleasing pasta dish. A bag of mixed salad greens and a bottle of salad dressing makes this a very quick and easy meal to take with you.

1 tablespoon olive or vegetable oil

1 medium onion, chopped (½ cup)

1 large clove garlic, finely chopped

2 jars (26 ounces each) four cheese–flavored tomato pasta sauce

1 can (15 ounces) tomato sauce

1 teaspoon dried Italian seasoning

2 packages (25 ounces each) frozen cheese-filled ravioli

2 cups shredded mozzarella cheese (8 ounces)

¼ cup chopped fresh parsley, if desired

Heat oil in 4-quart Dutch oven or 12-inch skillet over medium heat. Cook onion and garlic in oil about 4 minutes, stirring occasionally, until onion is tender. Stir in pasta sauce, tomato sauce and Italian seasoning.

Spray 5- to 6-quart slow cooker with cooking spray. Place 1 cup of the sauce mixture in cooker. Add 1 package frozen ravioli; top with 1 cup of the cheese. Top with remaining package of ravioli and 1 cup cheese. Pour remaining sauce mixture over top.

Cover and cook on low heat setting 5 hours 30 minutes to 6 hours 30 minutes. Sprinkle with parsley before serving. Ravioli will hold on low heat setting up to 30 minutes.

1 Serving: Calories 500 (Calories from Fat 160); Fat 18g (Saturated 8g); Cholesterol 175mg; Sodium 2110mg; Carbohydrate 57g (Dietary Fiber 5g); Protein 26g

Italian Tomato Sauce

About 4 cups

SLOW-COOKER SIZE:
3½- to 6-quart

PREP:
15 min

COOK:
Low 8 to 10 hours

Betty's Success Tip

This versatile sauce is perfect for meat loaf, meatballs or any variety of pasta. Use sauce immediately, or cover and refrigerate up to 2 weeks or freeze up to 1 year.

2 tablespoons olive or vegetable oil

1 medium onion, chopped (1 cup)

1 small green bell pepper, chopped (½ cup)

2 large cloves garlic, finely chopped

1 can (28 ounces) diced tomatoes, undrained

1 cans (8 ounces) tomato sauce

2 tablespoons chopped fresh or 2 teaspoons dried basil leaves

1 tablespoon chopped fresh or 1 teaspoon dried oregano leaves

½ teaspoon salt

½ teaspoon fennel seed

¼ teaspoon pepper

Mix all ingredients in 3½- to 6-quart slow cooker. Cover and cook on low heat setting 8 to 10 hours.

½ Cup: Calories 80 (Calories from Fat 35); Fat 4g (Saturated 1g); Cholesterol 0mg; Sodium 660mg; Carbohydrate 12g (Dietary Fiber 3g); Protein 2g

Southwest Vegetable Stew

10 servings

SLOW-COOKER SIZE:
6-quart

PREP:
30 min

COOK:
Low 5 to 6 hours

Betty's Success Tip

Pretty much anything goes in this recipe, so feel free to add your favorite beans and root vegetables. You may want to try garbanzo beans, whole green beans or sliced turnips or rutabaga.

Finishing Touch

Instead of sprinkling this hearty meatless stew with cilantro, you can top it with fresh chives or shredded or shavings of Parmesan cheese.

3 medium dark-orange sweet potatoes, peeled and cut into 1-inch pieces (4 cups)

8 small unpeeled red potatoes, cut into 1-inch pieces (4 cups)

4 medium carrots, cut into ½-inch pieces (3 cups)

2 medium parsnips, peeled and cut into ½-inch pieces (2½ cups)

1 medium green bell pepper, cut into ½-inch pieces (1½ cups)

1 medium onion, cut into ½-inch wedges (1 cup)

2 cloves garlic, finely chopped

2 cans (14½ ounces each) stewed tomatoes, undrained

¼ cup tomato paste

1½ teaspoons dried oregano leaves

1½ teaspoons ground cumin

1 teaspoon salt

¼ teaspoon pepper

¼ cup chopped fresh cilantro

Mix all ingredients except cilantro in 6-quart slow cooker.

Cover and cook on low heat setting 5 to 6 hours or until vegetables are tender. Spoon into shallow serving bowls; sprinkle with cilantro.

1 Serving: Calories 210 (Calories from Fat 0); Fat 0g (Saturated 0g); Cholesterol 0mg; Sodium 540mg; Carbohydrate 55g (Dietary Fiber 7g); Protein 5g

Lentils and Veggies

8 servings

SLOW-COOKER SIZE:
3½- to 4-quart

PREP:
15 min

COOK:
Low 4 to 6 hours

Betty's Success Tip

A popular ingredient in the Middle East and India, lentils are a good source of iron and phosphorus. Leftover cooked lentils can be frozen in an air-tight container for up to 2 months. Then reheat, covered, in a microwavable container until warm.

Finishing Touch

This lentil dish is extra delicious when topped with yogurt and shredded coconut to give it an Indian spin. You may also want to stir in a little ground red pepper before adding the toppings.

1 cup dried lentils (8 ounces), sorted and rinsed

2 medium carrots, sliced (1 cup)

1 medium onion, chopped (½ cup)

2 cloves garlic, finely chopped

1 teaspoon dried thyme leaves

¼ teaspoon pepper

2½ cups water

1 can (14½ ounces) diced tomatoes, undrained

1 teaspoon salt

Mix all ingredients except tomatoes and salt in 3½- to 4-quart slow cooker.

Cover and cook on low heat setting 4 to 6 hours or until lentils are tender.

Stir in tomatoes and salt.

1 Serving: Calories 75 (Calories from Fat 0); Fat 0g (Saturated 0g); Cholesterol 0mg; Sodium 380mg; Carbohydrate 18g (Dietary Fiber 6g); Protein 7g

Beans, Beans!

Cooking dried beans in a slow cooker can be tricky because of the variations in electrical power and the types of minerals found in your local water. Beans need sufficient heat to tenderize them; dried beans cooked on the low heat setting for 8 to 10 hours may not be tender. We found three ways to cook dried beans, and you can select the one that best fits your schedule. The most convenient way to cook a dried-bean recipe is to put all the ingredients into the slow cooker and cook on the high heat setting until the beans are tender. We used this method for most of the dried-bean recipes.

Another method is to cook the beans 2 to 3 hours on the high heat setting, then reduce to the low heat setting for 8 to 10 hours. This is a little less convenient because you have to be available after a couple of hours to reduce the heat setting.

A more traditional method for cooking dried beans is to first place the beans and water into the slow cooker. Cover and cook on the high heat setting 2 hours. Turn off the cooker, and let beans stand 8 to 24 hours. Change the water. Add remaining ingredients, and cook on the low heat setting 8 to 12 hours or until done. We used this method for the Old-Fashioned Baked Beans recipe on page 190 because this allows the flavors to blend and offers more of an oven-baked taste.

Lentil and Mixed-Vegetable Casserole

8 servings

SLOW-COOKER SIZE:
3½- to 6-quart

PREP:
5 min

COOK:
Low 2 to 2½ hours

FINISHING COOK TIME:
Low 30 min

Ingredient Substitution

We like the flavors and colors of the broccoli, cauliflower and carrots, but feel free to use any vegetable blend that you like and be creative with this casserole. The same goes for the flavor of the soup—cream of mushroom or cream of broccoli also would make a tasty dish.

Finishing Touch

Sprinkle a cup of shredded mozzarella cheese over the top of the casserole before serving. The heat of the dish will soften the cheese. Sliced process American cheese, cut into strips, or shredded process cheese loaf also works nicely because the cheese will melt on top of the hot dish.

1 pound dried lentils (2 cups), sorted and rinsed

2 cans (14½ ounces each) ready-to-serve vegetable broth

½ teaspoon salt

¼ teaspoon pepper

1 bag (16 ounces) frozen broccoli, cauliflower and carrots, thawed and drained

1 can (10¾ ounces) condensed golden mushroom soup

Mix lentils, broth, salt and pepper in 3½- to 6-quart slow cooker.

Cover and cook on low heat setting 2 to 2½ hours or until lentils are tender.

Stir in vegetables and soup.

Cover and cook on low heat setting about 30 minutes or until vegetable are tender.

1 Serving: Calories 185 (Calories from Fat 25); Fat 3g (Saturated 1g); Cholesterol 0mg; Sodium 880mg; Carbohydrate 38g (Dietary Fiber 14g); Protein 16g

White Beans with Sun-Dried Tomatoes

5 servings

SLOW-COOKER SIZE:
3½- to 6-quart

PREP:
10 min

COOK:
High 4 to 5 hours

Ingredient Substitution

Sun-dried tomatoes add a robust meaty flavor and a bit of chewiness to this dish. You can add a cup of finely chopped seeded fresh tomatoes instead of the sun-dried tomatoes if you want.

Serving Suggestion

Serve with a large crisp tossed green salad dressed with an olive oil-balsamic vinaigrette, along with slices of French baguette. A glass of red wine makes this a perfect meal.

1 pound dried great Northern beans (2 cups), sorted and rinsed

2 cloves garlic, crushed

6 cups water

1½ teaspoons dried basil leaves

1 teaspoon salt

¼ teaspoon pepper

¾ cup finely chopped sun-dried tomatoes in olive oil

1 can (2¼ ounces) sliced ripe olives, drained

Mix all ingredients except tomatoes and olives in 3½- to 6-quart slow cooker.

Cover and cook on high heat setting 4 to 5 hours or until beans are tender.

Stir in tomatoes and olives.

1 Serving: Calories 300 (Calories from Fat 35); Fat 4g (Saturated 1g); Cholesterol 0mg; Sodium 640mg; Carbohydrate 62g (Dietary Fiber 16g); Protein 23g

White Beans with Sun-Dried Tomatoes

Savory Garbanzo Beans with Vegetables

8 servings

SLOW-COOKER SIZE:
3½- to 6-quart

PREP:
15 min

COOK:
High 4 to 5 hours

FINISHING COOK TIME:
20 min

Betty's Success Tip

Sautéing the vegetables in olive oil before stirring them into the cooked beans not only enhances the flavor but also helps to reduce some of the liquid from the fresh mushrooms.

Ingredient Substitution

A drained 8-ounce can of sliced mushrooms can be used instead of the fresh mushrooms. You can skip the sautéing in step 3 and just add the canned mushrooms, carrots, onions and garlic to the cooked beans. Stir in a tablespoon of olive oil for added flavor.

1 pound dried garbanzo beans (2 cups), sorted and rinsed

5½ cups water

1 teaspoon salt

½ teaspoon pepper

2 tablespoons olive or vegetable oil

2 cups sliced mushrooms

1 cup shredded carrots (1½ medium)

4 medium green onions, thinly sliced (¼ cup)

2 cloves garlic, finely chopped

2 tablespoons lemon juice

1 to 2 tablespoons prepared horseradish

2 teaspoons mustard

Place beans, water, salt and pepper in 3½- to 6-quart slow cooker.

Cover and cook on high heat setting 4 to 5 hours or until beans are tender.

Heat oil in 12-inch skillet over medium heat. Cook mushrooms, carrots, onions, and garlic in oil about 5 minutes, stirring occasionally, until vegetables are tender. Stir vegetables into beans. Stir in remaining ingredients.

Cover and cook on high heat setting 15 minutes to blend flavors.

1 Serving: Calories 210 (Calories from Fat 65); Fat 7g (Saturated 1g); Cholesterol 0mg; Sodium 330mg; Carbohydrate 36g (Dietary Fiber 10g); Protein 11g

Tex-Mex Pinto Beans

6 servings

SLOW-COOKER SIZE:
3½- to 6-quart

PREP:
10 min

COOK:
High 7 to 9 hours

Ingredient Substitution

To make this easy recipe even easier, use ¼ teaspoon garlic powder or ½ teaspoon chopped garlic from a jar to save a few minutes.

Serving Suggestion

Nothing complements beans like hot corn bread slathered with butter. Add a big bowl of your favorite creamy cabbage salad and tall glasses of lemonade and feel like you're on a "picnic" at your supper table.

1 pound dried pinto beans (2 cups), sorted and rinsed

1 large onion, chopped (1 cup)

2 cloves garlic, finely chopped

6½ cups water

1 tablespoon chili powder

1½ teaspoons salt

½ teaspoon pepper

Mix all ingredients in 3½- to 6-quart slow cooker.

Cover and cook on high heat setting 7 to 9 hours or until beans are tender.

1 Serving: Calories 200 (Calories from Fat 10); Fat 1g (Saturated 0g); Cholesterol 0mg; Sodium 610mg; Carbohydrate 49g (Dietary Fiber 16g); Protein 15g

Spicy Black-Eyed Peas

8 servings

SLOW-COOKER SIZE:
3½- to 6-quart

PREP:
5 min

COOK:
High 3 to 4 hours

FINISHING COOK TIME:
High 10 min

Betty's Success Tip

We like the extra flavor of hot salsa that goes so well with black-eyed peas, but you use whichever salsa suits your family's taste—mild, medium or hot.

Serving Suggestion

Cooked greens, such as spinach, mustard or collards, are the perfect mate for black-eyed peas. Serve the greens with red wine vinegar to splash on top. Warm cornbread with molasses completes the meal.

1 pound dried black-eyed peas (2 cups), sorted and rinsed

1 medium onion, chopped (½ cup)

6 cups water

1 teaspoon salt

½ teaspoon pepper

¾ cup medium or hot salsa

Mix all ingredients except salsa in 3½- to 6-quart slow cooker.

Cover and cook on high heat setting 3 to 4 hours or until peas are tender.

Stir in salsa.

Cover and cook on high heat setting about 10 minutes or until hot.

1 Serving: Calories 145 (Calories from Fat 10); Fat 1g (Saturated 0g); Cholesterol 0mg; Sodium 360mg; Carbohydrate 35g (Dietary Fiber 11g); Protein 13g

Cuban Black Beans and Rice

6 servings

SLOW-COOKER SIZE:
3½- to 6-quart

PREP:
20 min

COOK:
High 6 to 8 hours

Serving Suggestion

Try serving these black beans with poached eggs instead of rice. Place a poached egg on top of each serving of beans. Spoon your favorite salsa or drizzle hot sauce onto the egg, and top it off with a sprinkle of shredded Cheddar cheese and chopped fresh cilantro.

Finishing Touch

Serve bowls of chopped red onion and hard-cooked eggs to sprinkle on top for a traditional black bean and rice dish.

1 pound dried black beans (2 cups), sorted and rinsed

1 large onion, chopped (1 cup)

1 large bell pepper, chopped (1½ cups)

5 cloves garlic, finely chopped

2 bay leaves

1 can (14½ ounces) diced tomatoes, undrained

5 cups water

2 tablespoons olive or vegetable oil

4 teaspoons ground cumin

2 teaspoons finely chopped jalapeño chile pepper

1 teaspoon salt

3 cups hot cooked rice, for serving

Mix all ingredients except rice in 3½- to 6-quart slow cooker.

Cover and cook on high heat setting 6 to 8 hours or until beans are tender and most of the liquid is absorbed. Remove bay leaves.

Serve beans over rice.

1 Serving: Calories 385 (Calories from Fat 55); Fat 6g (Saturated 1g); Cholesterol 0mg; Sodium 500mg; Carbohydrate 78g (Dietary Fiber 14g); Protein 19g

Barley–Pine Nut Casserole

5 servings

SLOW-COOKER SIZE:
3½- to 6-quart

PREP:
15 min

COOK:
Low 6 to 8 hours

Betty's Success Tip

Pearl barley, which is the most common form, is the perfect grain to cook in the slow cooker. The long, slow cooking produces barley that is tender but not gummy.

Ingredient Substitution

Pine nuts, or piñons, are the sweet edible seeds of pine trees that grow in the southwestern United States and in Mexico. Toasted, they add an interesting nutty flavor and texture to the casserole, but almonds can be substituted. Try the spicy eight-vegetable juice for a more robust flavor.

1 cup uncooked pearl barley

1½ cups eight-vegetable juice

½ teaspoon salt

¼ teaspoon pepper

2 medium stalks celery, sliced (1 cup)

1 medium bell pepper, chopped (1 cup)

1 medium onion, chopped (½ cup)

1 can (14½ ounces) ready-to-serve vegetable broth

4 medium green onions, sliced (¼ cup)

¼ cup pine nuts, toasted

Mix all ingredients except green onions and nuts in 3½- to 6-quart slow cooker.

Cover and cook on low heat setting 6 to 8 hours or until barley is tender.

Stir in green onions and nuts.

1 Serving: Calories 190 (Calories from Fat 35); Fat 4g (Saturated 1g); Cholesterol 0mg; Sodium 800mg; Carbohydrate 41g (Dietary Fiber 9g); Protein 6g

Three-Grain Medley

6 servings

SLOW-COOKER SIZE:
3½- to 6-quart

PREP:
10 min

COOK:
Low 4 to 6 hours

Betty's Success Tip

If you can't find wheat berries at your local market, check out any natural foods store.

Ingredient Substitution

Instead of the pimientos, soak sun-dried tomatoes in water until tender, then chop them and add to this grain mixture. Use about ¼ cup of the chopped tomatoes.

Serving Suggestion

Use this scrumptious grain filling to stuff bell pepper shells. Steam cleaned bell pepper halves (any color that you are in the mood for) just until tender so that they still hold their shape. Spoon the hot cooked grain mixture into the halves, and sprinkle with shredded Parmesan cheese.

⅔ cup uncooked wheat berries

½ cup uncooked pearl barley

½ cup uncooked wild rice

¼ cup chopped fresh parsley

¼ cup margarine or butter, melted

2 teaspoons finely shredded lemon peel

6 medium green onions, thinly sliced (6 tablespoons)

2 cloves garlic, finely chopped

2 cans (14½ ounces each) ready-to-serve vegetable broth

1 jar (2 ounces) diced pimientos, undrained

Mix all ingredients in 3½- to 6-quart slow cooker.

Cover and cook on low heat setting 4 to 6 hours or until liquid is absorbed. Stir before serving.

1 Serving: Calories 230 (Calories from Fat 70); Fat 8g (Saturated 0g); Cholesterol 0mg; Sodium 710mg; Carbohydrate 40g (Dietary Fiber 7g); Protein 6g

Mediterranean Bulgur and Lentils

8 servings

SLOW-COOKER SIZE:
3½- to 6-quart

PREP:
15 min

COOK:
Low 3 to 4 hours

FINISHING COOK TIME:
High 15 min

Serving Suggestion

You have a little of everything in one dish—grains, vegetables and cheese. A green salad made of tender Bibb lettuce is a nice addition. Serve with olive oil to drizzle on the greens and lemon wedges to squeeze over the top. Use warm pita bread wedges to scoop up every bit of this dish.

Finishing Touch

Before sprinkling the feta over this Mediterranean-inspired dish, stir together an 8-ounce container of plain yogurt and 1½ teaspoons dried mint leaves or 1 tablespoon chopped fresh mint leaves. Spoon over the dish, then top with the feta. You'll love the refreshing mint flavor.

1 cup uncooked bulgur or cracked wheat

½ cup dried lentils, sorted and rinsed

1 teaspoon ground cumin

¼ teaspoon salt

3 cloves garlic, finely chopped

1 can (15¼ ounces) whole kernel corn, drained

2 cans (14½ ounces each) ready-to-serve vegetable broth

2 medium tomatoes, chopped (1½ cups)

1 can (2¼ ounces) sliced ripe olives, drained

1 cup crumbled feta cheese

Mix all ingredients except tomatoes, olives and cheese in 3½- to 6-quart slow cooker.

Cover and cook on low heat setting 3 to 4 hours or until lentils are tender.

Stir in tomatoes and olives.

Cover and cook on high heat setting 15 minutes.

Top with cheese.

1 Serving: Calories 200 (Calories from Fat 55); Fat 6g (Saturated 3g); Cholesterol 15mg; Sodium 920mg; Carbohydrate 34g (Dietary Fiber 8g); Protein 10g

Bulgur Pilaf with Broccoli and Carrots

8 servings

SLOW-COOKER SIZE:
3½- to 6-quart

PREP:
20 min

COOK:
Low 6 to 8 hours

FINISHING COOK TIME:
High 15 min

Betty's Success Tip

Chop the broccoli into about ½-inch pieces, so they will be tender but still a little crisp when cooked. Or use 4 cups of thawed frozen chopped broccoli to save some time. Cut up large pieces so they all will cook in the same amount of time.

Ingredient Substitution

Cauliflower is less colorful but just as tasty. A light sprinkling of ground nutmeg over the melted cheese will add a delicate spicy flavor and a bit of color.

2 cups uncooked bulgur or cracked wheat

1 tablespoon margarine or butter, melted

1 teaspoon salt

4 medium carrots, shredded (2⅔ cups)

1 large onion, chopped (1 cup)

2 cans (14½ ounces each) ready-to-serve vegetable broth

4 cups chopped fresh broccoli

1 cup shredded Colby cheese (4 ounces)

Mix all ingredients except broccoli and cheese in 3½- to 6-quart slow cooker.

Cover and cook on low setting 6 to 8 hours or just until bulgur is tender.

Stir in broccoli. Sprinkle with cheese. Cover and cook on high setting about 15 minutes or until broccoli is tender and cheese is melted.

1 Serving: Calories 205 (Calories from Fat 65); Fat 7g (Saturated 3g); Cholesterol 15mg; Sodium 880mg; Carbohydrate 35g (Dietary Fiber 9g); Protein 10g

Substantial Sides and Vegetables

Garlic-Parmesan Smashed Potatoes

12 servings

SLOW-COOKER SIZE:
3½- to 4-quart

PREP:
20 min

COOK:
High 4 to 6 hours

HOLD TIME:
Low up to 2 hours

Betty's Success Tip

You've read it right—these potatoes are smashed, not mashed—which means that there should be some lumps left. Both the lumps and potato skins add robust texture, which you don't get with regular mashed potatoes. If you don't have a potato masher on hand, using a large fork will do the trick.

Ingredient Substitution

If you want to trim a few calories during the holidays, use fat-free half-and-half in this recipe instead of regular half-and-half. No one will guess because the potatoes will still be rich and tasty.

8 medium unpeeled russet potatoes, cut into ¾- to 1-inch pieces (8 cups)

2 cloves garlic, finely chopped

¼ cup butter or margarine

½ teaspoon salt

¼ teaspoon pepper

1 cup water

½ cup half-and-half

¾ cup shredded Parmesan cheese

¼ cup chopped fresh basil leaves

Place potatoes in 3½- to 4-quart slow cooker. Stir in garlic, butter, salt, pepper and water.

Cover and cook on high heat setting 4 to 6 hours or until potatoes are tender.

Do not drain potatoes. Mash potatoes slightly with potato masher. Add half-and-half and cheese; continue mashing until desired consistency and some lumps remain. Stir in basil just before serving. Potatoes will hold on low heat setting up to 2 hours.

1 Serving: Calories 165 (Calories from Fat 65); Fat 7g (Saturated 4g); Cholesterol 20mg; Sodium 250mg; Carbohydrate 21g (Dietary Fiber 2g); Protein 5g

Creamed Potatoes with Garden Peas

10 servings

3½- to 4-quart

PREP:
10 min

COOK:
High 3 to 4 hours

FINISHING COOK TIME:
High 20 to 30 min

Betty's Success Tip

The peas are added at the end so they maintain their texture and bright green color. If you don't have 30 minutes for them to warm through, just cook the peas separately in the microwave oven and stir in.

Finishing Touch

To make this luscious side dish even more appealing, sprinkle chopped fresh chives or chopped fresh or dried dill weed on top before serving.

2 pounds small red potatoes (2 to 3 inches in diameter), cut into ¼-inch slices (8 cups)

4 medium green onions, sliced (¼ cup)

2 cloves garlic, finely chopped

1 container (10 ounces) refrigerated Alfredo pasta sauce

½ cup half-and-half or milk

½ teaspoon salt

⅛ teaspoon pepper

1½ cups frozen green peas (from 1-pound bag)

Spray 3½- to 4-quart slow cooker with cooking spray. Layer half each of the potatoes, onions and garlic in cooker. Mix pasta sauce, half-and-half, salt and pepper; spoon half of mixture over potatoes and onions. Layer with remaining potatoes, onions, garlic and sauce mixture. Do not stir.

Cover and cook on high heat setting 3 to 4 hours.

About 30 minutes before serving, sprinkle peas over potato mixture. Cover and cook on high heat setting 20 to 30 minutes or until peas are hot. Stir gently before serving.

1 Serving: Calories 215 (Calories from Fat 100); Fat 11g (Saturated 7g); Cholesterol 30mg; Sodium 270mg; Carbohydrate 24g (Dietary Fiber 3g); Protein 5g

Scalloped Potatoes

8 servings

SLOW-COOKER SIZE:
3½- to 6-quart

PREP:
15 min

COOK:
Low 10 to 12 hours

Ingredient Substitution

Vary the taste by using whatever cream soup you have on hand, such as cream of mushroom, chicken or broccoli. You may want to add a thinly sliced small onion or ¼ teaspoon onion powder if you decide not to use the onion soup.

Finishing Touch

For the cheese lovers in your family, sprinkle about ½ cup of their favorite shredded cheese over the top of the potatoes. Cover and let stand a few minutes so the cheese becomes warm and melty.

6 medium potatoes (2 pounds), cut into ⅛-inch slices

1 can (10¾ ounces) condensed cream of onion soup

1 can (5 ounces) evaporated milk (⅔ cup)

1 jar (2 ounces) diced pimientos, undrained

½ teaspoon salt

¼ teaspoon pepper

Spray inside of 3½- to 6-quart slow cooker with cooking spray.

Mix all ingredients; pour into cooker.

Cover and cook on low heat setting 10 to 12 hours or until potatoes are tender.

1 Serving: Calories 155 (Calories from Fat 25); Fat 3g (Saturated 1g); Cholesterol 10mg; Sodium 460mg; Carbohydrate 30g (Dietary Fiber 2g); Protein 4g

Herbed Potatoes and Peppers

14 servings

SLOW-COOKER SIZE:
3½- to 4-quart

PREP:
15 min

COOK:
High 4 to 6 hours

Serving Suggestion

Refrigerate the leftovers, and serve them the next day as a delicious potato salad. Tangy and tomatoey, it makes a nice change from the usual mayonnaise-based potato salad and it's delicious with grilled chicken breast, hamburger patties or pork chops.

Finishing Touch

If you like your bell peppers with a bit of crunch, add them to the mixture during the last 15 minutes of cooking.

2 pounds small red potatoes, cut into eighths

1 medium green bell pepper, cut into strips

1 medium red bell pepper, cut into strips

2 cloves garlic, finely chopped

½ cup water

1½ teaspoons salt

1 teaspoon dried basil leaves

1 teaspoon dried oregano leaves

1 can (14½ ounces) diced tomatoes, undrained

Shredded Parmesan cheese, if desired

Place potatoes in 3½- to 4-quart slow cooker.

Layer bell peppers and garlic over potatoes. Pour water into cooker. Top with remaining ingredients except cheese, adding tomatoes last.

Cover and cook on high heat setting 4 to 6 hours or until potatoes are tender. Serve with cheese.

1 Serving: Calories 70 (Calories from Fat 0); Fat 0g (Saturated 0g); Cholesterol 0mg; Sodium 300mg; Carbohydrate 16g (Dietary Fiber 2g); Protein 2g

Hot German Potato Salad

6 servings

SLOW-COOKER SIZE:
3½- to 6-quart

PREP:
15 min

COOK:
Low 8 to 10 hours

Betty's Success Tip

We like to leave the skins on the potatoes because they are nutritious and add an interesting color to this hot salad. But you can peel the potatoes if you like.

Serving Suggestion

Create a simple German meal by serving this salad with grilled bratwurst or Polish sausage in buns. Crocks of dilled pickles or pickled beets and jars of mustard will add the final touch. To keep it simple, finish off the meal with crisp, juicy apples for dessert.

Finishing Touch

Add a touch of color and freshness by stirring in 3 tablespoons chopped fresh parsley with the bacon.

1 Serving: Calories 160 (Calories from Fat 20); Fat 2g (Saturated 1g); Cholesterol 5mg; Sodium 470mg; Carbohydrate 35g (Dietary Fiber 3g); Protein 4g

5 medium potatoes (about 1¾ pounds), cut into ¼-inch slices

1 large onion, chopped (1 cup)

⅓ cup water

⅓ cup cider vinegar

2 tablespoons all-purpose flour

2 tablespoons sugar

1 teaspoon salt

½ teaspoon celery seed

¼ teaspoon pepper

4 slices crisply cooked bacon, crumbled

Mix potatoes and onion in 3½- to 6-quart slow cooker. Mix remaining ingredients except bacon; pour into cooker.

Cover and cook on low heat setting 8 to 10 hours or until potatoes are tender.

Stir in bacon.

Smoky Cheese and Potato Bake

14 servings

SLOW-COOKER SIZE:
3½- to 4-quart

PREP:
10 min

COOK:
Low 5 to 6 hours

Betty's Success Tip

If curiosity is getting the better of you, and you want to see what's happening to the food in your slow cooker, don't give in! Just spin the slow cooker lid to dissipate the moisture rather than lifting it. You add time to the cooking process every time you lift the lid.

Ingredient Substitution

Vary the taste by using whatever creamed soup you have on hand, such as cream of onion, chicken or broccoli.

1 can (10¾ ounces) condensed cream of mushroom soup

1 container (8 ounces) sour cream (1 cup)

1 round (7 ounces) hickory-smoked Gouda cheese, cut into ½-inch cubes

⅓ cup drained roasted red bell pepper strips (from 7-ounce jar)

1 bag (32 ounces) frozen Southern-style cubed hash brown potatoes (8 cups), thawed

2 tablespoons chopped fresh chives

Spray 3½- to 4-quart slow cooker with cooking spray. Mix soup, sour cream and cheese in medium bowl. Gently stir in bell pepper strips.

Arrange half of the potatoes in cooker. Top with half of the sour cream mixture; spread evenly. Top with remaining potatoes and sour cream mixture, spreading evenly. Do not stir.

Cover and cook on low heat setting 5 to 6 hours. Sprinkle chives over potatoes before serving.

1 Serving: Calories 180 (Calories from Fat 70); Fat 8g (Saturated 5g); Cholesterol 25mg; Sodium 320mg; Carbohydrate 21g (Dietary Fiber 1g); Protein 6g

Sour Cream and Onion Potato Casserole

24 servings

SLOW-COOKER SIZE:
3½- to 4-quart

PREP:
5 min

COOK:
Low 5 to 6 hours

HOLD TIME:
Low up to 2 hours

Betty's Success Tip

Make sure you use melted butter or margarine in this recipe, because solid butter or margarine will not coat the hash browns as evenly.

Ingredient Substitution

Can't find chive and onion sour cream potato topper at your supermarket? Make your own by adding ½ cup chopped fresh or 3 tablespoons dried chives and 1 teaspoon onion salt to three 8-ounce containers of sour cream.

3 packages (5.2 ounces each) hash brown potato mix

3 tablespoons butter or margarine, melted

5 cups water

1 can (10¾ ounces) condensed cream of mushroom soup

2 containers (12 ounces each) chive and onion sour cream potato topper

2 cups shredded Cheddar and American cheese blend (8 ounces)

½ cup French-fried onions (from 2.8-ounce can)

Toss potatoes (dry) and butter in 3½- to 4-quart slow cooker. Stir in water, soup, potato topper and cheese.

Cover and cook on low heat setting 5 to 6 hours or until liquid is absorbed.

To serve, sprinkle onions on top. Potatoes will hold on low heat setting up to 2 hours.

1 Serving: Calories 140 (Calories from Fat 90); Fat 10g (Saturated 6g); Cholesterol 25mg; Sodium 410mg; Carbohydrate 8g (Dietary Fiber 1g); Protein 4g

Sweet Potatoes with Applesauce

6 servings

SLOW-COOKER SIZE:
2- to 3½-quart

PREP:
15 min

COOK:
Low 6 to 8 hours

Betty's Success Tip

The variety of sweet potatoes with dark orange skin is often labeled as "yams." The very light-colored sweet potatoes are not as sweet and are drier than the darker-skin ones. We like the darker-skin sweet potatoes (or "yams") for this dish because they not only make a richer colored dish but also a tastier, sweeter one.

Serving Suggestion

While the turkey roasts in the oven, cook this Thanksgiving favorite in the cooker. If your home is this year's holiday gathering spot for family and friends, you can double or triple this recipe and cook it in a 5- to 6-quart cooker. And it will stay warm for second helpings.

6 medium sweet potatoes or yams (2 pounds), peeled and cut into ½-inch cubes

1½ cups applesauce

⅔ cup packed brown sugar

3 tablespoons margarine or butter, melted

1 teaspoon ground cinnamon

½ cup chopped nuts, toasted

Place sweet potatoes in 2- to 3½-quart slow cooker. Mix remaining ingredients except nuts; spoon over potatoes.

Cover and cook on low heat setting 6 to 8 hours or until potatoes are very tender.

Sprinkle with nuts.

1 Serving: Calories 350 (Calories from Fat 115); Fat 13g (Saturated 2g); Cholesterol 0mg; Sodium 100mg; Carbohydrate 60g (Dietary Fiber 5g); Protein 3g

Sweet Potatoes with Orange-Pecan Butter

12 servings

SLOW-COOKER SIZE:
5- to 6-quart

PREP:
10 min

COOK:
Low 7 to 8 hours

Ingredient Substitution

If there's someone in your family who's not a fan of sweet potatoes, prepare this updated classic using half russet potatoes and half sweet potatoes instead.

Finishing Touch

The Orange-Pecan Butter can be pressed into a 1-cup mold that has been lined with plastic wrap. Cover with plastic wrap and refrigerate 2 hours or until firm. Unmold the butter onto a small serving plate.

12 unpeeled dark-orange sweet potatoes (6 to 8 ounces each)

2 tablespoons butter or margarine, melted

1 teaspoon seasoned salt

½ teaspoon coarsely ground pepper

Orange-Pecan Butter (below)

Pierce sweet potatoes with fork. Brush each potato with melted butter. Sprinkle with seasoned salt and pepper. Wrap potatoes individually in aluminum foil. Place in 5- to 6-quart slow cooker.

Cover and cook on low heat setting 7 to 8 hours or until tender.

Meanwhile, make Orange-Pecan Butter.

Remove potatoes from cooker; remove foil. Serve potatoes with Orange-Pecan Butter.

Orange-Pecan Butter

½ cup chopped pecans

½ cup butter or margarine, softened

¼ cup orange marmalade

1 tablespoon cream sherry, if desired

Heat oven to 375°. Place pecans in shallow baking pan. Bake 4 to 6 minutes or until toasted; cool slightly. Mix butter, marmalade, sherry and pecans in small bowl. Spoon into decorative serving bowl. Serve butter at room temperature. Store in refrigerator.

1 Serving: Calories 250 (Calories from Fat 110); Fat 12g (Saturated 6g); Cholesterol 25mg; Sodium 130mg; Carbohydrate 33g (Dietary Fiber 4g); Protein 3g

Candied Sweet Potatoes

12 servings

SLOW-COOKER SIZE:
3½- to 4-quart

PREP:
35 min

COOK:
Low 6 to 8 hours

FINISHING COOK TIME:
Low 10 min

Betty's Success Tip

Many varieties of sweet potatoes are sold in supermarkets. The sweet potatoes with darker skin (often labeled "yams") not only make a richer-colored dish, but also a tastier, sweeter one. The very light-colored sweet potatoes are not as sweet and are often drier.

Serving Suggestion

Put the emphasis on candied and marshmallow when passing this dish around the Thanksgiving table, and kids will have a hard time not trying a bite. Serve with turkey, cranberry sauce, mashed potatoes and gravy.

4 pounds dark-orange sweet potatoes (about 10), peeled and cut into 1-inch cubes

¾ cup butter or margarine

2 cups packed brown sugar

½ cup orange juice

1 tablespoon ground cinnamon

2 teaspoons grated lemon peel

2 teaspoons salt

½ teaspoon ground nutmeg

2 cups miniature marshmallows or 25 large marshmallows

Place sweet potatoes in 3½- to 4-quart slow cooker.

Place butter in medium microwavable bowl. Microwave uncovered on High about 1 minute or until melted. Stir in remaining ingredients except marshmallows; pour over sweet potatoes. Stir to coat sweet potatoes with butter mixture.

Cover and cook on low heat setting 6 to 8 hours or until potatoes are very tender.

Sprinkle marshmallows over potatoes. Cover and cook on low heat setting about 10 minutes or until marshmallows are melted. Serve with a slotted spoon.

1 Serving: Calories 405 (Calories from Fat 110); Fat 12g (Saturated 7g); Cholesterol 30mg; Sodium 500mg; Carbohydrate 72g (Dietary Fiber 4g); Protein 2g

Creamy Wild Rice

10 servings

SLOW-COOKER SIZE:
5- to 6-quart

PREP:
15 min

COOK:
Low 8 to 9 hours

Betty's Success Tip

Wash wild rice in water before cooking it. Place the rice in a bowl of cold water and swirl it around with your hand. When the water becomes cloudy, drain the rice. Repeat the process until the water remains clear.

Serving Suggestion

Do you have a chicken or turkey roasting in the oven? The flavors of this wild rice dish go perfectly with them and can be made in the cooker, so you don't have to crowd the oven. Open a can of cranberry sauce, cook some green beans in the microwave, mash some potatoes and dinner will be ready in no time.

1½ cups uncooked wild rice

2¼ cups water

½ teaspoon rubbed sage

½ teaspoon salt

¼ teaspoon pepper

1 medium onion, chopped (½ cup)

1 can (10¾ ounces) condensed cream of celery soup

1 can (10¾ ounces) condensed cream of mushroom soup

¼ cup chopped fresh parsley

Mix all ingredients except parsley in 5- to 6-quart slow cooker.

Cover and cook on low heat setting 8 to 9 hours or until wild rice is tender. Stir in parsley.

1 Serving: Calories 405 (Calories from Fat 115); Fat 13g (Saturated 2g); Cholesterol 0mg; Sodium 1360mg; Carbohydrate 69g (Dietary Fiber 11g); Protein 14g

Wild Rice with Cranberries

4 servings

SLOW-COOKER SIZE:
2- to 3½-quart

PREP:
15 min

COOK:
Low 6 to 8 hours

FINISHING COOK TIME:
15 min

Betty's Success Tip

Toasting the almonds not only enhances the flavor and color of the almonds but also helps prevent them from becoming soggy after they are stirred into the wild rice mixture.

Ingredient Substitution

Many supermarkets now carry a wide variety of dried fruits. Dried blueberries or cherries are a delicious substitute for the cranberries.

Serving Suggestion

Cooked broccoli spears are a tasty companion for wild rice and cranberries. Make an easy cheese sauce for the broccoli by melting some cubes of process cheese loaf in the microwave oven.

1½ cups uncooked wild rice

1 tablespoon margarine or butter, melted

½ teaspoon salt

¼ teaspoon pepper

4 medium green onions, sliced (¼ cup)

2 cans (14½ ounces each) ready-to-serve vegetable broth

1 can (4 ounces) sliced mushrooms, undrained

½ cup slivered almonds, toasted

⅓ cup dried cranberries

Mix all ingredients except almonds and cranberries in 2- to 3½-quart slow cooker.

Cover and cook on low heat setting 4 to 5 hours or until wild rice is tender.

Stir in almonds and cranberries.

Cover and cook on low heat setting 15 minutes.

1 Serving: Calories 150 (Calories from Fat 35); Fat 4g (Saturated 1g); Cholesterol 0mg; Sodium 560mg; Carbohydrate 26g (Dietary Fiber 2g); Protein 5g

Spanish Rice with Tomatoes and Peppers

10 servings

SLOW-COOKER SIZE:
3½- to 4-quart

PREP:
8 min

COOK:
Low 2 to 3 hours

Ingredient Substitution

Use ⅛ teaspoon garlic powder or ¼ teaspoon instant minced garlic in place of the fresh garlic, if needed.

Finishing Touch

This scrumptious side dish makes a great filling for burritos. Top with a dollop of sour cream, and garnish with a lime wedge or avocado slice before serving.

1 cup uncooked regular long-grain rice

1 cup water

1 medium onion, chopped (½ cup)

1 small green bell pepper, chopped (½ cup)

1 clove garlic, finely chopped

1 teaspoon chili powder

1 teaspoon ground cumin

½ teaspoon salt

1 can (14½ ounces) diced tomatoes, undrained

Spray 3½- to 4-quart slow cooker with cooking spray. Mix all ingredients except tomatoes in cooker. Top with tomatoes.

Cover and cook on low heat setting 2 to 3 hours or until rice and vegetables are tender and most of the liquid has been absorbed.

1 Serving: Calories 85 (Calories from Fat 0); Fat 0g (Saturated 0g); Cholesterol 0mg; Sodium 180mg; Carbohydrate 19g (Dietary Fiber 1g); Protein 2g

Sweet Maple Baked Beans

8 servings

SLOW-COOKER SIZE:
3½- to 4-quart

PREP:
2 hours

COOK:
Low 8 to 10 hours

Betty's Success Tip

Pure maple syrup may cost a little more, but it has much more flavor than maple-flavored syrup. Grade B, a dark amber and hearty-flavored maple syrup, makes especially delicious baked beans.

1 Serving: Calories 310 (Calories from Fat 70); Fat 8g (Saturated 1g); Cholesterol 0mg; Sodium 300mg; Carbohydrate 57g (Dietary Fiber 8g); Protein 11g

2 cups dried navy beans, sorted and rinsed

10 cups water

¾ cup water

1 medium onion, chopped (½ cup)

¾ cup real maple syrup

3 tablespoons packed brown sugar

2 teaspoons ground mustard

½ teaspoon ground ginger

1 teaspoon salt

Heat beans and 10 cups water to boiling in 6-quart Dutch oven; reduce heat. Cover and simmer 2 hours; drain.

Mix beans, ¾ cup water and the remaining ingredients in 3½- to 4-quart slow cooker.

Cover and cook on low heat setting 8 to 10 hours or until beans are very tender and most of the liquid has been absorbed.

Southwestern Pinto Beans

7 servings

SLOW-COOKER SIZE:
3½- to 4-quart

PREP:
2 hours 15 min

COOK:
Low 10 to 12 hours

FINISHING COOK TIME:
Low 15 to 30 min

Betty's Success Tip

Save the leftover chipotle chile peppers to add a fiery kick to salsa, tacos and other Mexican foods.

Serving Suggestion

You can vary the taste of this south-of-the-border–influenced side dish by using black beans instead of pinto beans. These Tex-Mex beans make a great side dish for grilled beef steak, pork chops or chicken.

4 cups water

1 cup dried pinto beans, sorted and rinsed

1 cup water

1 medium stalk celery, sliced (½ cup)

1 medium carrot, chopped (½ cup)

1 medium onion, chopped (½ cup)

2 cloves garlic, finely chopped

1 tablespoon chopped chipotle chile peppers in adobo sauce (from 7-ounce can)

1 teaspoon chili powder

½ teaspoon dried oregano leaves

2 teaspoons salt

1 can (6 ounces) tomato paste

Heat 4 cups water and the beans to boiling in 2-quart saucepan; reduce heat to low. Cover and simmer 2 hours.

Drain beans. Mix beans, 1 cup water and the remaining ingredients except salt and tomato paste in 3½- to 4-quart slow cooker.

Cover and cook on low heat setting 10 to 12 hours or until beans are tender.

Stir in salt and tomato paste. Cover and cook on low heat setting 15 to 30 minutes or until thoroughly heated. If bean mixture becomes too thick, stir in up to ¼ cup hot water, 1 tablespoon at a time, until desired consistency.

1 Serving: Calories 70 (Calories from Fat 0); Fat 0g (Saturated 0g); Cholesterol 0mg; Sodium 900mg; Carbohydrate 14g (Dietary Fiber 4g); Protein 3g

Easy Savory Baked Beans

18 servings

SLOW-COOKER SIZE:
3½- to 4-quart

PREP:
15 min

COOK:
High 1 hour, then Low 5 to 7 hours

Betty's Success Tip

The baked bean pot is the fore-runner of the slow cooker. The very first slow cookers were simple bean cookers and were even referred to as "beaneries."

Serving Suggestion

Spoon the beans over squares of hot corn bread or split corn bread muffins. Sprinkle with shredded Cheddar cheese and sliced green onion.

½ pound bacon, cut into ½-inch pieces

½ cup packed brown sugar

¼ cup cornstarch

1 teaspoon ground mustard

½ cup molasses

1 tablespoon white vinegar

4 cans (16 ounces each) baked beans

1 medium green bell pepper, chopped (1 cup)

1 medium onion, chopped (½ cup)

Cook bacon in 10-inch skillet over medium heat, stirring occasionally, until crisp. Drain, reserving 2 tablespoons drippings.

Mix cooked bacon, 2 tablespoons drippings and remaining ingredients in 3½- to 4-quart slow cooker.

Cover and cook on high heat setting 1 hour.

Turn to low heat setting; cook 5 to 7 hours to blend and develop flavors.

1 Serving: Calories 185 (Calories from Fat 25); Fat 3g (Saturated 1g); Cholesterol 10mg; Sodium 510mg; Carbohydrate 34g (Dietary Fiber 5g); Protein 6g

Country French White Beans

6 servings

SLOW-COOKER SIZE:
3½- to 4-quart

PREP:
12 min

SOAK:
10 hours

COOK:
High 3½ to 5 hours

Ingredient Substitution

Don't have any *herbes de Provence* on hand? Mix together 1 teaspoon dried thyme leaves, 1 teaspoon dried basil leaves, ½ teaspoon dried marjoram leaves and ½ teaspoon dried parsley flakes. Other herbs commonly used in *herbes de Provence* are fennel seed, lavender, rosemary and savory.

Serving Suggestion

This simple side dish will nicely complement herb-roasted chicken or roasted leg of lamb. Serve with a glass of red wine, and enjoy the flavors of France.

2 cups dried great Northern beans, sorted and rinsed

1 large onion, chopped (1 cup)

2 cloves garlic, finely chopped

2 cups water

1 tablespoon dried herbes de Provence

3 tablespoons olive or vegetable oil

2 teaspoons salt

½ cup chopped drained roasted red bell peppers (from 7-ounce jar)

Place beans in large bowl. Add enough water to cover by 2 inches. Let soak overnight, at least 10 hours.

Drain beans. Mix beans and remaining ingredients except bell peppers in 3½- to 4-quart slow cooker.

Cover and cook on high heat setting 3 hours 30 minutes to 5 hours or until beans are tender.

Stir bell peppers into beans in cooker.

1 Serving: Calories 250 (Calories from Fat 65); Fat 7g (Saturated 1g); Cholesterol 0mg; Sodium 800mg; Carbohydrate 42g (Dietary Fiber 10g); Protein 15g

Caribbean Black Beans

8 servings

SLOW-COOKER SIZE:
3½- to 4-quart

PREP:
10 min

COOK:
Low 5 to 6 hours

Betty's Success Tip

You're probably most familiar with pimientos as a stuffing in green olives. Pimientos can be purchased canned or bottled. They taste sweeter and more succulent than red bell peppers.

Serving Suggestion

This black bean dish tastes great as a meatless main dish with rice. Place a mound of hot rice in the middle of each individual shallow bowl and spoon the black bean mixture around the rice. Serve with plenty of chopped red onion and hard-cooked eggs to sprinkle on top.

2 cans (15 ounces each) black beans, rinsed and drained

½ cup water

1 medium green bell pepper, chopped (1 cup)

1 medium onion, chopped (½ cup)

1 teaspoon ground cumin

½ teaspoon salt

½ teaspoon garlic powder

1 jar (2 ounces) diced pimientos, drained

Mix all ingredients in 3½- to 4-quart slow cooker.

Cover and cook on low heat setting 5 to 6 hours to blend and develop flavors.

1 Serving: Calories 140 (Calories from Fat 10); Fat 1g (Saturated 0g); Cholesterol 0mg; Sodium 560mg; Carbohydrate 30g (Dietary Fiber 7g); Protein 10g

New Orleans–Style Red Beans

8 servings

SLOW-COOKER SIZE:
3½- to 4-quart

PREP:
10 min

COOK:
Low 4 to 6 hours

Betty's Success Tip

If you enjoy a bit of heat, shake in some red pepper sauce during the last hour of cooking, but not before, since hot sauce will become stronger-tasting and bitter over long, slow cooking. You can also pass a bottle of red pepper sauce at the table so everyone can season the beans as desired.

Serving Suggestion

Pair these savory beans with spicy andouille sausage or shrimp hot off the grill, heaping spoonfuls of hot rice and a side of fried okra for a southern-style dinner experience.

¼ cup sliced celery

2 cans (15½ ounces each) red kidney beans, drained

1 small green bell pepper, chopped (½ cup)

1 medium onion, chopped (½ cup)

2 cloves garlic, finely chopped

1 teaspoon dried thyme leaves

½ teaspoon salt

¼ teaspoon crushed red pepper flakes

1 can (8 ounces) tomato sauce

Red pepper sauce, if desired

Place celery in 3½- to 4-quart slow cooker. Layer remaining ingredients except pepper sauce over celery.

Cover and cook on low heat setting 4 to 6 hours or until desired consistency. Serve with pepper sauce.

1 Serving: Calories 135 (Calories from Fat 10); Fat 1g (Saturated 0g); Cholesterol 0mg; Sodium 600mg; Carbohydrate 29g (Dietary Fiber 8g); Protein 10g

Old-Fashioned Baked Beans

12 servings

SLOW-COOKER SIZE:
4- to 6-quart

PREP:
10 min

COOK:
High 2 hours

STAND:
24 hours

FINISHING COOK TIME:
Low 10 to 12 hours

Betty's Success Tip

Baked beans can be eaten as an entrée or served alongside a grilled veggie burger. To serve these beans as a side dish, you may want to cut the recipe in half and cook it in a 2- to 3½-quart slow cooker.

Ingredient Substitution

Dried navy beans are probably the most popular bean for old-fashioned baked beans, but you can use other beans. Great Northern, lima and pinto beans all will work because they cook in the same length of time.

2 pounds dried navy beans (4 cups), sorted and rinsed

9 cups water

⅔ cup packed brown sugar

⅔ cup molasses

1 tablespoon mustard

1 teaspoon salt

1 large onion, chopped (1 cup)

Place beans and water in 4- to 6-quart slow cooker.

Cover and cook on high heat setting 2 hours. Turn off heat; let stand 8 hours to 24 hours.

Stir in remaining ingredients.

Cover and cook on low heat setting 10 to 12 hours or until beans are very tender and most of the liquid is absorbed.

1 Serving: Calories 310 (Calories from Fat 10); Fat 1g (Saturated 0g); Cholesterol 0mg; Sodium 230mg; Carbohydrate 71g (Dietary Fiber 11g); Protein 15g

Southern-Style String Beans

10 servings

SLOW-COOKER SIZE:
3½- to 4-quart

PREP:
10 min

COOK:
Low 6 to 8 hours

Betty's Success Tip

Southern "string" beans are traditionally simmered in a ham broth made with a ham bone or ham hock until tender and very flavorful. They're considered a real treat in the South. This recipe uses smoked ham or pork chops because they're easier to find.

Serving Suggestion

Serve this summertime Southern side dish with fried chicken, fresh lemonade and coconut layer cake. It's like having a picnic at your dining room table.

½-pound boneless smoked ham or pork chops, cubed

1½ pounds fresh green beans, cut into 1- to 2-inch pieces

1 medium onion, cut into eighths

1 cup water

1 teaspoon salt

¼ teaspoon pepper

Mix all ingredients in 3½- to 4-quart slow cooker.

Cover and cook on low heat setting 6 to 8 hours or until beans are tender.

1 Serving: Calories 60 (Calories from Fat 20); Fat 2g (Saturated 1g); Cholesterol 10mg; Sodium 530mg; Carbohydrate 5g (Dietary Fiber 2g); Protein 5g

Honey-Cranberry Butternut Squash

6 servings

SLOW-COOKER SIZE:
6-quart

PREP:
20 min

COOK:
Low 5 to 6 hours

Betty's Success Tip

Butternut squash has the same shape as a lightbulb or pear—it's wider at one end than the other. It usually weighs between 2 and 3 pounds, and its shell is golden yellow to camel colored.

Serving Suggestion

When served with turkey and wild rice, this squash makes a satisfying and flavorful holiday meal. Add a fresh sliced orange and onion salad on Bibb lettuce, drizzled with raspberry vinaigrette. End the meal with parfait glasses filled with peppermint ice cream and hot fudge sauce, topped with a fresh mint leaf.

3 medium butternut squash (6 to 7 inches long)

⅓ cup frozen (thawed) cranberry-apple juice concentrate

⅓ cup honey

2 tablespoons butter or margarine, melted

¾ cup sweetened dried cranberries

3 tablespoons chopped crystallized ginger

¼ teaspoon salt

¼ cup water

¼ cup chopped walnuts

Cut each squash lengthwise in half; remove seeds. Mix juice concentrate, honey and butter in small bowl. Stir in cranberries and 2 tablespoons of the ginger. Spoon mixture evenly into each squash cavity; sprinkle with salt. Layer squash in 6-quart slow cooker. Carefully pour water into bottom of cooker.

Cover and cook on low heat setting 5 to 6 hours or until tender. Sprinkle walnuts and remaining 1 tablespoon ginger over squash halves.

1 Serving: Calories 300 (Calories from Fat 63); Fat 7g (Saturated 3g); Cholesterol 10mg; Sodium 135mg; Carbohydrate 57g (Dietary Fiber 4g); Protein 3g

French Vegetable Ratatouille

8 servings

SLOW-COOKER SIZE:
3½- to 6-quart

PREP:
20 min

COOK:
Low 6 to 8 hours

Ingredient Substitution

If you are a little short on time, a tablespoon of dried parsley flakes can be used instead of the fresh parsley, and ¼ teaspoon of garlic powder can be used for the garlic cloves.

Serving Suggestion

This vegetable medley, known as *ratatouille*, has long been a favorite in southern France, especially during the summer harvest season. Create a one-dish meal by serving ragout over cooked pasta. Sprinkle with grated Romano cheese, and accompany with French bread.

1 small eggplant (1 pound), peeled and cut into ½-inch cubes (about 5 cups)

4 medium tomatoes, cut into fourths

1 medium zucchini, sliced

1 medium green bell pepper, cut into strips

1 medium onion, sliced

2 cloves garlic, finely chopped

¼ cup chopped fresh parsley

2 tablespoons olive or vegetable oil

1 teaspoon salt

1 teaspoon dried basil leaves

¼ teaspoon pepper

Mix all ingredients in 3½ to 6 quart slow cooker.

Cover and cook on low heat setting 6 to 8 hours or until vegetables are tender.

1 Serving: Calories 70 (Calories from Fat 35); Fat 4g (Saturated 1g); Cholesterol 0mg; Sodium 300mg; Carbohydrate 10g (Dietary Fiber 3g); Protein 2g

Barley Casserole with Peas and Peppers

9 servings

SLOW-COOKER SIZE:
3½- to 4-quart

PREP:
10 min

COOK:
Low 5 to 6 hours

FINISHING COOK TIME:
High 15 to 20 min

Betty's Success Tip

Did you know? One cup of barley provides the same amount of protein as an 8-ounce glass of milk.

Ingredient Substitution

If you're trying to lower your sodium intake, use reduced-sodium chicken broth instead of the regular variety.

1 cup uncooked barley

½ cup water

2 tablespoons butter or margarine, melted

¾ teaspoon seasoned salt

½ teaspoon dried thyme leaves

¼ teaspoon pepper

1 medium onion, chopped (½ cup)

1 can (14 ounces) chicken broth

1 cup frozen green peas (from 1-pound bag)

¼ cup finely chopped drained roasted red bell peppers (from 7-ounce jar)

Mix all ingredients except peas and bell peppers in 3½- to 4-quart slow cooker.

Cover and cook on low heat setting 5 to 6 hours or until barley is tender.

Stir in peas and bell peppers. Cover and cook on high heat setting 15 to 20 minutes or until hot.

1 Serving: Calories 125 (Calories from Fat 25); Fat 3g (Saturated 2g); Cholesterol 5mg; Sodium 340mg; Carbohydrate 21g (Dietary Fiber 5g); Protein 4g

Red Cabbage with Apples

8 servings

SLOW-COOKER SIZE:
3½- to 6-quart

PREP:
15 min

COOK:
Low 6 to 8 hours

Betty's Success Tip

Shredding cabbage is easy if you use a long, sharp knife. Remove the tough outer leaves from the cabbage head. Cut the cabbage, through the core, into fourths. Remove the core, and cut the cabbage across the leaves into thin slices. The leaves will separate into long, thin pieces of cabbage. If you have a food processor with the slicing attachment, the work is even easier!

Ingredient Substitution

Apples with red cabbage is a popular combination, but you may want to add a cup of chopped dried apricots or pears instead of the apples for a different twist.

1 medium head red cabbage, coarsely shredded (8 cups)

2 medium tart red apples, sliced

2 tablespoons sugar

3 tablespoons water

3 tablespoons cider vinegar

1 tablespoon margarine or butter, melted

1 teaspoon salt

¼ teaspoon pepper

Mix all ingredients in 3½- to 6-quart slow cooker.

Cover and cook on low heat setting 6 to 8 hours or until cabbage is very tender.

1 Serving: Calories 70 (Calories from Fat 20); Fat 2g (Saturated 0g); Cholesterol 0mg; Sodium 330mg; Carbohydrate 14g (Dietary Fiber 3g); Protein 2g

Sherry Buttered Mushrooms

12 servings

SLOW-COOKER SIZE:
3½- to 4-quart

PREP:
15 min

COOK:
High 2 hours

HOLD TIME:
Up to 2 hours

Betty's Success Tip

These buttery mushrooms are the perfect accompaniment for beef. Serve them with an herbed roast or with grilled steaks. Or use them to dress up grilled hamburger patties.

Ingredient Substitution

If you prefer not to use sherry, substitute 3 tablespoons balsamic vinegar or apple juice or cider instead.

½ cup butter or margarine, melted

1 teaspoon beef base or beef bouillon granules

2 tablespoons chopped fresh chives

2 cloves garlic, finely chopped

3 tablespoons dry sherry

2 pounds fresh whole mushrooms

Mix butter and beef base in 3½- to 4-quart slow cooker. Add remaining ingredients; stir gently to coat mushrooms.

Cover and cook on high heat setting about 2 hours or until hot. Gently stir.

Serve with slotted spoon. Appetizers will hold on high heat setting up to 2 hours.

1 Serving: Calories 100 (Calories from Fat 70); Fat 8g (Saturated 4g); Cholesterol 20mg; Sodium 150mg; Carbohydrate 4g (Dietary Fiber 0g); Protein 2g

Cauliflower Curry

13 servings

SLOW-COOKER SIZE:
3½- to 4-quart

PREP:
15 min

COOK:
Low 4 to 6 hours

HOLD TIME:
Low 10 to 15 min

Betty's Success Tip

You may want to remove the skins of the tomatoes when making this dish. To do so, dip the tomato in boiling water for 1 minute, make a slit in the skin and slowly peel it off.

Finishing Touch

Serve small bowls of traditional curry dish toppers such as toasted shredded coconut, chopped peanuts and raisins. The saltiness of the peanuts and the sweetness of the coconut and raisins enhance the flavor of the curry powder.

4 cups cauliflowerets

3 medium tomatoes, seeded and coarsely chopped (2¼ cups)

1 medium onion, chopped (½ cup)

1 can (14 ounces) coconut milk (not cream of coconut)

1 tablespoon soy sauce

1½ teaspoons curry powder

⅓ teaspoon salt

½ teaspoon dried basil leaves

6 ounces baby spinach leaves

Mix cauliflowerets, tomatoes and onion in 3½- to 4-quart slow cooker. Mix remaining ingredients except spinach; pour over vegetables.

Cover and cook on low heat setting 4 to 6 hours or until cauliflowerets are tender.

Stir in spinach leaves. Cover and cook on low heat setting 10 to 15 minutes or until spinach is tender. Spoon into small bowls to serve.

1 Serving: Calories 90 (Calories from Fat 55); Fat 6g (Saturated 5g); Cholesterol 0mg; Sodium 200mg; Carbohydrate 7g (Dietary Fiber 2g); Protein 2g

Pineapple Carrots

6 servings

SLOW-COOKER SIZE:
3½- to 4-quart

PREP:
10 min

COOK:
High 4 to 5 hours

Betty's Success Tip

These bite-size, super-sweet carrots taste so good, your kids won't even realize what they're eating!

Serving Suggestion

The pineapple in this sweet side dish tastes wonderful when served with a ham main meal.

1 bag (16 ounces) baby-cut carrots

1 can (8 ounces) pineapple tidbits in juice, undrained

2 tablespoons packed brown sugar

2 tablespoons butter or margarine, melted

2 teaspoons grated orange peel

½ teaspoon salt

½ teaspoon ground cinnamon

¼ teaspoon ground nutmeg

Place carrots and pineapple in 3½- to 4-quart slow cooker. Mix remaining ingredients; pour over carrots and pineapple.

Cover and cook on high heat setting 4 to 5 hours or until carrots are tender.

1 Serving: Calories 110 (Calories from Fat 35); Fat 4g (Saturated 2g); Cholesterol 10mg; Sodium 250mg; Carbohydrate 18g (Dietary Fiber 3g); Protein 1g

The Ultimate Creamed Corn

5 servings

SLOW-COOKER SIZE:
3½- to 4-quart

PREP:
8 min

COOK:
High 2 to 3 hours

Betty's Success Tip

Patience is a virtue! Resist the urge to peek inside the slow cooker during the cooking process. Every time you lift the lid, you add 15 to 20 minutes to the cooking time.

Finishing Touch

To add crunch, sprinkle crushed crackers or corn chips over the top of this delicious, creamy side dish.

1 bag (1 pound) frozen whole kernel corn

2 packages (3 ounces each) cream cheese, cut into cubes

½ cup milk

¼ cup butter or margarine, melted

1 teaspoon sugar

½ teaspoon salt

⅛ teaspoon pepper

Spread corn over bottom of 3½- to 4-quart slow cooker. Top with cream cheese cubes. Mix remaining ingredients; pour over corn and cream cheese.

Cover and cook on high heat setting 2 to 3 hours or until creamy. Stir well before serving.

1 Serving: Calories 300 (Calories from Fat 200); Fat 22g (Saturated 14g); Cholesterol 65mg; Sodium 410mg; Carbohydrate 20g (Dietary Fiber 2g); Protein 6g

Greek-Style Veggies

16 servings

SLOW-COOKER SIZE:
3½- to 4-quart

PREP:
20 min

COOK:
Low 7 to 8 hours

Betty's Success Tip

You'll find many of the ingredients for this dish, such as zucchini, eggplant, red bell pepper, onions and mushrooms, at your local farmers' market.

Serving Suggestion

Make this vegetable-filled side dish a meal by serving over cooked rice or noodles. Warmed pita slices, followed by baklava for dessert, play up the Greek theme.

2 medium zucchini, cut into ½-inch slices (4 cups)

1 medium eggplant, peeled and cut into ½-inch cubes (4 cups)

1 medium red bell pepper, cut into strips

1 medium onion, chopped (½ cup)

1 package (8 ounces) whole mushrooms, cut into fourths

3 cloves garlic, finely chopped

1 can (28 ounces) tomato puree, undrained

1 can (2¼ ounces) sliced ripe olives, drained

2 teaspoons salt

2 teaspoons dried basil leaves

½ teaspoon dried thyme leaves

¼ teaspoon pepper

1 cup crumbled feta cheese, if desired

Mix all ingredients except cheese in 3½- to 4-quart slow cooker.

Cover and cook on low heat setting 7 to 8 hours or until vegetables are tender.

Top each serving with 1 tablespoon cheese.

1 Serving: Calories 60 (Calories from Fat 10); Fat 1g (Saturated 0g); Cholesterol 0mg; Sodium 530mg; Carbohydrate 10g (Dietary Fiber 3g); Protein 2g

Orange-Glazed Beets

6 servings

SLOW-COOKER SIZE:
3½- to 4-quart

PREP:
20 min

COOK:
Low 11 to 12 hours

FINISHING COOK TIME:
High 5 to 10 min

Betty's Success Tip

These sweet-and-sour beets are also referred to as Harvard beets. If you find beets with crisp, bright greens still attached, buy them because they'll be very fresh. Just make sure to remove the greens as soon as you get them home since they pull moisture from the beets.

Ingredient Substitution

In place of the cornstarch, use 2 tablespoons all-purpose flour or 4 teaspoons quick-cooking tapioca.

2 pounds beets, peeled and cut into ½-inch slices (3 cups)

½ cup orange juice

¼ cup cider vinegar

3 tablespoons honey

1 teaspoon salt

1 tablespoon cornstarch

1 tablespoon cold water

Mix all ingredients except cornstarch and water in 3½- to 4-quart slow cooker.

Cover and cook on low heat setting 11 to 12 hours or until beets are tender.

Mix cornstarch and water; stir into beets. Cook uncovered on high heat setting 5 to 10 minutes or until sauce has thickened.

1 Serving: Calories 95 (Calories from Fat 0); Fat 0g (Saturated 0g); Cholesterol 0mg; Sodium 470mg; Carbohydrate 22g (Dietary Fiber 2g); Protein 2g

Sweet
Endings

Caramel Rice Pudding

8 servings

SLOW-COOKER SIZE:
2- to 3½-quart

PREP:
5 min

COOK:
Low 3 to 4 hours

Betty's Success Tip

The sweetened condensed milk caramelizes during the long, slow cooking to give this rice pudding a pleasant caramel flavor and rich beige color. The evaporated milk and condensed milk also make a smooth, creamy pudding because they don't break down and separate like fresh milk would during the long cooking time.

Ingredient Substitution

This all-time favorite comfort food lends itself to a little flavor variety. Try chopped dried apricots, sweetened dried cherries or dried cranberries in place of the raisins.

3 cups cooked white rice

½ cup raisins

1 teaspoon vanilla

1 can (14 ounces) sweetened condensed milk

1 can (12 ounces) evaporated milk

1 tablespoon sugar

1 teaspoon ground cinnamon

Spray inside of 2- to 3½-quart slow cooker with cooking spray.

Mix all ingredients except sugar and cinnamon in cooker.

Cover and cook on low heat setting 3 to 4 hours or until liquid is absorbed. Stir pudding.

Sprinkle pudding with sugar and cinnamon. Serve warm.

1 Serving: Calories 385 (Calories from Fat 70); Fat 8g (Saturated 5g); Cholesterol 30mg; Sodium 140mg; Carbohydrate 68g (Dietary Fiber 1g); Protein 11g

Chocolate Rice Pudding

10 servings

SLOW-COOKER SIZE:
3½- to 6-quart

PREP:
10 min

COOK:
Low 2½ to 3 hours

Betty's Success Tip

We found that using uncooked rice made a rice pudding that was sticky instead of creamy. To save time at the last minute, cook the rice ahead and keep it in the refrigerator until you are ready to make the pudding.

Finishing Touch

Dress up this creamy chocolate rice pudding with a dollop of whipped cream, sliced toasted almonds and a long-stemmed maraschino cherry

4 cups cooked white rice

¾ cup sugar

¼ cup baking cocoa

3 tablespoons margarine or butter, melted

1 teaspoon vanilla

2 cans (12 ounces each) evaporated milk

Spray inside of 3½- to 6-quart slow cooker with cooking spray.

Mix all ingredients in cooker.

Cover and cook on low heat setting 2½ to 3 hours or until liquid is absorbed. Stir before serving.

Serve warm or chilled. To chill, cool about 2 hours, then spoon pudding into container; cover and refrigerate until chilled.

1 Serving: Calories 230 (Calories from Fat 65); Fat 7g (Saturated 3g); Cholesterol 10mg; Sodium 85mg; Carbohydrate 38g (Dietary Fiber 1g); Protein 5g

Triple Chocolate Bread Pudding

8 servings

SLOW-COOKER SIZE:
3½- to 6-quart

PREP:
10 min

COOK:
High 2½ to 3 hours

Ingredient Substitution

If chocolate bread isn't available, use French bread cubes. Double the chocolate chips to 1 cup so there is more chocolate flavor. It may not be triple chocolate, but it still will be triple delicious!

Finishing Touch

Turn this chocolate bread pudding into an Ultra Turtle Dessert. Top each serving with your favorite caramel sauce and a generous sprinkle of toasted pecans.

6 cups chocolate bread cubes (12 to 14 slices bread)

½ cup semisweet chocolate chips

1 cup fat-free cholesterol-free egg product

¾ cup warm water

1 teaspoon vanilla

½ teaspoon ground cinnamon

1 can (14 ounces) chocolate sweetened condensed milk

Spray inside of 3½- to 6-quart slow cooker with cooking spray.

Place bread cubes in cooker. Sprinkle with chocolate chips.

Mix remaining ingredients; pour over bread cubes and chocolate chips.

Cover and cook on high heat setting 2½ to 3 hours or until toothpick inserted in center comes out clean.

Serve warm.

1 Serving: Calories 455 (Calories from Fat 110); Fat 12g (Saturated 7g); Cholesterol 20mg; Sodium 260mg; Carbohydrate 74g (Dietary Fiber 3g); Protein 13g

Chocolate Fondue

2¼ cups fondue

SLOW-COOKER SIZE:
1- to 2½-quart

PREP:
5 min

COOK:
Low 45 to 60 min

HOLD TIME:
Low up to 2 hours

Ingredient Substitution

For a flavor twist, use any fruit-, coffee-, almond- or ginger-flavored liqueur; white crème de menthe; brandy or rum—the choices are endless.

Serving Suggestion

Chocolate makes anything taste sensational! Cubes of pound or angel food cake, large marshmallows, pretzels or rippled potato chips are a few more dipper ideas. What do you think would be good dipped in chocolate?

Finishing Touch

Place dishes of toasted coconut and chopped toasted nuts next to the fondue. Dip a piece of fruit into the chocolate, then into the coconut or nuts for the ultimate taste treat.

1 Tablespoon: Calories 55 (Calories from Fat 25); Fat 3g (Saturated 2g); Cholesterol 0mg; Sodium 0mg; Carbohydrate 6g (Dietary Fiber 0g); Protein 1g

1 package (12 ounces) semisweet chocolate chips (2 cups)

½ cup half-and-half

1 to 3 tablespoons orange-flavored liqueur, if desired

Fruit Dippers (below), for serving, if desired

Mix chocolate chips and half-and-half in 1- to 2½-quart slow cooker.

Cover and cook on low heat setting 45 to 60 minutes or until chocolate is melted. Stir until mixture is smooth. Stir in liqueur.

Serve with Fruit Dippers and wooden picks or fondue forks for dipping. Fondue will hold up to 2 hours.

Fruit Dippers

Select one or several of the following fruits: apple wedges, banana slices, kiwifruit wedges, melon balls, fresh or mandarin orange sections, pear wedges, pineapple chunks, strawberries. Dip apple wedges, banana slices and pear wedges in lemon or pineapple juice to help prevent them from turning dark.

Butterscotch-Rum Dip

3 cups dip

SLOW-COOKER SIZE:
1- to 2½-quart

PREP:
10 min

COOK:
Low 45 to 60 min

HOLD TIME:
Low up to 2 hours

Ingredient Substitution

Rum and butterscotch flavors blend nicely together. If you prefer not to use rum, however, add 2 teaspoons of rum extract. Or you can leave out the rum to make a delicious, nutty butterscotch dip—the choice is yours.

Serving Suggestion

Leftover dip? No problem. It keeps well in the refrigerator. Warm it and serve with pancakes or waffles. Top a slice of apple pie, pound cake or angel food cake with a scoop of ice cream, and pour warm butterscotch sauce over the top. In fact, this dip is so delicious, you might just want to make a batch to keep on hand.

2 packages (11 ounces each) butterscotch-flavored chips (4 cups total)

⅔ cup evaporated milk

⅔ cup walnuts, toasted and finely chopped

2 tablespoons rum

Apple and pear wedges, for serving, if desired

Mix butterscotch chips and evaporated milk in 1- to 2½-quart slow cooker.

Cover and cook on low heat setting 45 to 60 minutes or until chips are melted. Stir until mixture is smooth. Stir in walnuts and rum.

Serve with apple and pear wedges. Dip will hold up to 2 hours.

1 Tablespoon: Calories 90 (Calories from Fat 45); Fat 5g (Saturated 4g); Cholesterol 0mg; Sodium 15mg; Carbohydrate 10g (Dietary Fiber 0g); Protein 1g

Hot Fudge Sundae Cake

6 servings

SLOW-COOKER SIZE:
2- to 3½-quart

PREP:
15 min

COOK:
High 2 to 2½ hours

COOL:
30 to 40 min

Betty's Success Tip

We found that if you let the cake cool in the cooker before serving it, the sauce under the cake will thicken to a good consistency. If you eat it sooner, the sauce will be thinner but still delicious.

Finishing Touch

For a special treat, add ⅓ cup halved maraschino cherries with the nuts. Top with a scoop of your favorite ice cream. Tuck a long-stemmed maraschino cherry on top each serving to make this the best-ever sundae cake.

1 cup all-purpose flour

½ cup granulated sugar

2 tablespoons baking cocoa

2 teaspoons baking powder

½ teaspoon salt

½ cup milk

2 tablespoons vegetable oil

1 teaspoon vanilla

½ cup chopped nuts

¾ cup packed brown sugar

¼ cup baking cocoa

1½ cups hot water

Spray inside of 2- to 3½-quart slow cooker with cooking spray.

Mix flour, granulated sugar, 2 tablespoons cocoa, the baking powder and salt in medium bowl. Stir in milk, oil and vanilla until smooth. Stir in nuts. Spread batter evenly in bottom of cooker.

Mix brown sugar and ¼ cup cocoa in small bowl. Stir in hot water until smooth. Pour evenly over batter in cooker.

Cover and cook on high heat setting 2 to 2½ hours or until toothpick inserted in center comes out clean.

Turn off cooker. Let cake stand uncovered 30 to 40 minutes to cool slightly before serving.

Spoon warm cake into dessert dishes. Spoon sauce over top.

1 Serving: Calories 380 (Calories from Fat 110); Fat 12g (Saturated 2g); Cholesterol 0mg; Sodium 380mg; Carbohydrate 66g (Dietary Fiber 3g); Protein 5g

Hot Fudge Sundae Cake

Cinnamon-Raisin Bread Pudding

8 servings

SLOW-COOKER SIZE:
3½- to 6-quart

PREP:
10 min

COOK:
High 2½ to 3 hours

Betty's Success Tip

Using bread that is a day or two old is best; it will be firmer and drier than fresh bread. Bread that is too fresh and soft will give you a bread pudding that is too moist and soggy. We use an egg substitute because it is pasteurized, making it safe for long, slow cooking.

Serving Suggestion

Bread pudding is great for a brunch or weekend breakfast. Top each serving with a pat of butter to melt into the hot pudding, and pass a pitcher of warm maple syrup to drizzle on top. What a way to start the day!

6 cups cinnamon-raisin bread cubes (12 to 14 slices bread)

½ cup raisins

1 cup fat-free cholesterol-free egg product

¾ cup warm water

1 teaspoon vanilla

½ teaspoon ground cinnamon

1 can (14 ounces) sweetened condensed milk

Spray inside of 3½- to 6-quart slow cooker with cooking spray.

Place bread cubes in cooker. Sprinkle with raisins.

Mix remaining ingredients; pour over bread cubes and raisins.

Cover and cook on high heat setting 2½ to 3 hours or until toothpick inserted in center comes out clean.

Serve warm.

1 Serving: Calories 355 (Calories from Fat 65); Fat 7g (Saturated 4g); Cholesterol 25mg; Sodium 340mg; Carbohydrate 64g (Dietary Fiber 2g); Protein 11g

Blackberry Dumplings

6 servings

SLOW-COOKER SIZE:
3½- to 4-quart

PREP:
10 min

COOK:
Low 3 to 4 hours; High 1½ to 2 hours

FINISHING COOK TIME:
20 to 25 min

Betty's Success Tip

For light, fluffy dumplings, be sure the berry mixture is boiling before dropping the dough on top. If the mixture isn't hot enough, the tops of the dumplings will be wet and doughy. Dumplings need steam to rise during cooking, so don't lift the cover and peek because the steam will sneak out.

Ingredient Substitution

Any type of fresh or frozen berries can be used in this recipe. Try blueberries, strawberries, raspberries or a combination of two or three. If you use frozen berries, be sure to buy the bag of berries that aren't frozen in syrup.

1 package (14 ounces) frozen blackberries (3 cups), thawed and drained

⅓ cup sugar

⅓ cup water

1 teaspoon lemon juice

1 cup Bisquick Original baking mix

2 tablespoons sugar

⅓ cup milk

Ground cinnamon

Whipping (heavy) cream or vanilla ice cream, if desired

Mix blackberries, ⅓ cup sugar, the water and lemon juice in 3½- or 4-quart slow cooker.

Cover and cook on low heat setting 3 to 4 hours (or high heat setting 1½ to 2 hours) or until mixture is boiling.

Mix baking mix and 2 tablespoons sugar in small bowl. Stir in milk just until dry ingredients are moistened. Drop 6 spoonfuls of dough onto hot berry mixture. Sprinkle with cinnamon.

Cover and cook on high heat setting 20 to 25 minutes or until toothpick inserted in center of dumplings comes out clean.

To serve, spoon dumpling into dessert dish. Spoon berry mixture over dumpling. Top with whipping cream.

1 Serving: Calories 165 (Calories from Fat 25); Fat 3g (Saturated 1g); Cholesterol 0mg; Sodium 290mg; Carbohydrate 37g (Dietary Fiber 4g); Protein 2g

Cranberry Baked Apples

4 servings

SLOW-COOKER SIZE:
5- to 6-quart

PREP:
15 min

COOK:
Low 4 to 6 hours

Betty's Success Tip

We like to use a cooking apple that will hold its shape after it is cooked. Good selections are Rome Beauty, Golden Delicious, Beacon, San Rose and Wealthy apples. Granny Smith apples also are an excellent cooking apple, but they are quite tart, so you may want to increase the sugar by a tablespoon.

Ingredient Substitution

Dried cranberries are a natural with apples, but other dried fruits are just as tasty. Try dried cherries, mixed dried fruits or dark or golden raisins.

4 large cooking apples

⅓ cup packed brown sugar

¼ cup dried cranberries

½ cup cran-apple juice cocktail

2 tablespoons margarine or butter, melted

½ teaspoon ground cinnamon

¼ teaspoon ground nutmeg

Chopped nuts, if desired

Core apples. Fill centers of apples with brown sugar and cranberries. Place apples in 5- to 6-quart slow cooker.

Mix cran-apple juice and margarine; pour over apples. Sprinkle with cinnamon and nutmeg.

Cover and cook on low heat setting 4 to 6 hours or until apples are tender.

To serve, spoon apples into dessert dishes. Spoon sauce over apples. Sprinkle with nuts.

1 Serving: Calories 285 (Calories from Fat 65); Fat 7g (Saturated 1g); Cholesterol 0mg; Sodium 85mg; Carbohydrate 63g (Dietary Fiber 9g); Protein 1g

Maple-Sauced Pears

6 servings

SLOW-COOKER SIZE:
3½- to 5-quart

PREP:
10 min

COOK:
High 2 to 2½ hours

FINISHING COOK TIME:
High 10 min

Ingredient Substitution

For a honey of a pear, use ¼ cup honey instead of the maple syrup for a sweet change of pace.

Finishing Touch

For an elegant dessert, place each pear upright on a pretty dessert plate. Spoon the sauce around the pear, and sprinkle with chopped toasted nuts or coconut. Spoon a big dollop of soft whipped cream alongside the pear, and garnish the plate with a twisted orange slice.

6 pears

½ cup packed brown sugar

⅓ cup maple-flavored syrup

1 tablespoon margarine or butter, melted

1 teaspoon grated orange peel

⅛ teaspoon ground ginger

1 tablespoon cornstarch

2 tablespoons orange juice

Peel pears. Core pears from bottom, leaving stems attached. Place pears upright in 3½- to 5-quart slow cooker.

Mix remaining ingredients except cornstarch and orange juice; pour over pears.

Cover and cook on high heat setting 2 to 2½ hours or until tender.

Remove pears from cooker; place upright in serving dish or individual dessert dishes.

Mix cornstarch and orange juice; stir into sauce in cooker. Cover and cook on high heat setting about 10 minutes or until sauce is thickened. Spoon sauce over pears.

1 Serving: Calories 225 (Calories from Fat 25); Fat 3g (Saturated 0g); Cholesterol 0mg; Sodium 35mg; Carbohydrate 52g (Dietary Fiber 3g); Protein 1g

Chunky Cinnamon Applesauce

8 servings

SLOW-COOKER SIZE:
3½- to 6-quart

PREP:
20 min

COOK:
High 1½ to 2 hours

Betty's Success Tip

We liked the chunkiness of this applesauce, but if you and your family like a smoother sauce, use a potato masher to break up the apple pieces.

Serving Suggestion

Warm applesauce topped with a splash of heavy whipping cream makes a memorable homemade dessert. But applesauce also is good served with your favorite pork recipe or as a topping for pancakes or waffles.

8 medium Granny Smith apples or other tart cooking apples, peeled and cut into fourths

⅔ cup sugar

¾ cup apple juice

2 tablespoons margarine or butter, melted

1 teaspoon ground cinnamon

Mix all ingredients in 3½- to 6-quart slow cooker.

Cover and cook on high heat setting 1½ to 2 hours or until apples begin to break up. Stir well to break up larger pieces of apples.

Serve warm or chilled. To chill, cool about 2 hours, then spoon sauce into container; cover and refrigerate until chilled.

1 Serving: Calories 170 (Calories from Fat 25); Fat 3g (Saturated 1g); Cholesterol 0mg; Sodium 40mg; Carbohydrate 39g (Dietary Fiber 3g); Protein 0g

Dried Apricot-Cherry Compote

6 servings

SLOW-COOKER SIZE:
2- to 3½-quart

PREP:
5 min

COOK:
Low 8 to 10 hours

Ingredient Substitution

For a "golden" compote, use golden raisins instead of the dried cherries.

Serving Suggestion

This compote stands on its own for dessert, but it also makes a delicious topping for orange sherbet or vanilla or chocolate ice cream.

Finishing Touch

For an added hint of orange, stir a couple of tablespoons of orange-flavored liqueur into the compote before serving.

2 packages (6 ounces each) dried apricots

2 cans (5½ ounces each) apricot nectar

½ cup sweetened dried cherries

⅓ cup sugar

2 teaspoons grated orange peel

Mix all ingredients in 2- to 3½-quart slow cooker.

Cover and cook on low heat setting 8 to 10 hours.

Serve warm or chilled. To chill, cool about 2 hours, then spoon compote into container; cover and refrigerate until chilled.

1 Serving: Calories 235 (Calories from Fat 0); Fat 0g (Saturated 0g); Cholesterol 0mg; Sodium 10mg; Carbohydrate 65g (Dietary Fiber 9g); Protein 3g

Cherry Cobbler

6 servings

SLOW-COOKER SIZE:
2- to 3½-quart

PREP:
10 min

COOK:
High 1½ to 2 hours

Ingredient Substitution

Life is just a bowl of cherries—cobbler, that is. But peach, apple, blueberry or raspberry pie filling also would make a luscious cobbler. For a little extra crunch, stir ¼ cup toasted nuts into the batter before spreading over the pie filling—yummy.

Finishing Touch

Pass a pitcher of heavy whipping cream, half-and-half or eggnog, when it is available, to pour over bowls of warm cobbler. Sprinkle a little ground cinnamon or nutmeg on top for just a hint of spiciness.

1 can (21 ounces) cherry pie filling

1 cup all-purpose flour

¼ cup sugar

¼ cup margarine or butter, melted

½ cup milk

1½ teaspoons baking powder

½ teaspoon almond extract

¼ teaspoon salt

Spray inside of 2- to 3½-quart slow cooker with cooking spray.

Pour pie filling into cooker.

Beat remaining ingredients with spoon until smooth. Spread batter over pie filling.

Cover and cook on high heat setting 1½ to 2 hours or until toothpick inserted in center comes out clean.

1 Serving: Calories 270 (Calories from Fat 70); Fat 8g (Saturated 2g); Cholesterol 0mg; Sodium 330mg; Carbohydrate 49g (Dietary Fiber 2g); Protein 3g

Pear-Apple Sauce with Cherries

15 servings

SLOW-COOKER SIZE:
3½- to 4-quart

PREP:
30 min

COOK:
Low 7 to 8 hours

FINISHING COOK TIME:
High 15 to 30 min

Betty's Success Tip

After 7 hours in the slow cooker, the apples and the pears become quite tender and form a chunky-style sauce, even without mashing.

6 medium apples, peeled and chopped

6 medium pears, peeled and chopped

¾ cup sugar

½ cup apple juice

3 teaspoons grated orange peel

¼ teaspoon ground allspice

1 package (5 ounces) sweetened dried cherries (1 cup)

Mix apples, pears, sugar, apple juice, 2 teaspoons of the orange peel and the allspice in 3½- to 4-quart slow cooker.

Cover and cook on low heat setting 7 to 8 hours or until fruit is tender.

Mash fruit with potato masher. Stir in remaining 1 teaspoon orange peel and the cherries. Cook uncovered on high heat setting 15 to 30 minutes or until desired consistency. Cool slightly. Serve warm or cool.

1 Serving: Calories 140 (Calories from Fat 0); Fat 0g (Saturated 0g); Cholesterol 0mg; Sodium 0mg; Carbohydrate 35g (Dietary Fiber 3g); Protein 0g

Part 2
Relax While It Cooks
Oven Recipes

Sometimes using the oven to bake casseroles, meat and vegetable dishes is as convenient as a slow cooker. One-dish meals are convenient and a breeze to prepare. Simply assemble all the ingredients, place them in a baking dish and supper is ready to go into the oven. Some of the recipes in this section can be started early in the day—or even the night before—and refrigerated until dinnertime. Others may even be assembled and then frozen for later use. Look for *Betty's Secret Tips* for directions to make these recipes ahead of time.

Finally, to put the perfect finish on any meal, this section includes easy-to-prepare desserts—some that can be baked in the oven alongside your dinner, others that require no cooking at all and can be assembled and chilled in advance.

◄ **Country-Style Chicken**

Oven Meals Made Simple

Follow these techniques for easy meals the whole family will enjoy.

Secrets to Oven-Baking Success

Baking dinner in the oven doesn't have to require lots of time and attention. A whole meal may be made in one dish, making this meal method simple and easy.

When assembling one-dish meals, feel free to experiment with flavors and ingredients. If a recipe calls for dried basil but your family prefers oregano, make the switch. If you are out of celery but have plenty of carrots and onions, add a bit more of these to fill out the recipe. Many of the following recipes include ingredient substitutions; here are a few basics:

- Dishes calling for frozen vegetable mixes may easily be altered by using a different veggie mix; just be sure the package size is the same.

- Substitute chicken broth, apple juice or water for the white wine in recipes.

- Beef broth makes a great substitute for red wine in beef dishes.

- Use balsamic vinegar or apple juice in place of sherry.

- Add zest to dishes by using chili sauce or mesquite-flavored ketchup instead of the original ketchup.

- Finely crushed cracker crumbs or cornflakes will work in place of dry bread crumbs.

- Easily replace one type of canned bean for another. Some good exchanges are pinto or cannellini for kidney beans, black-eyed peas or kidney for black beans.

- Out of onions? Substitute 1 teaspoon onion powder or 1 tablespoon instant minced onion for 1 medium onion.

- Substitute your favorite semi-hard cheese such as Cheddar, Monterey Jack or Swiss for the cheese in recipes.

Recipe Shortcuts for Casseroles and Oven Dinners

The following ingredients are often used in many of the recipes. Keep them on hand for last-minute suppers.

- Canned vegetables such as green beans, peas, corn or mixed vegetables

- Canned soups such as Cheddar cheese, broccoli cheese or golden corn, and cream soups such as asparagus, celery, mushroom or onion

- Canned or jarred gravies (chicken, beef, turkey, mushroom)

- Frozen chopped onions—store-bought or from your freezer

- Frozen vegetables

- Frozen or precooked lasagna sheets from the freezer case

- Crunchy toppings such as seasoned bread crumbs, croutons or flavored potato chips

- Frozen potato nuggets or potato wedges

- Quicker-cooking pasta such as orzo, elbow macaroni, small shells or vermicelli

- Instant rice or potatoes

Cooking Ahead of Time

If you'd like to be a weekend cook with dinner ready from the freezer, check out the tips that follow for some tricks you'll like to share.

- Plan to prepare and cook only high-quality foods for freezing. Freezing can keep flavor, color and texture but cannot improve original food quality if it's not there to begin with.

- Use safe-handling food practices during preparation, cooking and freezing.

- Once food is cooked, cool it quickly to warm (about 100°F) before freezing to retain the best quality and flavor. The slower that food freezes, the larger the ice crystals are, which makes the food mushy when thawed. A quantity of hot food added to a freezer will also make the freezer work harder and create moisture and could partially thaw already-frozen foods. Cooling the food down quickly before freezing is especially important for moist foods like soups, stews and sauces. The amount of time it takes to cool food quickly depends on the kind and quantity of food. Stir the food every 15 minutes.

- Refrigerate food uncovered in a shallow container.

- Carefully transfer food from the cooking pan into a large shallow pan such as a cake pan or roasting pan in a sinkful of ice.

- **Refrigerate perishable foods** such as meats, eggs, dairy products, fruits or vegetables until ready to freeze.

- **Use airtight,** moisture-vaporproof containers and materials specifically designed for food storage that can withstand freezer temperatures of 0°F and below.

- **Properly package foods** for best results. Allow about ¼- to ½-inch headspace for expansion, especially important for chunky soups, stews and sauces.

- **Be sure to label** all packages and containers before freezing.

- **If you've seen** dry, discolored surfaces on frozen foods, you're familiar with "freezer burn." Unprotected exposure to cold air shortens storage life and impairs quality and flavor. Pack food tightly, with the container almost full to eliminate as much air as possible.

- **"Shrink-wrap" foods** packaged in freezer bags with either of these methods: Press out as much air as possible before sealing; close the bag except for a ½-inch opening; insert a drinking straw and suck out any remaining air until the bag "shrinks" around the food; quickly slip out the straw and seal the bag completely. Or close the bag except for a ½-inch opening; submerge the filled bag in a container of water, pushing the air out of the bag; seal the bag.

- **When freezing foods in a container** where the lid or wrap is more than ¼ inch above the surface of the food, place aluminum foil or plastic wrap directly on top of the food before covering to seal out the air. Remove before baking, carefully using a hot wet towel if necessary.

- **Adding unfrozen food** to the freezer can significantly increase its temperature. To maintain ideal freezing temperatures and efficiency, do not freeze more than about $\frac{1}{10}$ of the capacity of the freezer at one time, or freezing will be slow. Set the thermostat to −10°F to speed freezing; once the food is frozen (usually 24 hours), reset the temperature to 0°F.

- **Allow space around** the food for the air to circulate.

- **When freezing several** packages at once, place them in a single layer in the coldest part of the freezer directly on the freezer shelf, leaving space between for air circulation, until solidly frozen. Once frozen, the packages can be stacked.

- **To quick-freeze foods,** arrange in a single layer, not touching, on a cookie sheet or jelly roll pan. Freeze uncovered or covered with an inverted pan until solid (12 to 24 hours). Package and freeze so pieces can be used as needed.

- **Purchase wire baskets** to place in your freezer to help keep it organized, and designate each for certain types of food.

Put the Freeze on Casseroles

Don't freeze your assets! When you're freezing casseroles but need the dish for other uses, try this easy method. Line casserole and lasagna dishes with heavy-duty foil, allowing enough extra foil to completely seal food with a double fold. Freeze food right in the casserole or lasagna dish until completely frozen. Remove food, and wrap again with foil, or place in plastic freezer bag; label and date for future use. Casseroles and lasagna can either be thawed in the refrigerator or placed frozen in a cold oven. To cook, place it in the same casserole or dish that the mixture was frozen in—foil and all! If baking from the frozen state, allow an extra 15 to 30 minutes for cooking.

Cook Now for Later

Leftover pasta or rice, whether planned or not, can be a real time-saver during the week when every minute counts to get an evening meal on the table.

Make extra pasta, rice or barley and refrigerate or freeze. (To prevent pasta from sticking, toss it with a small amount of oil.) Cooked pasta, rice or other grains can be covered and stored in the refrigerator for up to 5 days. To freeze, place desired amount in resealable plastic freezer bags or containers with lids, label and date. Freeze up to 6 months and thaw in refrigerator before using.

There are 3 ways to reheat pasta, rice and other grains—note that frozen pasta and grains must be thawed first.

- Place in rapidly boiling water for up to 2 minutes. Drain and serve immediately.
- Place in colander and pour boiling water over it until heated through. Drain and serve immediately.

- Place in microwave-safe dish or container. Microwave tightly covered on High for 1 to 3 minutes or until heated through. Serve immediately.

Extra-Quick Cooking Tricks

- When making a pasta dish that will be mixed with frozen vegetables, simply add the vegetables to the boiling pasta during the last several minutes of cooking for crisp-tender vegetables. Add vegetables earlier in the process for softer vegetables. Drain pasta and vegetables in a colander, and continue with the recipe. Or if you don't want to cook your vegetables at all, place them in the bottom of the colander, and when the pasta is cooked, just pour the hot water and pasta right over the vegetables—they will thaw instantly!

- Measuring honey or syrup? Spray measuring spoons and cups with cooking spray first—that sticky stuff will slide right out!

- Want meat loaf in a hurry? Instead of baking a whole loaf at once, press the uncooked meat loaf mixture into muffin tins—you'll cut the baking time in half!

- How do you serve hard ice cream without using a hammer and chisel? Use an electric knife to cut slices, or soften very hard ice cream in the refrigerator for 10 to 20 minutes before serving.

- To "frost" cupcakes in a hurry, dip cupcake tops into whipped topping or whipped cream, then sprinkle with nuts, miniature chocolate chips or candy sprinkles.

- Have you ever needed softened butter or margarine in a hurry but didn't want to microwave it because it might get too soft or melt? Get out the cheese grater, and grate the stick of butter or margarine against the large or small holes! Keep the paper or foil on, and roll it up on the stick as you go to avoid greasy hands.

223

Beef and Pork Oven Dinners

Saucy Italian Steak

6 servings

PREP:
10 min

COOK:
5 min

BAKE:
1½ hours

Betty's Success Tip

Italian green beans are flatter and wider than regular green beans, and they are usually available frozen.

1½-pound beef round steak, ¾ to 1 inch thick

2 tablespoons all-purpose flour

¼ teaspoon pepper

1 tablespoon olive or vegetable oil

1 jar (14 ounces) fat-free spaghetti sauce (any variety)

1 package (9 ounces) frozen Italian or regular cut green beans

¼ cup sliced ripe olives

Heat oven to 375°. Remove fat from beef. Mix flour and pepper; rub over both sides of beef, shaking off excess. Cut beef into 6 serving pieces.

Heat oil in 12-inch nonstick skillet over medium heat. Cook beef in oil about 5 minutes, turning once, until brown. Place beef in ungreased rectangular baking dish, 11 × 7 × 1½ inches. Pour spaghetti sauce over beef. Cover and bake 1½ hours or until beef is tender. During last 30 minutes of cooking, place frozen green beans in sauce around beef. Cover and continue to bake as directed. Sprinkle with olives.

1 Serving: Calories 175 (Calories from Fat 55); Fat 6g (Saturated 2g); Cholesterol 55mg; Sodium 300mg; Carbohydrate 10g (Dietary Fiber 2g); Protein 22g

Robust London Broil

4 servings

PREP:
10 min

CHILL:
24 hours

BROIL:
10 min

1 pound high-quality beef flank steak, 1 inch thick

½ cup dry white wine or beef broth

¼ cup soy sauce

¼ cup water

1 tablespoon molasses

2 cloves garlic, finely chopped

Cut both sides of beef in diamond pattern ⅛ inch deep. Place beef in shallow baking dish.

Mix remaining ingredients; pour over beef. Cover tightly and refrigerate at least 6 hours but no longer than 24 hours, turning beef occasionally.

About 15 minutes before serving, set oven control to broil. Remove beef from marinade; discard marinade. Place beef on rack in broiler pan. Broil with top 2 to 3 inches from heat about 5 minutes or until brown; turn. Broil about 5 minutes longer for medium (160°). Cut beef across grain at slanted angle into thin slices.

1 Serving: Calories 190 (Calories from Fat 70); Fat 8g (Saturated 3g); Cholesterol 60mg; Sodium 1090mg; Carbohydrate 6g (Dietary Fiber 0g); Protein 24g

Brisket with Cranberry Gravy

6 to 8 servings

PREP:
5 min

COOK TIME:
2 hours

1 Serving: Calories 310 (Calories from Fat 70); Fat 8g (Saturated 3g); Cholesterol 65mg; Sodium 690mg; Carbohydrate 36g (Dietary Fiber 2g); Protein 26g

2- to 2½-pound fresh beef brisket (not corned beef)

½ teaspoon salt

1 can (16 ounces) whole-berry cranberry sauce

1 can (15 ounces) tomato sauce

1 medium onion, chopped (½ cup)

Rub surface of beef with salt. Place beef in 10-inch skillet.

Mix cranberry sauce, tomato sauce and onion; pour over beef. Heat to boiling over medium-high heat. Stir; reduce heat to low. Cover and simmer 1 hour 30 minutes to 2 hours or until beef is tender.

To serve, cut beef across grain into thin slices. Serve with gravy.

Beef Brisket Barbecue

12 servings

PREP:
8 min

BAKE:
3 hours

4- to 5-pound well-trimmed lean fresh beef brisket (not corned)

1 teaspoon salt

½ cup ketchup

¼ cup white vinegar

1 tablespoon Worcestershire sauce

1½ teaspoons liquid smoke

¼ teaspoon pepper

1 medium onion, finely chopped (½ cup)

1 bay leaf

Heat oven to 325°.

Rub surface of beef with salt. Place in ungreased rectangular pan, 13 × 9 × 2 inches. Mix remaining ingredients; pour over beef. Cover and bake about 3 hours or until beef is tender.

Cut thin diagonal slices across grain at an angle from 2 or 3 "faces" of beef. Spoon any remaining pan juices over sliced beef, if desired. Remove bay leaf.

1 Serving: Calories 210 (Calories from Fat 60); Fat 6g (Saturated 2); Cholesterol 60mg; Sodium 430mg; Carbohydrate 3g (Dietary Fiber 0g); Protein 33g

Beefy Baked Chili

6 servings

PREP:
10 min

COOK:
2 min

BAKE:
4 hours

Betty's Success Tip

Instead of ground beef, this hearty chili features chunks of tender beef. It's the perfect chili to make when you want to entertain because you just pop it in the oven and let it slowly cook for several hours, until it's savory and full of flavor.

1½ cups dried pinto beans

6 cups water

1½ pounds boneless beef chuck, tip or round steak, cut into 1-inch pieces

1 teaspoon chili powder

1 tablespoon cumin seed

1½ teaspoons salt

1½ teaspoons ground red pepper

3 medium onions, chopped

3 cloves garlic, finely chopped

3 cans (8 ounces each) tomato sauce

Heat oven to 325°.

Heat beans and water to boiling in 4-quart ovenproof Dutch oven. Boil 2 minutes.

Stir remaining ingredients into bean mixture. Cover and bake until beef and beans are tender, about 4 hours; stir. Garnish with sour cream, chopped onion and shredded Cheddar cheese, if desired.

1 Serving: Calories 370 (Calories from Fat 50g); Fat 6g (Saturated 2g); Cholesterol 50mg; Sodium 127mg; Carbohydrates 43g (Dietary Fiber 11g); Protein 38g

Mexican Beef and Bean Casserole

4 servings

PREP:
10 min

COOK:
10 min

BAKE:
50 min

1 pound lean ground beef

2 cans (15 to 16 ounces each) pinto or kidney beans, rinsed and drained

1 can (8 ounces) tomato sauce

½ cup thick-and-chunky salsa

1 teaspoon chili powder

1 cup shredded Monterey Jack cheese (4 ounces)

Heat oven to 375°.

Cook beef in 10-inch skillet over medium heat 8 to 10 minutes, stirring occasionally, until brown; drain.

Mix beef, beans, tomato sauce, salsa and chili powder in ungreased 2-quart casserole.

Cover and bake 40 to 45 minutes, stirring once or twice, until hot and bubbly. Sprinkle with cheese. Bake uncovered about 5 minutes or until cheese is melted.

1 Serving: Calories 585 (Calories from Fat 235); Fat 26g (Saturated 12g); Cholesterol 90mg; Sodium 1030mg; Carbohydrate 62g (Dietary Fiber 20g); Protein 46g

Tortilla Casserole

6 servings

PREP:
25 min

COOK:
10 min

BAKE:
40 min

STAND:

10 min

1 pound ground beef

1 medium onion, chopped (½ cup)

1 jar (8 ounces) green or red salsa (1 cup)

½ cup sour cream

1 can (10¾ ounces) condensed cream of chicken soup

1 jar (2 ounces) sliced pimientos, drained

6 corn tortillas (6 to 8 inches), cut into 1-inch strips

2 cups shredded Cheddar cheese (8 ounces)

Heat oven to 350°.

Cook beef and onion in 10-inch skillet over medium heat 8 to 10 minutes, stirring occasionally, until beef is brown; drain.

Spread ½ cup of the salsa in bottom of ungreased square baking dish, 8 × 8 × 2 inches. Mix remaining salsa, sour cream, soup and pimientos. Layer half of the tortilla strips, beef mixture, soup mixture and cheese on salsa; repeat.

Bake uncovered 30 to 40 minutes or until hot and bubbly. Let stand 10 minutes. Garnish with olives, if desired.

1 Serving: Calories 465 (Calories from Fat 280); Fat 31g (Saturated 16g); Cholesterol 100mg; Sodium 940mg; Carbohydrate 21g (Dietary Fiber 2g); Protein 27g

Fiesta Taco Casserole

6 servings

PREP:
10 min

COOK:
10 min

BAKE:
30 min

1 pound ground beef

1 can (15 to 16 ounces) spicy chili beans, undrained

1 cup salsa

2 cups coarsely broken tortilla chips

½ cup sour cream

4 medium green onions, sliced (½ cup)

1 medium tomato, chopped (¾ cup)

1 cup shredded Cheddar or Monterey Jack cheese (4 ounces)

Tortilla chips, if desired

Shredded lettuce, if desired

Salsa, if desired

Heat oven to 350°.

Cook beef in 10-inch skillet over medium heat 8 to 10 minutes, stirring occasionally, until brown; drain. Stir in beans and 1 cup salsa. Heat to boiling, stirring occasionally.

Place broken tortilla chips in ungreased 2-quart casserole. Top with beef mixture. Spread with sour cream. Sprinkle with onions, tomato and cheese. Bake uncovered 20 to 30 minutes or until hot and bubbly. Arrange tortilla chips around edge of casserole. Serve with lettuce and salsa.

1 Serving: Calories 390 (Calories from Fat 170g); Fat 19g (Saturated 9g); Cholesterol 55mg; Sodium 750mg; Carbohydrate 30g (Dietary Fiber 5g); Protein 27g

Baked Taco Sandwich

4 servings

PREP:
8 min

COOK:
10 min

BAKE:
30 min

STAND:
2 min

Betty's Success Tip

To make ahead, cover unbaked sandwich tightly with aluminum foil and refrigerate no longer than 24 hours.

About 45 minutes before serving, heat oven to 450°. Bake in covered pan about 25 minutes or until golden brown. Immediately sprinkle with cheese. Let stand 1 to 2 minutes or until cheese is melted. Serve with sour cream, lettuce and tomatoes.

1 pound ground beef

1 envelope (1¼ ounces) taco seasoning mix

1 cup Bisquick Original baking mix

⅓ cup cold water

¾ cup shredded Cheddar cheese (3 ounces)

Sour cream, if desired

Shredded lettuce, if desired

Chopped tomatoes, if desired

Grease square pan, 8 × 8 × 2 inches.

Cook beef as directed on envelope of taco seasoning mix.

Mix baking mix and cold water until smooth; spread in pan. Spread beef mixture over dough.

Heat oven to 450°. Bake uncovered 25 to 30 minutes or until edges are golden brown and toothpick inserted in center comes out clean. Immediately sprinkle with cheese. Let stand 1 to 2 minutes or until cheese is melted. Serve with sour cream, lettuce and tomatoes.

1 Serving: Calories 485 (Calories from Fat 270); Fat 30g (Saturated 14g); Cholesterol 95mg; Sodium 980mg; Carbohydrate 26g (Dietary Fiber 1g); Protein 29g

German-Style Meat Loaf

6 servings

PREP:
10 min

BAKE:
40 min

STAND:
5 min

Serving Suggestion

Before baking, try spreading the meat loaf with a mixture of ¼ cup each packed brown sugar and spicy brown mustard. Serve the meat loaf with spaetzle, the traditional German noodle side dish. You'll find dried spaetzle in the pasta section of the supermarket.

Ingredient Substitution

For a change of pace, ½ cup dry bread crumbs or ¾ cup quick-cooking oats can be substituted for the 3 slices bread.

1½ pounds diet-lean or extra-lean ground beef

1 cup low-calorie beer, nonalcoholic beer or skim milk

¼ cup fat-free cholesterol-free egg product or 2 egg whites, slightly beaten

2 tablespoons packed brown sugar

2 tablespoons spicy brown mustard

1 teaspoon onion salt

3 slices rye or pumpernickel bread, torn into small pieces

1 can (8 ounces) sauerkraut, very well drained and chopped

Heat oven to 350°. Mix all ingredients. Spread mixture in ungreased square pan, 9 × 9 × 2 inches. Insert meat thermometer so tip is in center of meat loaf.

Bake uncovered about 40 minutes or until no longer pink in center and juice is clear (meat thermometer should reach at least 160°). Let stand 5 minutes before serving.

1 Serving: Calories 250 (Calories from Fat 120); Fat 13g (Saturated 5g); Cholesterol 70mg; Sodium 350mg; Carbohydrate 9g (Dietary Fiber 1g); Protein 25g

Healthy Meat Loaf

6 servings

PREP:
15 min

BAKE:
1 hour

Betty's Success Tip

Ground turkey isn't necessarily less fatty than ground beef; check the label to see what percentage of fat it contains. Ground turkey breast is the leanest ground turkey product—it's 99 percent fat free.

1 Serving: Calories 225 (Calories from Fat 90); Fat 10g (Saturated 4g); Cholesterol 70mg; Sodium 390mg; Carbohydrate 9g (Dietary Fiber 1g); Protein 26g

¾ **pound ground turkey breast**

¾ **pound extra-lean ground beef**

1 **large onion, finely chopped (1 cup)**

½ **cup soft bread crumbs**

2 **tablespoons ketchup or tomato puree**

2 **tablespoons Dijon mustard**

½ **teaspoon salt**

¼ **cup fat-free cholesterol-free egg product or 2 egg whites**

2 **cloves garlic, finely chopped**

Heat oven to 375°. Spray loaf pan, 8½ × 4½ × 2½ inches, with cooking spray. Mix all ingredients. Spread in pan. Bake uncovered about 1 hour or until no longer pink in center and juice is clear (meat thermometer should reach at least 160°). Drain immediately.

Meat Loaf

6 servings

PREP:
15 min

BAKE:
1¼ hours

STAND:
5 min

Betty's Success Tip

For variety, try a mixture of ½ pound each ground beef, ground pork and ground turkey. (Cook to 180° if ground turkey is used.)

Ingredient Substitution

For a change of pace, ½ cup dry bread crumbs or ¾ cup quick-cooking oats can be substituted for the 3 slices bread.

1½ pounds extra-lean ground beef

1 cup milk

1 tablespoon Worcestershire sauce

1 teaspoon chopped fresh or ¼ teaspoon dried sage leaves

½ teaspoon salt

½ teaspoon ground mustard (dry)

¼ teaspoon pepper

1 clove garlic, finely chopped or ⅛ teaspoon garlic powder

1 large egg

3 slices bread, torn into small pieces

1 small onion, chopped (¼ cup)

½ cup ketchup, chili sauce or barbecue sauce

Heat oven to 350°.

Mix all ingredients except ketchup. Spread mixture in ungreased loaf pan, 8½ × 4½ × 2½ inches or 9 × 5 × 3 inches, or shape into 9 × 5-inch loaf in ungreased rectangular pan, 13 × 9 × 2 inches. Spread ketchup over top.

Insert meat thermometer so tip is in center of loaf. Bake uncovered 1 hour to 1 hour 15 minutes or until thermometer reads 170°. Let stand 5 minutes; remove from pan.

1 Serving: Calories 280 (Calories from Fat 120g); Fat 17g (Saturated 5g); Cholesterol 110mg; Sodium 590mg; Carbohydrate 15g (Dietary Fiber 1g); Protein 25g

Mini Meat Loaves

4 servings

PREP:
15 min

BAKE:
25 min

Betty's Success Tip

This recipe can also be used for meatballs. Shape and cut meat mixture as directed, except shape into balls. Cook meatballs in 10-inch skillet over medium heat about 20 minutes, turning occasionally, until no longer pink in center and juice is clear.

1 pound extra-lean ground beef

½ cup dry bread crumbs

¼ cup milk

½ teaspoon salt

½ teaspoon Worcestershire sauce, if desired

1 small onion, finely chopped

1 egg

Heat oven to 400°.

Mix all ingredients. Pat mixture in rectangle, 9 × 3 inches, in ungreased rectangular baking dish. Cut into 1½-inch squares; separate squares slightly.

Bake uncovered about 25 minutes or until brown and no longer pink in center and juice is clear.

1 Serving: Calories 290 (Calories from Fat 110g); Fat 13g (Saturated 5g); Cholesterol 95mg; Sodium 500mg; Carbohydrate 14g (Dietary Fiber 1g); Protein 27g

Giant Oven Burger

6 servings

PREP:
10 min

BAKE:
50 min

STAND:
5 min

Betty's Success Tip

This easy baked burger is fun to make and to eat. Serve it with your favorite baked potato chips and carrot and celery sticks for healthy crunch.

1 pound diet-lean or extra-lean ground beef

1 small bell pepper, finely chopped (½ cup)

1 small onion, finely chopped (¼ cup)

1 tablespoon prepared horseradish

1 tablespoon mustard

½ teaspoon salt

⅓ cup chili sauce or ketchup

1 unsliced round loaf Italian or sourdough bread (8 inches in diameter)

Heat oven to 350°. Mix all ingredients except chili sauce and bread. Press beef mixture in ungreased pie plate, 9 × 1¼ inches. Spread chili sauce over top.

Bake uncovered 45 to 50 minutes or until no longer pink in center and juice is clear (meat thermometer should reach at least 160°); drain. Let stand 5 minutes. Cut bread horizontally in half. Carefully place burger between halves. Cut into wedges.

1 Serving: Calories 195 (Calories from Fat 80); Fat 9g (Saturated 3g); Cholesterol 45mg; Sodium 510mg; Carbohydrate 12g (Dietary Fiber 1g); Protein 17g

Hamburger-Cabbage Casserole

6 servings

PREP:
10 min

COOK:
10 min

BAKE:
45 min

1 pound lean ground beef

1 large onion, chopped (1 cup)

½ cup uncooked instant rice

½ teaspoon salt

½ teaspoon pepper

1 can (10¾ ounces) condensed tomato soup

¼ cup water

4 cups coleslaw mix or shredded cabbage

Heat oven to 400°.

Cook beef and onion in 10-inch skillet over medium heat 8 to 10 minutes, stirring occasionally, until beef is brown; drain. Stir in remaining ingredients. Spoon into ungreased 2-quart casserole. Cover and bake 45 minutes or until hot and bubbly.

1 Serving: Calories 240 (Calories from Fat 110); Fat 12g (Saturated 5g); Cholesterol 45mg; Sodium 570mg; Carbohydrate 19g (Dietary Fiber 2g); Protein 16g

Corn Bread Beef Bake

6 servings

PREP:
10 min

COOK:
10 min

BAKE:
40 min

Betty's Success Tip

A cast-iron skillet works well for this casserole. However, if you don't have one, any oven-proof skillet works just fine.

1 pound lean ground beef

1 medium onion, chopped (½ cup)

1 can (14½ ounces) Mexican-style stewed tomatoes, undrained

1 can (15 ounces) black beans, rinsed and drained

1 can (8 ounces) tomato sauce

½ cup frozen corn

2 teaspoons chili powder

1 can (11½ ounces) refrigerated corn bread twists

Heat oven to 350°.

Cook beef and onion in 10-inch ovenproof skillet over medium heat 8 to 10 minutes, stirring occasionally, until beef is brown; drain.

Stir in tomatoes, beans, tomato sauce, corn and chili powder; heat to boiling. Immediately top with corn bread twists left in round shape (do not unwind), pressing down gently. Bake uncovered 35 to 40 minutes or until corn bread is golden brown.

1 Serving: Calories 395 (Calories from Fat 155); Fat 17g (Saturated 7g); Cholesterol 85mg; Sodium 530mg; Carbohydrate 43g (Dietary Fiber 6g); Protein 24g

Pizza Casserole

6 servings

PREP:
15 min

COOK:
10 min

BAKE:
30 min

STAND:
5 min

4 cups uncooked wagon wheel pasta (8 ounces)

½ pound diet-lean or extra-lean ground beef

¼ cup sliced ripe olives

1 can (4 ounces) mushroom pieces and stems, drained

1 jar (26 to 28 ounces) fat-free tomato pasta sauce

1 cup shredded reduced-fat mozzarella cheese (4 ounces)

Heat oven to 350°. Cook and drain pasta as directed on package. While pasta is cooking, cook beef in 10-inch skillet over medium-high heat, stirring frequently, until brown; drain. Mix pasta, beef and remaining ingredients except cheese in ungreased 2½-quart casserole.

Cover and bake about 30 minutes or until hot. Sprinkle with cheese. Cover and let stand about 5 minutes or until cheese is melted.

1 Serving: Calories 310 (Calories from Fat 80); Fat 9g (Saturated 4g); Cholesterol 30mg; Sodium 630mg; Carbohydrate 41g (Dietary Fiber 3g); Protein 19g

Manicotti

7 servings

PREP:
40 min

BAKE:
1½ hours

Red Sauce (below)

2 packages (10 ounces each) frozen chopped spinach, thawed

2 cups small-curd creamed cottage cheese

⅓ cup grated Parmesan cheese

¼ teaspoon ground nutmeg

¼ teaspoon pepper

14 uncooked manicotti shells

2 tablespoons grated Parmesan cheese

Make Red Sauce. Heat oven to 350°.

Squeeze spinach to drain; spread on paper towels and pat dry. Mix spinach, cottage cheese, the ⅓ cup Parmesan cheese, nutmeg and pepper.

Spread about one-third of the sauce in ungreased rectangular baking dish, 13 × 9 × 2 inches. Fill uncooked manicotti shells with spinach mixture. Place shells in sauce in dish. Pour remaining sauce evenly over shells, covering shells completely. Sprinkle with the 2 tablespoons Parmesan cheese.

Cover and bake about 1 hour 30 minutes or until shells are tender.

Red Sauce

1 pound lean ground beef

1 large onion, chopped (1 cup)

2 large cloves garlic, finely chopped

1 can (28 ounces) whole tomatoes, undrained

1 can (8 ounces) mushroom pieces and stems, drained

¼ cup chopped fresh parsley

1 tablespoon chopped fresh or 1 teaspoon dried basil leaves

1 teaspoon salt

Cook beef, onion and garlic in 10-inch skillet over medium heat 8 to 10 minutes, stirring occasionally, until beef is brown; drain. Stir in remaining ingredients, breaking up tomatoes with a fork or snipping with kitchen scissors. Heat to boiling; reduce heat. Cover and simmer 10 minutes.

1 Serving: Calories 380 (Calories from Fat 125); Fat 14g (Saturated 7g); Cholesterol 50mg; Sodium 720mg; Carbohydrate 39g (Dietary Fiber 5g); Protein 30g

Applesauce Meat Squares and Spaghetti

6 servings

PREP:
10 min

BAKE:
15 min

COOK:
20 min

Betty's Success Tip

Cutting the meat into squares is much quicker than forming individual meatballs. To make ahead of time, cover the meat squares tightly and refrigerate for no longer than 2 days.

1 pound lean ground beef

½ cup dry bread crumbs

½ cup applesauce

1 tablespoon instant minced onion

¾ teaspoon garlic salt

¼ teaspoon pepper

1 jar (26 to 28 ounces) spaghetti sauce

3 cups hot cooked spaghetti

Heat oven to 400°.

Mix all ingredients except spaghetti sauce and spaghetti. Press mixture evenly in ungreased rectangular pan, 11 × 7 × 1½ inches. Cut into 1¼-inch squares.

Bake uncovered about 15 minutes or until no longer pink in center and juice is clear; drain. Separate squares.

Mix meat squares and spaghetti sauce in 3-quart saucepan. Heat to boiling; reduce heat to low. Simmer uncovered about 15 minutes, stirring occasionally, until hot. Serve over spaghetti.

1 Serving: Calories 395 (Calories from Fat 155); Fat 17g (Saturated 6g); Cholesterol 45mg; Sodium 1070mg; Carbohydrate 43g (Dietary Fiber 3g); Protein 20g

Pepperoni Pizza–Hamburger Pie

6 servings

PREP:
20 min

BAKE:
30 min

STAND:
5 min

1 pound lean ground beef

⅓ cup dry bread crumbs

1½ teaspoons chopped fresh or ½ teaspoon dried oregano leaves

¼ teaspoon salt

1 large egg

½ cup sliced mushrooms

1 small green bell pepper, chopped (½ cup)

⅓ cup chopped pepperoni (2 ounces)

¼ cup sliced ripe olives

1 cup spaghetti sauce

1 cup shredded mozzarella cheese (4 ounces)

Heat oven to 400°.

Mix beef, bread crumbs, oregano, salt and egg. Press mixture evenly against bottom and side of ungreased pie plate, 9 × 1¼ inches.

Sprinkle mushrooms, bell pepper, pepperoni and olives into beef-lined plate. Pour spaghetti sauce over toppings.

Bake uncovered about 25 minutes or until beef is no longer pink in center and juice is clear; carefully drain. Sprinkle with cheese. Bake about 5 minutes longer or until cheese is light brown. Let stand 5 minutes before cutting.

1 Serving: Calories 335 (Calories from Fat 190); Fat 21g (Saturated 8g); Cholesterol 95mg; Sodium 740mg; Carbohydrate 14g (Dietary Fiber 1g); Protein 24g

Spaghetti Pie

6 servings

PREP:
10 min

COOK:
16 min

BAKE:
45 min

STAND:
5 min

Betty's Success Tip

If you hold your uncooked spaghetti together in a bundle, 4 ounces is about as big around as the size of a quarter.

4 ounces uncooked spaghetti

½ pound lean ground beef

1 small green bell pepper, chopped (½ cup)

1 small onion, chopped (¼ cup)

1 jar (14 ounces) spaghetti sauce

1 teaspoon chili powder

½ teaspoon salt

¼ teaspoon pepper

2 large eggs

1 cup small-curd creamed cottage cheese

½ cup shredded mozzarella cheese (2 ounces)

Heat oven to 375°. Grease pie plate, 10 × 1½ inches. Cook spaghetti as directed on package.

While spaghetti is cooking, cook beef, bell pepper and onion in 10-inch skillet over medium heat 8 to 10 minutes, stirring occasionally, until beef is brown; drain. Stir in spaghetti sauce, chili powder, salt and pepper. Cook 5 to 6 minutes, stirring occasionally, until sauce is thickened.

Drain spaghetti. Place spaghetti in pie plate; gently press on bottom and 1 inch up side of pie plate.

Mix eggs and cottage cheese; spread evenly over spaghetti. Spoon beef mixture over cottage cheese mixture. Sprinkle with mozzarella cheese.

Bake 35 to 45 minutes or until center is set. Let stand 5 minutes before cutting.

1 Serving: Calories 310 (Calories from Fat 115); Fat 13g (Saturated 5g); Cholesterol 100mg; Sodium 760mg; Carbohydrate 30 (Dietary Fiber 2g); Protein 20g

Veal and Potato Strata
with Roasted Peppers

6 servings

PREP:
10 min

COOK:
25 min

BAKE:
25 min

Betty's Success Tip

If you can't find tenderized veal cutlets already packaged in the meat case, ask the butcher to tenderize slices of veal for you.

1½ pounds tenderized boneless veal cutlets

1 bag (1 pound, 4 ounces) refrigerated shredded hash brown potatoes

1 jar (12 ounces) roasted red bell peppers, drained

½ teaspoon salt

3 medium onions, cut lengthwise in half, then cut crosswise into thin slices

3 cloves garlic, finely chopped

½ teaspoon dried oregano leaves

½ teaspoon cracked black pepper

4 ounces feta cheese, crumbled (⅔ cup)

Heat oven to 350°. Spray rectangular baking dish, 13 × 9 × 2 inches, with cooking spray. Remove fat from veal. Cut veal into 6 serving pieces.

Layer potatoes and bell peppers in dish. Sprinkle salt over potatoes. Cover and bake 15 minutes. While potatoes are baking, spray 12-inch nonstick skillet with cooking spray; heat over medium-high heat. Cook veal in skillet about 5 minutes, turning once, until slightly pink in center. Remove veal from skillet.

Cook onions and garlic in same skillet over medium heat about 5 minutes, stirring frequently, until onions are tender.

Place veal on potato mixture. Layer onion mixture over veal. Sprinkle with oregano and pepper. Sprinkle with feta. Cover and bake 20 to 25 minutes or until heated through.

1 Serving: Calories 295 (Calories from Fat 70); Fat 8g (Saturated 4g); Cholesterol 90mg; Sodium 640mg; Carbohydrate 36g (Dietary Fiber 4g); Protein 24g

Veal and Potato Strata with Roasted Peppers

Stuffed Peppers

6 servings

PREP:
15 min

COOK:
15 min

BAKE:
1 hour

6 large bell peppers (any color)

1 pound lean ground beef

2 tablespoons chopped onion

1 cup cooked rice

1 teaspoon salt

1 clove garlic, finely chopped

1 can (15 ounces) tomato sauce

¾ cup shredded mozzarella cheese (3 ounces)

Cut thin slice from stem end of each bell pepper to remove top of pepper. Remove seeds and membranes; rinse peppers. Cook peppers in enough boiling water to cover in 4-quart Dutch oven about 5 minutes; drain.

Cook beef and onion in 10-inch skillet over medium heat 8 to 10 minutes, stirring occasionally, until beef is brown; drain. Stir in rice, salt, garlic and 1 cup of the tomato sauce; cook until hot.

Heat oven to 350°.

Stuff peppers with beef mixture. Stand peppers upright in ungreased square baking dish, 8 × 8 × 2 inches. Pour remaining tomato sauce over peppers.

Cover and bake 45 minutes. Uncover and bake about 15 minutes longer or until peppers are tender. Sprinkle with cheese.

1 Serving: Calories 290 (Calories from Fat 125); Fat 14g (Saturated 6g); Cholesterol 50mg; Sodium 930mg; Carbohydrate 24g (Dietary Fiber 4g); Protein 21g

Italian Sausage Lasagna

8 servings

PREP:
1 hour 10 min

BAKE:
45 min

STAND:
15 min

Betty's Success Tip

To make ahead, cover the un-baked lasagna with aluminum foil and refrigerate no longer than 24 hours or freeze no longer than 2 months. Bake covered 45 minutes; uncover and bake refrigerated lasagna 15 to 20 minutes longer or frozen lasagna 35 to 45 minutes longer until hot and bubbly.

Ingredient Substitution

For easy Italian Sausage Lasagna, substitute 4 cups (from 48-ounce jar) spaghetti sauce with meat for the first 8 ingredients (do not use thick or extra-thick varieties).

1 pound bulk Italian sausage or lean ground beef

1 medium onion, chopped (½ cup)

1 clove garlic, finely chopped

3 tablespoons chopped fresh parsley

1 tablespoon chopped fresh or 1 teaspoon dried basil leaves

1 teaspoon sugar

1 can (14½ ounces) whole tomatoes, undrained

1 can (15 ounces) tomato sauce

8 uncooked lasagna noodles (from 16-ounce box)

1 container (15 ounces) ricotta cheese or small-curd creamed cottage cheese (2 cups)

½ cup grated Parmesan cheese

1 tablespoon chopped fresh or 1½ teaspoons dried oregano leaves

2 cups shredded mozzarella cheese (8 ounces)

Cook sausage, onion and garlic in 10-inch skillet over medium heat, stirring occasionally, until sausage is no longer pink; drain.

Stir in 2 tablespoons of the parsley, the basil, sugar, tomatoes and tomato sauce, breaking up tomatoes with a fork or snipping with kitchen scissors. Heat to boiling, stirring occasionally; reduce heat. Simmer uncovered about 45 minutes or until slightly thickened.

Heat oven to 350°. Cook noodles as directed on package.

While noodles are cooking, mix ricotta cheese, ¼ cup of the Parmesan cheese, the oregano and remaining 1 tablespoon parsley.

Drain noodles. Spread ½ of the sausage mixture (about 2 cups) in un-greased rectangular baking dish, 13 × 9 × 2 inches. Top with 4 noodles. Spread ½ of the cheese mixture (about 1 cup) over noodles. Sprinkle with ½ of the mozzarella cheese. Repeat layers, ending with mozzarella and the remaining ¼ cup Parmesan cheese.

Cover and bake 30 minutes. Uncover and bake about 15 minutes longer or until hot and bubbly. Let stand 15 minutes before cutting.

1 Serving: Calories 450 (Calories from Fat 200); Fat 22g (Saturated 11g); Cholesterol 70mg; Sodium 1220mg; Carbohydrate 36g (Dietary Fiber 3g); Protein 30g

Easy Lasagna

8 to 10 servings

PREP:
20 min

CHILL:
24 hours

BAKE:
1 hour

STAND:
15 min

Betty's Success Tip

To make ahead, cover unbaked lasagna tightly with aluminum foil and refrigerate no longer than 24 hours or freeze no longer than 2 months. About 1½ hours (2 hours if frozen) before serving, heat oven to 350°. Bake in covered pan 45 minutes. Uncover and bake 15 to 20 minutes longer or until hot and bubbly (35 to 45 minutes if frozen). Sprinkle with mozzarella cheese. Let stand 15 minutes before cutting.

2 cups ricotta or small-curd creamed cottage cheese

½ cup grated Parmesan cheese

2 tablespoons chopped fresh parsley

1 tablespoon chopped fresh or 1½ teaspoons dried oregano leaves

2 jars (28 ounces each) spaghetti sauce

12 uncooked lasagna noodles

2 cups shredded mozzarella cheese (8 ounces)

¼ cup grated Parmesan cheese

Shredded mozzarella cheese, if desired

Mix ricotta cheese, ½ cup Parmesan cheese, the parsley and oregano.

Spread 2 cups spaghetti sauce in ungreased rectangular pan, 13 × 9 × 2 inches; top with 4 noodles. Spread cheese mixture over noodles. Spread with 2 cups spaghetti sauce and top with 4 noodles; repeat with 2 cups spaghetti sauce and 4 noodles. Sprinkle with 2 cups mozzarella cheese. Spread with remaining spaghetti sauce. Sprinkle with ¼ cup Parmesan cheese.

To complete recipe and serve now, heat oven to 350°. Cover with aluminum foil and bake 30 minutes. Uncover and bake about 30 minutes longer or until hot and bubbly. Sprinkle with mozzarella cheese. Let stand 15 minutes before cutting.

1 Serving: Calories 455 (Calories from Fat 190); Fat 21g (Saturated 9g); Cholesterol 40mg; Sodium 1710mg; Carbohydrate 47g (Dietary Fiber 4g); Protein 24g

Easy Lasagna

Sausage and Cheese Squares

8 servings

PREP:
12 min

CHILL:
24 hours

BAKE:
35 min

1 can (8 ounces) refrigerated crescent rolls

16 refrigerated smoked cocktail sausage links

1 large bell pepper, coarsely chopped (1½ cups)

1½ cups shredded Monterey Jack cheese (6 ounces)

1 can (10¾ ounces) condensed cream of onion soup

4 eggs

Unroll crescent roll dough. Place dough in bottom of ungreased rectangular baking dish, 11 × 7 × 1½ inches. Press seams closed and push dough 1 inch up sides of baking dish.

Arrange sausage evenly on dough. Sprinkle with bell pepper and 1 cup of the cheese.

Beat soup and eggs until blended; pour over ingredients in baking dish. Sprinkle with remaining cheese.

Heat oven to 350°. Bake uncovered 30 to 35 minutes or until knife inserted in center comes out clean.

1 Serving: Calories 350 (Calories from Fat 215); Fat 24g (Saturated 10g); Cholesterol 150mg; Sodium 1070mg; Carbohydrate 19g (Dietary Fiber 1g); Protein 15g

Sausage and Cheese Squares

Caribbean Pork Roast

8 servings

PREP:
20 min

MARINATE:
4 hours

ROAST:
1½ hours

STAND:
15 min

Betty's Success Tip

Allspice isn't a blend of numerous spices, as its name implies but is a single spice. Popular in Caribbean cuisine, allspice tastes like a combination of cinnamon, nutmeg and clove.

2- to 2½-pound pork boneless center loin roast

1 cup orange juice

½ cup lime juice

1½ teaspoons ground cumin

1½ teaspoons red pepper sauce

¾ teaspoon ground allspice

1 medium green bell pepper, cut into eighths

1 medium onion, cut into fourths

4 cloves garlic, finely chopped

Salt and pepper to taste

1½ teaspoons sugar

½ teaspoon salt

Remove fat from pork. Pierce pork deeply all over with meat fork or skewer. Place pork in heavy resealable plastic food-storage bag. Place remaining ingredients except salt and pepper, sugar and ½ teaspoon salt in blender or food processor. Cover and blend on medium speed until smooth. Pour blended mixture over pork. Seal bag; place in dish. Refrigerate, turning bag occasionally, at least 4 hours but no longer than 24 hours.

Heat oven to 325°. Remove pork from marinade; refrigerate marinade. Sprinkle pork with salt and pepper to taste. Place pork on rack in shallow roasting pan. Insert meat thermometer so tip is in center of thickest part of pork and does not rest in fat. Roast uncovered 1 hour to 1 hour 30 minutes for medium doneness (160°). Remove pork from pan. Cover and let stand about 15 minutes before slicing.

Pour marinade into 1½-quart saucepan. Stir in sugar and ½ teaspoon salt. Heat to boiling; reduce heat. Simmer uncovered about 5 minutes, stirring occasionally, until mixture thickens slightly. Serve sauce with pork.

1 Serving: Calories 165 (Calories from Fat 65); Fat 7g (Saturated 3g); Cholesterol 50mg; Sodium 480mg; Carbohydrate 8g (Dietary Fiber 1g); Protein 19g

Zesty Pork Tenderloin

6 servings

PREP:
5 min

MARINATE:
24 hours

ROAST:
29 min

¼ cup ketchup

1 tablespoon sugar

1 tablespoon dry white wine or water

1 tablespoon hoisin sauce

1 clove garlic, finely chopped

2 pork tenderloins (about ¾ pound each)

Mix all ingredients except pork in shallow glass or plastic dish. Add pork; turn to coat with marinade. Cover and refrigerate at least 1 hour but no longer than 24 hours, turning pork occasionally.

Heat oven to 425°. Place pork on rack in shallow roasting pan. Insert meat thermometer horizontally so tip is in thickest part of pork.

Roast uncovered 27 to 29 minutes or until thermometer reads 160° or pork is slightly pink in center.

1 Serving: Calories 155 (Calories from Fat 35); Fat 4g (Saturated 2g); Cholesterol 65mg; Sodium 170mg; Carbohydrate 6g (Dietary Fiber 0g); Protein 24g

Italian Roasted Pork Tenderloin

6 servings

PREP:
10 min

ROAST:
35 min

2 pork tenderloins, about ¾ pound each

1 teaspoon olive or vegetable oil

½ teaspoon salt

½ teaspoon fennel seed, crushed

¼ teaspoon pepper

1 clove garlic, finely chopped

Heat oven to 375°. Spray roasting pan rack with cooking spray. Remove fat from pork. Mash remaining ingredients into a paste. Rub paste on pork.

Place pork on rack in shallow roasting pan. Insert meat thermometer so tip is in thickest part of pork. Roast uncovered about 35 minutes for medium doneness (160°).

1 Serving: Calories 140 (Calories from Fat 45); Fat 5g (Saturated 2g); Cholesterol 65mg; Sodium 240mg; Carbohydrate 0g (Dietary Fiber 0g); Protein 24g

Pork with Stuffed Yams

4 servings

PREP:
10 min

BAKE:
1½ hours

Serving Suggestion

All you need to complete this hearty meal is a simple side dish of your favorite cooked green vegetable.

2 medium yams or sweet potatoes

4 pork loin or rib chops, about ¾ inch thick (about 1½ pounds)

½ teaspoon salt

¼ teaspoon paprika

⅛ teaspoon garlic powder

⅛ teaspoon pepper

½ cup orange juice

2 tablespoons orange juice

½ cup chopped apple

2 tablespoons finely chopped onion

2 tablespoons finely chopped celery

Heat oven to 350°. Pierce yams with fork to allow steam to escape. Bake 55 to 60 minutes or until tender. Remove fat from pork chops. About 30 minutes before yams are done, place pork in ungreased rectangular pan, 13 × 9 × 2 inches. Mix salt, paprika, garlic powder and pepper; sprinkle half of the salt mixture over pork. Turn pork; sprinkle with remaining salt mixture. Pour ½ cup orange juice into pan. Cover and bake 30 minutes.

Cut each yam lengthwise in half. Scoop out pulp, leaving ¼-inch shell. Mash pulp until no lumps remain. Beat in 2 tablespoons orange juice until light and fluffy. Stir in apple, onion and celery. Fill shells with pulp mixture.

Move pork to one end of pan; place yams in other end of pan. Bake uncovered about 30 minutes or until yams are hot and pork is slightly pink when cut near bone.

1 Serving: Calories 280 (Calories from Fat 90); Fat 10g (Saturated 4g); Cholesterol 75mg; Sodium 350mg; Carbohydrate 21g (Dietary Fiber 2g); Protein 28g

Almond-Stuffed Pork Chops

4 servings

PREP:
15 min

CHILL:
48 hours

BROIL:
25 min

½ cup chicken broth

¼ cup uncooked quick-cooking brown rice

2 tablespoons finely chopped dried apricots

2 tablespoons slivered almonds, toasted

2 teaspoons chopped fresh or ¾ teaspoon dried marjoram leaves

2 tablespoons chopped fresh parsley

4 pork loin chops, 1 inch thick (about 2 pounds)

¼ cup apricot preserves

Mix broth, rice, apricots, almonds and marjoram in 1½-quart saucepan. Heat to boiling; reduce heat to low. Cover and simmer about 10 minutes or until rice is tender. Stir in parsley.

Cut a 3-inch pocket in each pork chop, cutting from fat side almost to bone. Spoon about 2 tablespoons rice mixture into each pocket. Secure pockets with toothpicks.

Set oven control to broil. Place pork on rack in broiler pan. Broil with tops 5 to 6 inches from heat 10 minutes; turn. Broil 10 to 15 minutes longer for medium doneness (160°).

Heat preserves; brush over pork.

1 Serving: Calories 285 (Calories from Fat 90); Fat 10g (Saturated 3g); Cholesterol 65mg; Sodium 150mg; Carbohydrate 25g (Dietary Fiber 1g); Protein 25g

Yummy Pork Chops

4 servings

PREP:
5 min

BAKE:
50 min

Ingredient Substitution

For a bit of a kick, substitute chili sauce or chili puree with garlic for the ketchup.

4 pork loin chops, ½ inch thick (about 1¼ pounds)

3 tablespoons reduced-sodium soy sauce

3 tablespoons ketchup

2 teaspoons honey

Heat oven to 350°. Remove fat from pork. Place pork in ungreased square baking dish, 8 × 8 × 2 inches. Mix remaining ingredients; pour over pork.

Cover and bake about 45 minutes or until pork is slightly pink when cut near bone. Uncover and bake 5 minutes longer.

1 Serving: Calories 190 (Calories from Fat 70); Fat 8g (Saturated 3g); Cholesterol 65mg; Sodium 570mg; Carbohydrate 7g (Dietary Fiber 0g); Protein 23g

High on the Hog

Pork is 50 percent leaner than it was 20 years ago. The leanest pork cuts, in descending order, are:

- Boneless loin roast and chops
- Top loin roast
- Tenderloin
- Top loin chops

- Loin chops
- Boneless ham
- Canadian-style bacon

Spicy Asian Pork Ribs

4 to 6 servings

PREP:
15 min

BAKE:
1½ hours

COOK:
2 min

Serving Suggestion

Serve these luscious ribs on a pretty platter, and garnish with fresh orange wedges and parsley.

4 pounds pork loin back ribs

¼ cup orange marmalade

2 tablespoons hoisin sauce

1 tablespoon soy sauce

¼ teaspoon ground mustard

Heat oven to 350°.

Cut ribs into serving pieces. Place meaty sides up in shallow roasting pan.

Mix remaining ingredients in 1-quart saucepan. Brush pork generously with some of the marmalade mixture.

Cover and bake 1 hour. Brush with marmalade mixture. Cover and bake 15 to 30 minutes longer or until pork is tender.

Heat remaining marmalade mixture to boiling. Boil 1 minute, stirring constantly. Serve with pork.

1 Serving: Calories 920 (Calories from Fat 600); Fat 67g (Saturated 24g); Cholesterol 265mg; Sodium 570mg; Carbohydrate 16g (Dietary Fiber 1g); Protein 64g

Saucy Ribs

6 servings

PREP:
10 min

BAKE:
2¼ hours

COOK:
1 min

4½ pounds pork loin back ribs or pork spareribs

Spicy Barbecue Sauce (below)

Heat oven to 325°. Prepare desired sauce.

Cut ribs into serving pieces. Place meaty sides up on rack in a shallow roasting pan. Bake uncovered 1 hour to 1 hour 30 minutes; brush with sauce. Bake uncovered about 45 minutes longer, brushing frequently with sauce, until tender.

Heat any remaining sauce to boiling, stirring constantly; boil and stir 1 minute. Serve sauce with ribs.

Spicy Barbecue Sauce

⅓ cup margarine, butter or spread

2 tablespoons white vinegar

2 tablespoons water

1 teaspoon sugar

½ teaspoon garlic powder

½ teaspoon onion powder

½ teaspoon pepper

Dash of ground red pepper (cayenne)

Heat all ingredients in 1-quart saucepan over medium heat, stirring frequently, until margarine is melted.

1 Serving: Calories 580 (Calories from Fat 450); Fat 50g (Saturated 17); Cholesterol 135mg; Sodium 250mg; Carbohydrate 2g (Dietary Fiber 0g); Protein 29g

Harvest Bean Casserole

6 servings

PREP:
12 min

BAKE:
35 min

Ingredient Substitution

Use either spicy or regular sausage—whichever suits your household—for this hearty casserole.

1 pound bulk pork breakfast sausage

1 can (28 ounces) baked beans

2 baking apples, thinly sliced

1 can (18 ounces) vacuum-packed sweet potatoes

3 medium green onions, sliced (⅓ cup)

Heat oven to 375°.

Cook sausage in 10-inch skillet over medium heat 8 to 10 minutes, stirring occasionally, until no longer pink; drain.

Place sausage in ungreased rectangular baking dish, 11 × 7 × 1½ inches. Stir in baked beans. Arrange apple slices over sausage mixture. Slice sweet potatoes over apples.

Cover and bake 30 to 35 minutes or until apples are tender. Sprinkle with onions.

1 Serving: Calories 355 (Calories from Fat 80); Fat 9g (Saturated 3g); Cholesterol 55mg; Sodium 1310mg; Carbohydrate 50g (Dietary Fiber 8g); Protein 26g

Glazed Baked Ham
20 servings

PREP:
10 min

BAKE:
1½ hours

STAND:
15 min

6-pound fully cooked smoked bone-in ham

Brown Sugar–Orange Glaze or Pineapple Glaze (below)

Heat oven to 325°. Place ham on rack in shallow roasting pan. Insert meat thermometer in thickest part of ham. Bake uncovered 1 hour 30 minutes or until thermometer reads 135° to 140°.

Make desired glaze. Brush glaze over ham during last 45 minutes of baking.

Remove ham from oven, cover with tent with aluminum foil and let stand 10 to 15 minutes for easier carving.

Brown Sugar–Orange Glaze

½ cup packed brown sugar

2 tablespoons orange or pineapple juice

½ teaspoon ground mustard

Mix all ingredients.

Pineapple Glaze

1 cup packed brown sugar

1 tablespoon cornstarch

¼ teaspoon salt

1 can (8 ounces) crushed pineapple in syrup, undrained

2 tablespoons lemon juice

1 tablespoon yellow mustard

Mix brown sugar, cornstarch and salt in 1-quart saucepan. Stir in pineapple, lemon juice and mustard. Cook over medium heat, stirring constantly, until mixture thickens and boils. Boil and stir 1 minute.

1 Serving: Calories 125 (Calories from Fat 35); Fat 4g (Saturated 1g); Cholesterol 40mg; Sodium 890mg; Carbohydrate 7g (Dietary Fiber 0g); Protein 15g

Ham and Potato Bake

8 servings

PREP:
10 min

BAKE:
1 hour

Betty's Success Tip

To make ahead, cover unbaked mixture tightly and refrigerate at least 4 hours but no longer than 24 hours. About 1¼ hours before serving, heat oven to 350°. Bake uncovered 50 to 60 minutes or until top is light brown and center is set.

Ingredient Substitution

If you'd like a spicier dish, increase red pepper sauce to ½ teaspoon.

1 package (1 pound 4 ounces) refrigerated shredded hash brown potatoes

1 cup chopped fully cooked ham

1 cup seasoned croutons

1 can (11 ounces) condensed Cheddar cheese soup

4 eggs

½ cup milk

¼ teaspoon red pepper sauce

Grease rectangular baking dish, 11 × 7 × 1½ inches. Spread potatoes in baking dish. Sprinkle with ham and croutons.

Beat soup, eggs, milk and pepper sauce until blended. Pour over ingredients in baking dish. Bake uncovered 50 to 60 minutes or until top is light brown and center is set.

Heat oven to 350°.

1 Serving: Calories 190 (Calories from Fat 70); Fat 8g (Saturated 4g); Cholesterol 125mg; Sodium 680mg; Carbohydrate 20g (Dietary Fiber 1g); Protein 11g

Bread on the Side

In a rush? Round out your meal with these easy ideas.

- **Dropped biscuits** with butter or honey
- **Garlic bread sprinkled** with chopped parsley or oregano
- **Pita** or toast triangles spread with savory-flavored cream cheese
- **Breadsticks,** plain, herbed or Parmesan cheese
- **Flour tortillas** sprinkled with Monterey Jack cheese, melted and rolled
- **English muffins** or crumpets, toasted and sprinkled with shredded Parmesan cheese
- **Pizza crust shell,** heated and cut into wedges.

Impossible Ham and Swiss Pie

6 to 8 servings

PREP:
10 min

BAKE:
40 min

COOL:
5 min

2 cups cut-up fully cooked smoked ham

1 cup shredded natural Swiss cheese (4 ounces)

⅓ cup sliced green onions or chopped onion

2 cups milk

4 eggs

1 cup Bisquick Original baking mix

¼ teaspoon salt, if desired

⅛ teaspoon pepper

Heat oven to 400°.

Grease glass pie plate, 10 × 1½ inches. Sprinkle ham, cheese and onions in pie plate.

Stir remaining ingredients with fork until blended. Pour into pie plate. Bake 35 to 40 minutes or until knife inserted in center comes out clean. Cool 5 minutes. Garnish with tomato slices and green bell pepper rings.

1 Serving: Calories 320 (Calories from Fat 150); Fat 17g (Saturated 8g); Cholesterol 190mg; Sodium 940mg; Carbohydrates 19g (Dietary Fiber 1g), Protein 24g

Ham and Egg Bake

8 servings

PREP:
10 min

BAKE:
50 min

Betty's Success Tip

This is a perfect dish to make ahead. Just cover and refrigerate no longer than 24 hours; increase bake time to 55 to 60 minutes.

6 cups frozen (not thawed) hash brown potatoes

2 cups diced, fully cooked smoked ham

2 cups shredded Swiss cheese (8 ounces)

1 jar (7 ounces) roasted red bell peppers, drained and chopped

1 jar (4½ ounces) sliced mushrooms, drained

6 large eggs

⅓ cup milk

1 cup small-curd, creamed cottage cheese

¼ teaspoon pepper

Heat oven to 350°. Grease rectangular baking dish, 13 × 9 × 2 inches, with shortening.

Sprinkle 3 cups of the potatoes evenly in baking dish. Layer with ham, Swiss cheese, bell peppers and mushrooms. Sprinkle remaining potatoes over mushrooms.

Beat eggs, milk, cottage cheese and pepper with fork or wire whisk until blended. Pour egg mixture over potatoes. Bake uncovered 45 to 50 minutes or until light golden brown and set in center.

1 Serving: Calories 350 (Calories from Fat 140); Fat 17g (Saturated 8g); Cholesterol 210mg; Sodium 770mg; Carbohydrate 33g (Dietary Fiber 3g); Protein 28g

Ham Loaf

8 servings

PREP:
15 min

BAKE:
1½ hours

STAND:
5 min

1½ pounds ground fully cooked ham

1 small onion, finely chopped (¼ cup)

½ cup dry bread crumbs

¼ cup finely chopped green bell pepper

½ cup milk

½ teaspoon ground mustard

¼ teaspoon pepper

2 large eggs

Heat oven to 350°.

Mix all ingredients. Spread mixture in ungreased loaf pan, 9 × 5 × 3 or 8½ × 4½ × 2½ inches.

Insert meat thermometer so tip is in center of loaf. Bake uncovered about 1 hour 30 minutes or until thermometer reads 170°.

Let stand 5 minutes; remove from pan.

1 Serving: Calories 205 (Calories from Fat 90); Fat 10g (Saturated 3g); Cholesterol 105mg; Sodium 1360mg; Carbohydrate 7g (Dietary Fiber 0g); Protein 22g

Quiche Lorraine

6 servings

PREP:
10 min

BAKE:
45 min

STAND:
10 min

1 prepared 9-inch piecrust shell

8 slices bacon, crisply cooked and crumbled

1 cup shredded natural Swiss cheese (4 ounces)

⅓ cup finely chopped onion

4 large eggs

2 cups whipping (heavy) cream

¼ teaspoon salt

¼ teaspoon pepper

⅛ teaspoon ground red pepper (cayenne)

Heat oven to 425°.

Prepare pastry. Ease into quiche dish, 9 × 1½ inches, or pie plate, 9 × 1¼ inches.

Sprinkle bacon, cheese and onion in pastry-lined quiche dish. Beat eggs slightly; beat in remaining ingredients. Pour into quiche dish. Bake 15 minutes. Reduce oven temperature to 300°. Bake about 30 minutes longer or until knife inserted in center comes out clean. Let stand 10 minutes before cutting.

1 Serving: Calories 550 (Calories from Fat 420); Fat 47g (Saturated26); Cholesterol 280mg; Sodium 500mg; Carbohydrate 16g (Dietary Fiber 1g); Protein 15g

Chili Dog Wraps

5 servings

PREP:
5 min

BAKE:
25 min

10 corn or flour tortillas (6 to 8 inches in diameter)

10 hot dogs

1 can (15 to 16 ounces) chili

2 cups salsa

1 cup shredded Cheddar or Monterey Jack cheese (4 ounces)

Heat oven to 350°. Grease rectangular baking dish, 13 × 9 × 2 inches.

Soften tortillas as directed on package. Place 1 hot dog and 3 table-spoons chili on each tortilla. Roll up tortillas; place seam side down in baking dish. Spoon salsa over tortillas.

Cover and bake 20 minutes. Sprinkle with cheese. Bake uncovered about 5 minutes longer or until cheese is melted.

1 Serving: Calories 550 (Calories from Fat 325); Fat 36g (Saturated 15g); Cholesterol 65mg; Sodium 2190mg; Carbohydrate 41g (Dietary Fiber 7g); Protein 22g

Poultry and Fish Entrées

Chicken-Potato Roast

6 servings

PREP:
20 min

ROAST:
1¼ hours

STAND:
10 min

Betty's Success Tip

For a savory, herb flavor, add dried rosemary or sage to the margarine mixture before brushing it on the chicken.

3- to 3½-pound whole broiler-fryer chicken

1 medium apple, cut into fourths

1 medium onion, cut into fourths

2 cloves garlic, cut into fourths

3 unpeeled medium baking potatoes, cut into fourths

2 tablespoons margarine, melted

1 teaspoon dried thyme leaves

1 teaspoon paprika

½ teaspoon salt

Heat oven to 375°. Fold wings of chicken across back with tips touching. Place apple, onion and garlic in body cavity. Tie or skewer drumsticks to tail. Place chicken, breast side up, on rack in shallow roasting pan.

Cut potatoes crosswise about ¾ of the way through into ¼-inch slices. Place on rack around chicken. Mix remaining ingredients; brush over chicken and potatoes. Insert meat thermometer in chicken so tip is in thickest part of inside thigh muscle and does not touch bone.

Roast uncovered 1 hour to 1 hour 15 minutes, brushing chicken and potatoes with margarine mixture every 30 minutes, until thermometer reads 180° and juice of chicken is no longer pink when center of thigh is cut. Let chicken stand 10 minutes before carving; keep potatoes warm. Discard apple, onion and garlic. Remove and discard chicken skin.

1 Serving: Calories 340 (Calories from Fat 155); Fat 17g (Saturated 5g); Cholesterol 85mg; Sodium 330mg; Carbohydrate 21g (Dietary Fiber 2g); Protein 28g

Country-Style Chicken

6 servings

PREP:
25 min

BAKE:
2 hours

COOK:
5 min

Betty's Success Tip

Leaving the skin on the chicken during the baking time helps lock in flavorful juices and keeps the meat both tender and moist.

3- to 3½-pound whole broiler-fryer chicken

1 tablespoon margarine

1 can (10½ ounces) condensed chicken broth

¾ teaspoon chopped fresh or ¼ teaspoon dried thyme leaves

¼ teaspoon pepper

8 medium carrots, cut into fourths

8 whole small white onions

4 medium turnips, cut into fourths

½ cup dry white wine or chicken broth

2 tablespoons cold water

1 tablespoon cornstarch

Chopped fresh thyme, if desired

Fold wings of chicken across back with tips touching. Tie or skewer drumsticks to tail. Melt margarine in ovenproof nonstick Dutch oven over medium heat. Cook chicken in margarine until brown on all sides; drain.

Heat oven to 375°. Pour broth over chicken in Dutch oven. Sprinkle with thyme and pepper. Insert meat thermometer in chicken so tip is in thickest part of inside thigh muscle and does not touch bone. Cover and bake 45 minutes.

Arrange carrots, onions and turnips around chicken. Cover and bake 1 hour to 1 hour 15 minutes or until thermometer reads 180° and juice of chicken is no longer pink when center of thigh is cut. Remove chicken and vegetables from Dutch oven; keep warm.

Skim fat from pan drippings in Dutch oven. Stir wine into juices. Heat to boiling. Mix cold water and cornstarch; stir into wine mixture. Heat to boiling, stirring constantly. Boil and stir 1 minute. Remove and discard chicken skin. Serve chicken and vegetables with sauce. Sprinkle with thyme.

1 Serving: Calories 330 (Calories from Fat 145); Fat 16g (Saturated 5g); Cholesterol 85mg; Sodium 480mg; Carbohydrate 22g (Dietary Fiber 6g); Protein 31g

Country-Style Chicken

Rosemary-Lemon Chicken

6 servings

PREP:
20 min

ROAST:
1½ hours

STAND:
10 min

2 large shallots or 1 small onion, finely chopped (¼ cup)

1 garlic clove, finely chopped

1 teaspoon grated lemon peel

½ teaspoon dried rosemary leaves, crumbled

½ teaspoon salt

¼ teaspoon pepper

3- to 3½-pound whole broiler-fryer chicken

1 medium lemon, cut in half

½ teaspoon paprika

Heat oven to 350°. Mix all ingredients except chicken, lemon and paprika. Gently loosen breast skin from chicken with fingers, reaching as far back as possible without tearing skin. Spread herb mixture over breast meat; cover with skin. Squeeze lemon halves over outside of chicken and inside body cavity; place lemon halves in cavity.

Fold wings of chicken across back with tips touching. Tie or skewer drumsticks to tail. Sprinkle paprika over chicken. Place chicken, breast side up, on rack in shallow roasting pan. Insert meat thermometer in chicken so tip is in thickest part of inside thigh muscle and does not touch bone.

Roast uncovered about 1 hour to 1 hour 30 minutes or until thermometer reads 180° and juice of chicken is no longer pink when center of thigh is cut. Let stand 10 minutes before carving. Remove and discard chicken skin and lemon.

1 Serving: Calories 230 (Calories from Fat 115); Fat 13g (Saturated 4g); Cholesterol 85mg; Sodium 280mg; Carbohydrate 1g (Dietary Fiber 0g); Protein 27g

Wine-Sauced Chicken

6 servings

PREP:
10 min

ROAST:
1¼ hours

COOK:
30 min

STAND:
10 min

3- to 3½-pound whole broiler-fryer chicken

1 cup dry red wine or grape juice

1 tablespoon chopped fresh or 1 teaspoon dried basil leaves

½ teaspoon salt

1 medium onion, finely chopped (½ cup)

2 large cloves garlic, finely chopped

1 can (8 ounces) tomato sauce

Heat oven to 375°. Fold wings of chicken across back with tips touching. Tie or skewer drumsticks to tail. Place chicken, breast side up, on rack in shallow roasting pan. Insert meat thermometer in chicken so tip is in thickest part of inside thigh muscle and does not touch bone.

Roast uncovered 1 hour to 1 hour 15 minutes or until thermometer reads 180° and juice of chicken is no longer pink when center of thigh is cut. Let stand 10 minutes before carving. Remove and discard chicken skin.

While chicken is roasting, mix remaining ingredients in 1½-quart saucepan. Heat to boiling, stirring occasionally; reduce heat to low. Cover and simmer 30 minutes. Serve with chicken.

1 Serving: Calories 250 (Calories from Fat 115); Fat 13g (Saturated 4g); Cholesterol 85mg; Sodium 510mg; Carbohydrate 5g (Dietary Fiber 1g); Protein 27g

Thyme-Baked Chicken with Vegetables

6 servings

PREP:
15 min

BAKE:
1¾ hours

3- to 3½-pound whole broiler-fryer chicken

6 medium carrots, cut into 1-inch pieces

4 medium stalks celery, cut into 1-inch pieces

3 medium baking potatoes, cut into 1½-inch pieces

2 medium onions, cut into wedges

2 tablespoons butter or stick margarine, melted

4 teaspoons chopped fresh or 1 teaspoon dried thyme leaves

Heat oven to 375°.

Fold wings of chicken across back with tips touching. Tie or skewer drumsticks to tail. Place chicken, breast side up, in shallow roasting pan. Insert meat thermometer so tip is in thickest part of inside thigh muscle and does not touch bone.

Bake uncovered 45 minutes. Arrange carrots, celery, potatoes and onions around chicken. Mix butter and thyme; drizzle over chicken and vegetables.

Cover and bake 45 to 60 minutes or until thermometer reads 180° and juice of chicken is no longer pink when center of thigh is cut.

1 Serving: Calories 355 (Calories from Fat 155); Fat 17g (Saturated 6g); Cholesterol 95mg; Sodium 160mg; Carbohydrate 26g (Dietary Fiber 4g); Protein 29g

Spicy Jamaican Chicken and Potatoes

6 servings

PREP:
15 min

BAKE:
1¼ hours

STAND:
15 min

Fast & Low-Fat Jamaican Jerk Seasoning (below)

3- to 3½-pound whole broiler-fryer chicken

2 tablespoons vegetable oil

3 medium baking potatoes, cut lengthwise into fourths

Make Fast & Low-Fat Jamaican Jerk Seasoning below.

Heat oven to 375°. Line roasting pan with aluminum foil.

Place chicken, breast side up, on rack in roasting pan. Brush 1 tablespoon of the oil over chicken. Rub 2 tablespoons of the seasoning into chicken skin. Insert meat thermometer so tip is in thickest part of inside thigh muscle and does not touch bone.

Brush remaining 1 tablespoon oil over potatoes. Sprinkle with remaining seasoning mix. Place potatoes on rack around chicken.

Roast uncovered 1 hour to 1 hour 15 minutes or until potatoes are tender, thermometer reads 180° and juice of chicken is no longer pink when center of thigh is cut. Let chicken stand about 15 minutes for easiest carving.

Fast & Low-Fat Jamaican Jerk Seasoning

1 tablespoon instant minced onion

2 teaspoons dried thyme leaves

1 teaspoon ground allspice

1 teaspoon ground pepper

½ teaspoon salt

½ teaspoon ground cinnamon

¼ teaspoon ground red pepper (cayenne)

Mix all ingredients in storage container with tight-fitting lid.

Store in cool, dry place up to 6 months. Stir before each use.

1 Serving: Calories 325 (Calories from Fat 170); Fat 18g (Saturated 4g); Cholesterol 85mg; Sodium 280mg; Carbohydrate 12g (Dietary Fiber 1g); Protein 28g

Oven-Fried Chicken

6 servings

PREP:
10 min

BAKE:
1 hour

Ingredient Substitution

For crunchy Oven-Fried Chicken, substitute 1 cup corn-flake crumbs for the ½ cup flour. Dip chicken into ¼ cup butter or stick margarine, melted, before coating with crumb mixture.

¼ **cup butter or stick margarine**

½ **cup all-purpose flour**

1 **teaspoon paprika**

½ **teaspoon salt**

¼ **teaspoon pepper**

3- **to 3½-pound cut-up broiler-fryer chicken**

Heat oven to 425°. Melt butter in rectangular pan, 13 × 9 × 2 inches, in oven.

Mix flour, paprika, salt and pepper. Coat chicken with flour mixture. Place chicken, skin side down, in pan.

Bake uncovered 30 minutes. Turn chicken; bake about 30 minutes longer or until juice is no longer pink when centers of thickest pieces are cut.

1 Serving: Calories 320 (Calories from Fat 180); Fat 20g (Saturated 8g); Cholesterol 100mg; Sodium 320mg; Carbohydrate 7g (Dietary Fiber 0g); Protein 28g

Zesty Italian Chicken

6 servings

PREP:
5 min

BAKE:
1 hour

3- to 3½-pound cut-up broiler-fryer chicken

¼ cup mayonnaise or salad dressing

¼ cup zesty Italian dressing

2 tablespoons chopped fresh basil

1 tablespoon chopped fresh oregano

1 teaspoon chopped fresh rosemary

Heat oven to 375°. Place chicken, skin side down, in ungreased rectangular pan, 13 × 9 × 2 inches.

Mix remaining ingredients; brush half of mayonnaise mixture on chicken. Cover and bake 30 minutes. Turn chicken; brush with remaining mayonnaise mixture. Bake uncovered about 30 minutes longer or until juice of chicken is no longer pink when centers of thickest pieces are cut. (If chicken browns too quickly, cover with aluminum foil.)

1 Serving: Calories 375 (Calories from Fat 245); Fat 27g (Saturated 6g); Cholesterol 105mg; Sodium 220mg; Carbohydrate 2g (Dietary Fiber 0g); Protein 31g

Honey-Mustard Chicken

6 servings

PREP:
10 min

BAKE:
1 hour

3- to 3½-pound cut-up broiler-fryer chicken

⅓ cup country-style Dijon mustard

3 tablespoons honey

1 tablespoon mustard seed

½ teaspoon pepper

Heat oven to 375°. Place chicken, skin side down, in ungreased rectangular pan, 13 × 9 × 2 inches. Mix remaining ingredients; brush over chicken.

Cover and bake 30 minutes. Turn chicken; brush with mustard mixture. Bake uncovered about 30 minutes longer or until juice of chicken is no longer pink when centers of thickest pieces are cut. (If chicken begins to brown too quickly, cover with aluminum foil.) Discard any remaining mustard mixture.

1 Serving: Calories 285 (Calories from Fat 135); Fat 15g (Saturated 4g); Cholesterol 85mg; Sodium 250mg; Carbohydrate 10g (Dietary Fiber 0g); Protein 28g

Herbed Baked Chicken Breasts

6 servings

PREP:
15 min

BAKE:
35 min

6 boneless, skinless chicken breast halves (about 1¾ pounds)

½ cup fat-free mayonnaise or salad dressing

1 teaspoon garlic salt

1 tablespoon chopped fresh or 1 teaspoon dried marjoram leaves

2 teaspoons chopped fresh or ½ teaspoon dried rosemary leaves

2 teaspoons chopped fresh or ½ teaspoon dried thyme leaves

1 cup cornflakes cereal, crushed (½ cup)

½ teaspoon paprika

Heat oven to 375°. Spray rectangular pan, 13 × 9 × 2 inches, with cooking spray. Remove fat from chicken.

Mix mayonnaise, garlic salt, marjoram, rosemary and thyme; set aside. Mix cereal and paprika. Spread rounded tablespoon of mayonnaise mixture over both sides of each chicken breast half; coat evenly with cereal mixture. Place chicken in pan.

Bake uncovered 30 to 35 minutes or until juice of chicken is no longer pink when centers of thickest pieces are cut.

1 Serving: Calories 175 (Calories from Fat 35); Fat 4g (Saturated 1g); Cholesterol 5mg; Sodium 650mg; Carbohydrate 8g (Dietary Fiber 0g); Protein 27g

Chicken with Orange-Pecan Rice

4 servings

PREP:
5 min

BAKE:
45 min

Serving Suggestion

This is the dish for easy enter-taining. Complete the meal with asparagus spears, sliced tomatoes and your favorite dinner rolls.

1 package (6.25 ounces) fast-cooking long grain and wild rice

2 cups orange juice

¼ cup chopped pecans

1 jar (2 ounces) diced pimientos, drained

4 skinless boneless chicken breast halves (about 1 pound)

Chopped fresh parsley, if desired

Heat oven to 350°. Grease square pan, 8 × 8 × 2 inches.

Mix rice, seasoning packet included in rice mix, orange juice, pecans and pimientos in pan. Place chicken on rice.

Cover and bake 35 to 45 minutes or until liquid is absorbed and juice of chicken is no longer pink when centers of thickest pieces are cut. Sprinkle with parsley.

1 Serving: Calories 285 (Calories from Fat 70); Fat 8g (Saturated 2g); Cholesterol 60mg; Sodium 60mg; Carbohydrate 27g (Dietary Fiber 1g); Protein 27g

Golden Potato-Coated Baked Chicken

4 servings

PREP:
10 min

BAKE:
25 min

Serving Suggestion

For a fresh-tasting accompaniment to this crispy chicken, sprinkle chopped fresh basil leaves over sliced roma (plum) tomatoes. Then drizzle on Italian dressing.

4 skinless, boneless chicken breast halves (about 1 pound)

1 egg white

2 tablespoons water

¼ cup mashed potato mix (dry)

1 tablespoon cornstarch

2 teaspoons Italian seasoning

¼ teaspoon ground red pepper (cayenne)

Butter-flavored cooking spray

Heat oven to 425°. Spray 12-inch pizza pan or jelly roll pan, 15½ × 10½ × 1 inch, with cooking spray. Remove fat from chicken.

Mix egg white and water. Mix potato mix, cornstarch, Italian seasoning and red pepper in a second bowl. Dip chicken into egg white mixture, then coat with potato mixture. Place in pan so pieces don't touch. Spray chicken lightly with cooking spray.

Bake uncovered about 25 minutes or until juice of chicken is no longer pink when centers of thickest pieces are cut (do not turn chicken while baking).

1 Serving: Calories 160 (Calories from Fat 35); Fat 4g (Saturated 1g); Cholesterol 70mg; Sodium 80mg; Carbohydrate 5g (Dietary Fiber 0g); Protein 26g

Super-Easy Chicken Manicotti

7 servings

PREP:
12 min

CHILL:
24 hours

BAKE:
1 hour

Betty's Success Tip

Just say "no" to the time-consuming task of cooking and stuffing manicotti shells and use our clever new technique: Simply insert chicken breast tenders into uncooked manicotti shells! Smother with sauce, olives and cheese; cover and refrigerate 24 hours to help "soften" the pasta.

1 jar (30 ounces) spaghetti sauce

1 teaspoon garlic salt

1½ pounds chicken breast tenders

14 uncooked manicotti shells (8 ounces)

1 can (2½ ounces) sliced ripe olives, drained

2 cups shredded mozzarella cheese (8 ounces)

Spread about ⅓ of the spaghetti sauce in ungreased rectangular baking dish, 13 × 9 × 2 inches.

Sprinkle garlic salt on chicken. Insert chicken into uncooked manicotti shells, stuffing from each end of shell to fill if necessary. Place shells on spaghetti sauce in dish.

Pour remaining spaghetti sauce evenly over shells, covering completely. Sprinkle with olives and cheese. Cover unbaked manicotti tightly with aluminum foil and refrigerate no longer than 24 hours.

About 1 hour before serving, heat oven to 350°. Bake in covered baking dish about 1 hour or until shells are tender.

1 Serving: Calories 405 (Calories from Fat 145); Fat 16g (Saturated 7g); Cholesterol 30mg; Sodium 1430mg; Carbohydrate 43g (Dietary Fiber 4g); Protein 26g

Rice and Onion Chicken Casserole

4 servings

PREP:
10 min

BAKE:
1 hour

1 can (10¾ ounces) condensed cream of mushroom soup

1 soup can of milk

¾ cup uncooked regular long-grain rice

1 can (4 ounces) mushroom stems and pieces, undrained

1 envelope (about 1½ ounces) onion soup mix

4 skinless boneless chicken breast halves (about 1 pound)

Heat oven to 350°.

Mix mushroom soup and milk; reserve ½ cup soup mixture. Mix remaining soup mixture, the rice, mushrooms and half of the dry onion soup mix; spoon into ungreased rectangular baking dish, 11 × 7 × 1½ inches.

Place chicken on rice mixture. Pour reserved soup mixture over chicken. Sprinkle with remaining dry onion soup mix.

Cover and bake 45 minutes. Uncover and bake **about 15 minutes** longer or until chicken is no longer pink when centers of thickest pieces are cut.

1 Serving: Calories 405 (Calories from Fat 100); Fat 11g (Saturated 4g); Cholesterol 70mg; Sodium 1710mg; Carbohydrate 46g (Dietary Fiber 2g); Protein 32g

Zesty Roasted Chicken and Potatoes

6 servings

PREP:
10 min

BAKE:
35 min

Betty's Success Tip

Serve this family favorite with a super-quick salad. Simply pick up prepared salad greens at your local fast-food restaurant or supermarket, toss them with your favorite dressing, and you'll have a meal on the table in a snap!

6 skinless boneless chicken breast halves

1 pound small red potatoes, cut in quarters

⅓ cup mayonnaise or salad dressing

3 tablespoons Dijon mustard

½ teaspoon pepper

2 cloves garlic, crushed

Chopped fresh chives, if desired

Heat oven to 350°. Grease jelly roll pan, 15½ × 10½ × 1 inch.

Place chicken and potatoes in pan. Mix remaining ingredients except chives; brush over chicken and potatoes.

Bake uncovered 30 to 35 minutes or until potatoes are tender and juice of chicken is no longer pink when centers of thickest pieces are cut. Sprinkle with chives.

1 Serving: Calories 380 (Calories from Fat 200); Fat 22g (Saturated 5g); Cholesterol 90mg; Sodium 240mg; Carbohydrate 17g (Dietary Fiber 1g); Protein 29g

Chicken with Basil-Seasoned Vegetables

4 servings

PREP:
10 min

COOK:
26 min

2 pounds chicken drumsticks

1 can (14½ ounces) ready-to-serve chicken broth

1 can (5½ ounces) spicy eight-vegetable juice

1½ teaspoons dried basil leaves

½ teaspoon cracked black pepper

1 bag (16 ounces) frozen green beans, potatoes, onions and red peppers, thawed

2 tablespoons cornstarch

Hot cooked noodles, if desired

Spray 12-inch nonstick skillet with cooking spray; heat over medium heat. Cook chicken in skillet about 10 minutes, turning occasionally, until brown on all sides. Remove chicken from skillet; keep warm.

Reserve 2 tablespoons of the broth. Add remaining broth, the vegetable juice, basil and pepper to skillet. Heat to boiling; reduce heat. Arrange chicken in broth mixture. Add vegetables. Cover and simmer about 15 minutes, stirring occasionally, until juice of chicken is no longer pink when centers of thickest pieces are cut. Remove chicken; keep warm.

Mix reserved 2 tablespoons broth and the cornstarch; stir into vegetable mixture. Heat to boiling, stirring constantly. Boil and stir 1 minute. Serve over chicken and noodles.

1 Serving: Calories 300 (Calories from Fat 110); Fat 12g (Saturated 4g); Cholesterol 90mg; Sodium 630mg; Carbohydrate 17g (Dietary Fiber 3g); Protein 34g

Gingered Apricot Chicken Breasts

4 servings

PREP:
5 min

CHILL:
24 hours

BAKE:
20 min

COOK:
1 min

1 can (5½ ounces) apricot nectar

2 tablespoons dry white wine or apricot nectar

2 tablespoons soy sauce

1 tablespoon vegetable oil

1 teaspoon grated gingerroot or ¼ teaspoon ground ginger

4 skinless boneless chicken breast halves (about 1 pound)

2 teaspoons cornstarch

Mix all ingredients except chicken and cornstarch in heavy-duty plastic food-storage bag.

Add chicken to bag, turning to coat. Seal bag tightly and refrigerate at least 1 hour but no longer than 24 hours.

Heat oven to 375°. Grease square pan, 8 × 8 × 2 inches. Remove chicken from marinade; reserve marinade. Place chicken in pan. Bake uncovered about 20 minutes or until juice is no longer pink when centers of thickest pieces are cut.

Mix marinade and cornstarch in 1-quart saucepan. Heat to boiling; boil and stir 1 minute. Serve over chicken.

1 Serving: Calories 195 (Calories from Fat 65); Fat 7g (Saturated 2g); Cholesterol 60mg; Sodium 570mg; Carbohydrate 8g (Dietary Fiber 0g); Protein 25g

Southwestern Drumsticks

4 servings

PREP:
20 min

BAKE:
45 min

Serving Suggestion

For a little extra fiber, toss in ¼ cup of oat bran with the cornmeal mixture.

2 pounds chicken drumsticks

⅔ cup yellow cornmeal

1 teaspoon ground cumin

1 teaspoon chili powder

¼ teaspoon salt

⅓ cup buttermilk

¼ teaspoon red pepper sauce

Cooking spray

1 cup thick-and-chunky salsa, if desired

Heat oven to 400°. Spray rectangular pan, 13 × 9 × 2 inches, with cooking spray. Remove skin and fat from chicken.

Mix cornmeal, cumin, chili powder and salt in heavy resealable plastic food-storage bag. Mix buttermilk and pepper sauce in medium bowl. Dip chicken into buttermilk mixture, then shake in bag to coat with cornmeal mixture. Place in pan. Spray chicken lightly with cooking spray.

Bake uncovered 40 to 45 minutes or until juice of chicken is no longer pink when centers of thickest pieces are cut. Serve with salsa.

1 Serving: Calories 220 (Calories from Fat 55); Fat 6g (Saturated 2g); Cholesterol 90mg; Sodium 240mg; Carbohydrate 19g (Dietary Fiber 2g); Protein 25g

Quick Coatings for Chicken and Fish

Try these quick coatings for chicken or fish. Dip chicken or fish in melted margarine, salad dressing, mayonnaise or mustard; then coat with desired crumbs and bake or cook in skillet.

- Bread crumbs mixed with dry salad dressing mix
- Bread crumbs mixed with Parmesan cheese
- Bread crumbs mixed with dry seasoning mixes
- Cornmeal mixed with chili powder, Cajun or Creole seasoning
- Crushed cereal
- Crushed corn chips
- Crushed crackers
- Crushed potato chips
- Crushed tortilla chips
- Seasoned bread crumbs

Chicken-Linguine Casserole

6 servings

PREP:
10 min

BAKE:
43 min

1 package (9 ounces) refrigerated linguine

2 cups cut-up cooked chicken

1 cup frozen onions, celery, bell pepper and parsley (from 16-ounce package)

1 can (10¾ ounces) condensed cream of chicken soup

1 cup chicken broth

½ cup shredded Cheddar cheese (2 ounces)

Heat oven to 350°. Grease square pan, 8 × 8 × 2 inches.

Place uncooked linguine in large colander and rinse with hot water 15 seconds; drain. Mix linguine, chicken, vegetables, soup and broth in pan.

Bake uncovered 35 to 40 minutes or until bubbly around edges. Sprinkle with cheese. Bake uncovered about 3 minutes longer or until cheese is melted.

1 Serving: Calories 340 (Calories from Fat 90); Fat 10g (Saturated 4g); Cholesterol 55mg; Sodium 630mg; Carbohydrate 39g (Dietary Fiber 1g); Protein 24g

Chicken Enchiladas

6 servings

Betty's Success Tip

Fresh cilantro and parsley will
keep up to a week in the
refrigerator if they are wrapped
in a slightly damp towel and
placed in a sealed plastic bag.
Just before using, wash the
fresh herbs, and dry them with
a paper towel.

1 cup bottled mild green sauce or salsa

¼ cup cilantro sprigs

¼ cup parsley sprigs

1 tablespoon lime juice

2 cloves garlic

2 cups chopped cooked chicken or turkey

¾ cup shredded reduced-fat mozzarella cheese (3 ounces)

6 fat-free flour tortillas (6 to 8 inches in diameter)

1 medium lime, cut into wedges

Heat oven to 350°. Spray rectangular baking dish, 11 × 7 × 1½ inches,
with cooking spray. Place green sauce, cilantro, parsley, lime juice and
garlic in blender or food processor. Cover and blend on high speed
about 30 seconds or until smooth. Reserve half of mixture.

Mix remaining sauce mixture, the chicken and ¼ cup of the cheese.
Spoon about ¼ cup chicken mixture onto each tortilla. Roll tortilla
around filling; place seam side down in baking dish.

Pour reserved sauce mixture over enchiladas. Sprinkle with remaining
½ cup cheese. Bake uncovered 20 to 25 minutes or until hot. Serve with
lime wedges.

1 Serving: Calories 235 (Calories from Fat 55); Fat 6g (Saturated 3g); Cholesterol 50mg; Sodium
570mg; Carbohydrate 27g (Dietary Fiber 2g); Protein 20g

Saturday Night Supper

4 servings

PREP:
15 min

BAKE:
30 min

Serving Suggestion

An easy casserole that kids—
and adults—both would like.
Try serving with milk and
fresh fruit.

1 pound ground turkey

2 cups frozen mixed vegetables

1 can (15 ounces) Italian-style tomato sauce

1½ cups cooked small pasta shells or elbow macaroni

¾ teaspoon garlic salt

¼ teaspoon pepper

¼ cup grated Parmesan cheese

Heat oven to 400°.

Cook turkey in 10-inch skillet over medium heat 8 to 10 minutes, stirring occasionally, until no longer pink; drain.

Spoon turkey into ungreased 2-quart casserole. Stir in vegetables, tomato sauce, pasta, garlic salt and pepper. Cover and bake about 30 minutes or until vegetables are tender; stir. Sprinkle with cheese.

1 Serving: Calories 370 (Calories from Fat 125);
Fat 14g (Saturated 5g); Cholesterol 80mg;
Sodium 1020mg; Carbohydrate 35g (Dietary
Fiber 5g); Protein 31g

Wild Rice and Turkey Casserole

6 servings

PREP:
10 min

BAKE:
1 hour 5 minutes

Betty's Success Tip

This dish is a great way to use up those Thanksgiving leftovers. If you like, toss in chopped vegetables, such as carrots or celery, for a healthy and hearty one-dish meal.

2 cups cut-up cooked **turkey**

2¼ cups boiling water

⅓ cup skim milk

1 small onion, chopped (¼ cup)

1 can (10¾ ounces) condensed **cream of mushroom soup**

1 package (6.2 ounces) fast-cooking long-grain and wild-rice mix

Heat oven to 350°. Mix all ingredients, including contents of seasoning packet from rice mix, in ungreased 2-quart casserole.

Cover and bake 45 to 50 minutes or until rice is tender. Uncover and bake 10 to 15 minutes longer or until liquid is absorbed.

1 Serving: Calories 170 (Calories from Fat 65); Fat 7g (Saturated 2g); Cholesterol 40mg; Sodium 500mg; Carbohydrate 12g (Dietary Fiber 0g); Protein 15g

Tarragon-Pimiento Turkey Rolls

4 servings

PREP:
12 min

CHILL:
24 hours

BAKE:
25 min

Betty's Success Tip

A great party dish! This recipe
is easy to double or triple.

1 pound uncooked turkey breast slices, about ¼ inch thick

1 package (3 ounces) cream cheese, softened

2 tablespoons chopped fresh or 2 teaspoons dried tarragon leaves

1 jar (2 ounces) diced pimientos, drained

½ teaspoon garlic pepper

1 tablespoon margarine, butter or spread, melted

2 tablespoons dry bread crumbs

Spread each turkey slice with cream cheese. Sprinkle with tarragon,
pimientos and garlic pepper.

Roll up each slice from short side; secure with toothpicks. Brush rolls
with margarine. Sprinkle with bread crumbs. Grease square pan,
8 × 8 × 2 inches. Place unbaked rolls, seam sides down, in pan. Cover
tightly and refrigerate at least 8 hours but no longer than 24 hours.

About 35 minutes before serving, heat oven to 425°. Bake rolls uncovered about 25 minutes or until turkey is no longer pink in center.

1 Serving: Calories 255 (Calories from Fat 125);
Fat 14g (Saturated 6g); Cholesterol 90mg;
Sodium 190mg; Carbohydrate 4g (Dietary
Fiber 0g); Protein 28g

Italian Turkey Rolls

4 servings

PREP:
15 min

BAKE:
30 min

Betty's Success Tip

To make ahead, cover tightly and refrigerate at least 8 hours but no longer than 24 hours. About 1 hour before serving, heat oven to 375°. Bake turkey roll uncovered about 45 minutes or until turkey is no longer pink in center.

2 slices provolone cheese (2½ ounces), cut in half

4 thin slices pastrami

4 uncooked turkey breast slices, about ¼ inch thick

⅓ cup Italian-style dry bread crumbs

¼ cup grated Romano or Parmesan cheese

2 tablespoons finely chopped fresh parsley

¼ cup milk

Grease square pan, 8 × 8 × 2 inches.

Place piece of provolone cheese and slice of pastrami on each turkey slice. Fold long sides of each turkey slice over pastrami. Roll up turkey from short side; secure with toothpick.

Mix bread crumbs, Romano or Parmesan cheese and parsley. Dip turkey rolls into milk, then coat evenly with bread crumb mixture. Place seam sides down in pan.

Heat oven to 425°. Bake uncovered about 30 minutes or until turkey is no longer pink in center.

1 Serving: Calories 245 (Calories from Fat 115); Fat 13g (Saturated 6g); Cholesterol 70mg; Sodium 550mg; Carbohydrate 8g (Dietary Fiber 0g); Protein 24g

Fish and Vegetable Packets

4 servings

PREP:
12 min

BAKE:
20 min

4 lean fish fillets (about 4 ounces each)

1 package (16 ounces) frozen broccoli, cauliflower and carrots, thawed

1 tablespoon chopped fresh or 1 teaspoon dried dill weed

½ teaspoon salt

¼ teaspoon pepper

¼ cup dry white wine or chicken broth

Heat oven to 450°.

Place each fish fillet on a 12-inch square of aluminum foil. Top each fish fillet with one-fourth of the vegetables. Sprinkle with dill weed, salt and pepper. Drizzle 1 tablespoon wine over each mound of vegetables.

Fold up sides of foil to make a tent; fold top edges over to seal. Fold in sides, making a packet; fold to seal. Place packets on ungreased cookie sheet.

Bake about 20 minutes or until vegetables are crisp-tender and fish flakes easily with fork.

1 Serving: Calories 130 (Calories from Fat 20); Fat 2g (Saturated 0g); Cholesterol 60mg; Sodium 400mg; Carbohydrate 7g (Dietary Fiber 2g); Protein 23g

Tuna-Macaroni Casserole

6 servings

PREP:
15 min

BAKE:
40 min

1 package (7 ounces) elbow macaroni (2 cups)

2 cups grated Cheddar cheese (8 ounces)

1 medium onion, finely chopped (½ cup)

1 can (6 ounces) tuna, drained

1 can (10¾ ounces) condensed cream of mushroom or celery soup

1 soup can of milk

Heat oven to 350°. Grease 2-quart casserole.

Cook and drain macaroni as directed on package.

Mix macaroni and remaining ingredients in casserole. Bake uncovered 30 to 40 minutes or until hot and bubbly.

1 Serving: Calories 410 (Calories from Fat 180); Fat 20g (Saturated 11g); Cholesterol 50mg; Sodium 770mg; Carbohydrate 34g (Dietary Fiber 1g); Protein 25g

Tuna-Broccoli Casserole

4 servings

PREP:
11 min

BAKE:
40 min

1½ cups uncooked small pasta shells (6 ounces)

1 package (10 ounces) frozen broccoli cuts, thawed

1 can (6 ounces) tuna, drained

1 can (10¾ ounces) condensed Cheddar cheese soup

1 soup can of milk

1 cup crushed potato chips

Heat oven to 350°. Grease 2-quart casserole.

Mix all ingredients except potato chips in casserole. Sprinkle with potato chips. Bake uncovered 30 to 40 minutes or until hot and bubbly.

1 Serving: Calories 480 (Calories from Fat 155); Fat 17g (Saturated 7g); Cholesterol 30mg; Sodium 880mg; Carbohydrate 59g (Dietary Fiber 4g); Protein 27g

Lobster Chow Mein Bake

4 servings

PREP:
10 min

BAKE:
25 min

Ingredient Substitution

If you'd prefer, use refrigerated imitation crabmeat chunks in place of the lobster.

¾ cup reduced-fat mayonnaise or salad dressing

1 tablespoon all-purpose flour

1 tablespoon reduced-sodium soy sauce

1 can (14 to 16 ounces) fancy mixed Chinese vegetables, drained

1 can (8 ounces) sliced water chestnuts, drained

1 package (8 ounces) refrigerated imitation lobster chunks

1 medium stalk celery, sliced (½ cup)

Chow mein noodles, if desired

Heat oven to 350°. Mix mayonnaise, flour and soy sauce in 1½-quart casserole. Stir in remaining ingredients except noodles.

Cover and bake about 25 minutes or until heated through. Sprinkle with noodles.

1 Serving: Calories 265 (Calories from Fat 145); Fat 16g (Saturated 3g); Cholesterol 30mg; Sodium 1000mg; Carbohydrate 22g (Dietary Fiber 4g); Protein 12g

Creamy Crab au Gratin

4 servings

PREP:
15 min

COOK:
5 min

BAKE:
15 min

Serving Suggestion

Steam some fresh pea pods to serve alongside this dish.

1½ cups sliced mushrooms (4 ounces)

2 medium stalks celery, sliced (1 cup)

1 can (14½ ounces) ready-to-serve chicken broth

¾ cup fat-free half-and-half

3 tablespoons all-purpose flour

½ teaspoon red pepper sauce

2 packages (8 ounces each) refrigerated imitation crabmeat chunks or 2 cups chopped cooked crabmeat

1 cup soft bread crumbs (about 1½ slices bread)

Heat oven to 400°. Lightly spray rectangular baking dish, 11 × 7 × 1½ inches, with cooking spray.

Spray 3-quart saucepan with cooking spray; heat over medium heat. Cook mushrooms and celery in saucepan about 4 minutes, stirring constantly, until celery is tender. Stir in broth. Heat to boiling; reduce heat.

Beat half-and-half, flour and pepper sauce with wire whisk until smooth; stir into vegetable mixture. Heat to boiling, stirring constantly. Boil and stir 1 minute. Stir in crabmeat.

Spoon crabmeat mixture into baking dish. Top with bread crumbs. Bake uncovered about 15 minutes or until heated through.

1 Serving: Calories 200 (Calories from Fat 20); Fat 2g (Saturated 1g); Cholesterol 35mg; Sodium 1540mg; Carbohydrate 24g (Dietary Fiber 1g); Protein 23g

Crab and Artichoke Bake

4 servings

PREP:
10 min

COOK:
1 min

BAKE:
25 min

Ingredient Substitution

This classy casserole tastes delicious with a variety of vegetables. Besides the artichokes, you can make it with frozen (thawed) cut asparagus, cauliflower or Italian-style green beans.

2 cups skim milk

¼ cup all-purpose flour

1 teaspoon chicken bouillon granules

1 teaspoon ground mustard (dry)

¼ teaspoon pepper

1 cup shredded reduced-fat mozzarella cheese (4 ounces)

1 package (9 ounces) frozen artichoke hearts, thawed

1 package (8 ounces) refrigerated imitation crabmeat chunks

Heat oven to 425°. Gradually stir milk into flour in 2-quart saucepan. Stir in bouillon granules, mustard and pepper. Heat to boiling, stirring constantly. Boil and stir 1 minute; remove from heat. Stir in ½ cup of the cheese until melted. Stir in artichokes and crabmeat.

Pour mixture into ungreased 1½-quart casserole. Sprinkle with remaining ½ cup cheese. Bake uncovered about 25 minutes or until hot and bubbly and cheese is golden brown.

1 Serving: Calories 235 (Calories from Fat 55); Fat 6g (Saturated 4g); Cholesterol 35mg; Sodium 1210mg; Carbohydrate 24g (Dietary Fiber 3g); Protein 24g

One-Crust Tuna-Vegetable Pie

4 servings

PREP:
10 min

BAKE:
30 min

STAND:
5 min

Betty's Success Tip

To make ahead, cover unbaked pie tightly and refrigerate no longer than 24 hours. About 50 minutes before serving, heat oven to 375°. Bake uncovered 40 to 45 minutes or until hot and bubbly and crust is golden brown. Let stand at least 5 minutes before cutting.

2 cups frozen mixed vegetables

1 can (9¼ ounces) tuna, drained

4 medium green onions, sliced (½ cup)

½ cup sour cream

1 can (11 ounces) condensed Cheddar cheese soup

1 cup Bisquick Original baking mix

¼ cup cold water

Layer frozen vegetables, tuna and onions in ungreased square baking dish, 8 × 8 × 2 inches. Mix sour cream and soup; spread over top.

Mix baking mix and cold water; beat vigorously 20 strokes. On lightly floured surface, pat dough into 9-inch square. Place on soup mixture; cut slits to allow steam to escape.

Heat oven to 375°. Bake uncovered 25 to 30 minutes or until hot and bubbly and crust is golden brown. Let stand at least 5 minutes before cutting.

1 Serving: Calories 395 (Calories from Fat 155); Fat 17g (Saturated 9g); Cholesterol 245mg; Sodium 350mg; Carbohydrate 49g (Dietary Fiber 0g); Protein 12g

Baked Fish Fillets

4 servings

PREP:
5 min

BAKE:
20 min

Betty's Success Tip

Check fish for doneness by placing a fork in the thickest part of the fish, then gently twisting the fork. The fish will flake easily when it's done.

1 pound sole, orange roughy or other delicate fish fillets, about ¾ inch thick

2 tablespoons butter or stick margarine, melted

1 tablespoon lemon juice

¼ teaspoon salt

¼ teaspoon paprika

Heat oven to 375°. Spray rectangular pan, 13 × 9 × 2 inches, with cooking spray.

Cut fish into 4 serving pieces; place in pan. If fish has skin, place skin side down. Tuck under any thin ends for more even cooking.

Mix remaining ingredients; drizzle over fish.

Bake uncovered 15 to 20 minutes or until fish flakes easily with fork. Remove skin from fish before serving if desired.

1 Serving: Calories 130 (Calories from Fat 65); Fat 7g (Saturated 1g); Cholesterol 45mg; Sodium 300mg; Carbohydrate 0g (Dietary Fiber 0g); Protein 17g

Crispy Baked Catfish

4 servings

PREP:
10 min

BAKE:
18 min

1 pound catfish, trout or other medium-firm fish fillets

¼ cup yellow cornmeal

¼ cup dry bread crumbs

1 teaspoon chili powder

½ teaspoon paprika

½ teaspoon garlic salt

¼ teaspoon pepper

¼ cup French or ranch dressing

Heat oven to 450°. Spray broiler pan rack with cooking spray.

If fish fillets are large, cut into 4 serving pieces. Mix remaining ingredients except dressing. Lightly brush dressing on all sides of fish. Coat fish with cornmeal mixture.

Place fish on rack in broiler pan. Bake uncovered 15 to 18 minutes or until fish flakes easily with fork.

1 Serving: Calories 220 (Calories from Fat 70); Fat 8g (Saturated 1g); Cholesterol 60mg; Sodium 410mg; Carbohydrate 14g (Dietary Fiber 1g); Protein 24g

Selecting Fish

When buying fish, put your senses of sight, smell and touch into action.

Fresh Whole Fish, Fillets or Steaks

- Eyes should be bright, clear and slightly bulging; only a few fish such as walleye have naturally cloudy eyes.
- Gills should be bright pink to red and have no slime on them.
- Scales should be bright with a sheen. Avoid fish with any darkening around the edges or brown or yellowish discoloration.
- Flesh should be shiny, firm and elastic. It will spring back when touched.
- Fish should smell fresh and mild, not fishy or like ammonia.

Frozen Fish

- Package should be tightly wrapped and frozen solid with little or no gap between packaging and fish.
- There should be no dark, icy or dry spots—these are signs of freezer burn.
- The package should be odor-free.

Flounder Florentine

4 servings

PREP:
8 min

BAKE
30 min

2 packages (10 ounces each) frozen chopped spinach, thawed and squeezed to drain

1 pound flounder or other whitefish fillets, about ½ inch thick

¼ teaspoon salt

½ cup roasted red bell peppers (from 7-ounce jar)

¼ cup chopped fresh or 2 teaspoons dried basil leaves

1 tablespoon milk

⅛ teaspoon red pepper sauce

Heat oven to 400°.

Spread spinach evenly in ungreased rectangular pan, 11 × 7 × 2 inches. Arrange fish on spinach. Sprinkle with salt.

Place bell peppers, basil, milk and pepper sauce in blender or food processor. Cover and blend on high speed about 15 seconds or until smooth; pour over fish.

Cover and bake 25 to 30 minutes or until fish flakes easily with fork.

1 Serving: Calories 130 (Calories from Fat 20); Fat 2g (Saturated 0g); Cholesterol 55mg; Sodium 300mg; Carbohydrate 7g (Dietary Fiber 2g); Protein 23g

Shrimp Supreme

4 servings

PREP:
8 min

BAKE:
45 min:

1 package (5.3 ounces) mushroom and wild-rice mix

1 package (3 ounces) cream cheese, softened

2 medium stalks celery, sliced (1 cup)

1 small red bell pepper, chopped (½ cup)

3 medium green onions, sliced (⅓ cup)

1¼ cups hot water

1½ teaspoons lemon juice

¾ pound uncooked peeled and deveined medium shrimp, thawed if frozen

Heat oven to 425°.

Mix rice mix, with seasoning packet and remaining ingredients except shrimp in ungreased 1½-quart casserole.

Cover and bake 30 minutes. Stir in shrimp. Cover and bake about 15 minutes longer or until shrimp are pink and firm.

1 Serving: Calories 200 (Calories from Fat 90); Fat 10g (Saturated 6g); Cholesterol 145mg; Sodium 490mg; Carbohydrate 13g (Dietary Fiber 1g); Protein 16g

Seafood Casserole

4 servings

PREP:
10 min

CHILL:
24 hours

BAKE:
45 min

Betty's Success Tip

The frozen vegetable mixture used in this recipe is a great time-saver for soups, stews and casseroles.

4 cups herb-seasoned stuffing cubes

½ pound frozen uncooked peeled and deveined medium shrimp, thawed if frozen

1 package (8 ounces) refrigerated imitation crabmeat chunks

1 cup frozen onions, celery, bell pepper and parsley (from 16-ounce package)

1¼ cups vegetable or chicken broth

2 tablespoons margarine, butter or spread, melted

Mix stuffing cubes, shrimp, crabmeat and vegetables in 2-quart casserole.

Stir in broth and margarine. Cover unbaked casserole tightly and refrigerate at least 8 hours but no longer than 24 hours.

About 1 hour before serving, heat oven to 350°. Bake covered casserole about 45 minutes or until center is hot.

1 Serving: Calories 270 (Calories from Fat 80); Fat 9g (Saturated 2g); Cholesterol 90mg; Sodium 900mg; Carbohydrate 30g (Dietary Fiber 2g); Protein 19g

Oven-Poached Halibut

4 servings

PREP:
5 min

BAKE:
25 min

Betty's Success Tip

Like most varieties of fish, halibut is naturally low in fat. Halibut has a firm eating texture and is mild flavored.

4 halibut, swordfish or tuna fillets, about 1 inch thick (about 1½ pounds)

¼ teaspoon salt

4 sprigs dill weed

4 slices lemon

4 black peppercorns

¼ cup dry white wine or chicken broth

Heat oven to 450°. Place fish in ungreased rectangular baking dish, 11 × 7 × 1½ inches. Sprinkle with salt. Place dill weed sprig and lemon slice on each. Top with peppercorns. Pour wine over fish. Bake uncovered 20 to 25 minutes or until fish flakes easily with fork.

1 Serving: Calories 140 (Calories from Fat 20); Fat 2g (Saturated 0g); Cholesterol 90mg; Sodium 290mg; Carbohydrate 1g (Dietary Fiber 0g); Protein 30g

Mediterranean Sole with Ratatouille

4 servings

PREP:
10 min

COOK:
28 min

Betty's Success Tip

Fennel, with a celery-like bulb, is eaten as a vegetable. It has a very subtle anise flavor and is rich in vitamin A.

1 medium red or green bell pepper, chopped (1 cup)

1 medium onion, cut into 8 wedges and separated

1 small bulb fennel, thinly sliced

1 small eggplant (1 pound), peeled and cut into ½-inch cubes

1 can (14½ ounces) diced tomatoes with garlic and onion, undrained

2 teaspoons chopped fresh or 1 teaspoon dried oregano leaves

4 sole, orange roughy or other lean fish fillets, about ¼ inch thick (about ¾ pound)

2 teaspoons chopped fresh or 1 teaspoon dried oregano leaves

Feta cheese, if desired

Spray 12-inch nonstick skillet with cooking spray; heat over medium heat. Cook bell pepper, onion and fennel in skillet about 5 minutes, stirring frequently, until vegetables are crisp-tender.

Stir in eggplant, tomatoes and 2 teaspoons oregano; reduce heat to medium-low. Cover and cook 15 minutes, stirring frequently.

Beginning from narrow end, roll up each fillet and secure with toothpicks; sprinkle with remaining oregano. Place fish rolls, seam sides down, in eggplant mixture. Cover and cook about 8 minutes or until fish flakes easily with fork.

Remove fish to serving platter, using slotted spoon. Remove toothpicks from fish. Serve eggplant mixture with fish. Sprinkle with cheese.

1 Serving: Calories 175 (Calories from Fat 20); Fat 2g (Saturated 1g); Cholesterol 55mg; Sodium 400mg; Carbohydrate 23g (Dietary Fiber 6g); Protein 22g

Oven-Baked Meatless Main Dishes

Rice and Cheese Casserole

4 servings

PREP:
10 min

BAKE:
45 min

1 cup uncooked instant rice

1 package (8 ounces) shredded process cheese (2 cups)

2 cups packaged shredded carrots

4 medium green onions, chopped (¼ cup)

2 eggs

¼ cup milk

⅓ cup dry bread crumbs

1 tablespoon margarine, butter or spread, melted

Heat oven to 350°. Grease square pan, 8 × 8 × 2 inches.

Prepare rice as directed on package.

Mix rice, cheese, carrots, onions, eggs and milk in pan. Sprinkle with bread crumbs. Drizzle with margarine. Bake uncovered 40 to 45 minutes or until knife inserted in center comes out clean.

1 Serving: Calories 435 (Calories from Fat 215); Fat 24g (Saturated 13g); Cholesterol 160mg; Sodium 980mg; Carbohydrate 38g (Dietary Fiber 3g); Protein 20g

Mexican Rice and Bean Bake

6 servings

PREP:
10 min

BAKE:
35 min

STAND:
5 min

2 cups cooked brown or white rice

2 eggs

1½ cups picante sauce or salsa

1 cup shredded Cheddar cheese (4 ounces)

1 can (15 to 16 ounces) pinto beans, drained

¼ teaspoon chili powder

Heat oven to 350°. Grease square baking dish, 8 × 8 × 2 inches.

Mix rice, eggs, ½ cup of the picante sauce and ½ cup of the cheese; press in bottom of baking dish.

Mix beans and remaining 1 cup picante sauce; spoon over rice mixture. Sprinkle with remaining ½ cup cheese and the chili powder.

Bake uncovered 30 to 35 minutes or until cheese is melted and bubbly. Let stand 5 minutes before serving.

1 Serving: Calories 260 (Calories from Fat 90); Fat 10g (Saturated 5g); Cholesterol 90mg; Sodium 700mg; Carbohydrate 35g (Dietary Fiber 7g); Protein 14g

Chili con Queso Casserole

6 servings

PREP:
8 min

BAKE:
40 min

Betty's Success Tip

To make ahead, cover unbaked casserole tightly and refrigerate no longer than 24 hours.

2 cans (4 ounces each) mild chopped green chile peppers, drained

2 large tomatoes, seeded and chopped (2 cups)

2 cups shredded Cheddar cheese (8 ounces)

1 cup Bisquick Original baking mix

½ cup sour cream

3 eggs

Grease square pan, 8 × 8 × 2 inches.

Sprinkle chiles and tomato evenly in pan.

Beat remaining ingredients with wire whisk or hand beater until smooth; pour over top.

Heat oven to 375°. Bake uncovered 35 to 40 minutes or until knife inserted in center comes out clean.

1 Serving: Calories 325 (Calories from Fat 200); Fat 22g (Saturated 12g); Cholesterol 160mg; Sodium 890mg; Carbohydrate 18g (Dietary Fiber 1g); Protein 15g

Cheese and Chiles Bake

4 servings

PREP:
10 min

BAKE:
25 min

¾ cup shredded reduced-fat Cheddar cheese (3 ounces)

¾ cup shredded reduced-fat mozzarella cheese (3 ounces)

1 can (4 ounces) chopped green chile peppers, drained

1 cup skim milk

½ cup fat-free cholesterol-free egg product

1 cup Bisquick Reduced Fat baking mix

½ teaspoon onion powder

Heat oven to 425°. Spray square pan, 8 × 8 × 2 inches, with cooking spray. Sprinkle ½ cup of the Cheddar cheese, the mozzarella cheese and the chile peppers in pan.

Place remaining ingredients except ¼ cup Cheddar in blender or food processor. Cover and blend on high speed about 30 seconds or until smooth. Pour into pan.

Bake uncovered about 25 minutes or until toothpick inserted in center comes out clean. Sprinkle with remaining ¼ cup Cheddar cheese. Cut into squares. Serve warm.

1 Serving: Calories 235 (Calories from Fat 65); Fat 7g (Saturated 4g); Cholesterol 15mg; Sodium 700mg; Carbohydrate 26g (Dietary Fiber 1g); Protein 18g

Mushroom and Spinach Lasagna

6 servings

PREP:
25 min

BAKE:
1 hour

STAND:
10 min

Betty's Success Tip

Check out your freezer case for precooked uncut sheets of lasagna noodles, or the dried pasta section for precooked lasagna noodles. Use the precooked noodles just as you would traditional cooked noodles.

1 package (8 ounces) lasagna noodles

1¼ cups fat-free ricotta cheese

½ cup fat-free cholesterol-free egg product or 4 egg whites

1 cup chopped mushrooms (4 ounces)

1 large onion, chopped (1 cup)

1 package (10 ounces) frozen chopped spinach, thawed and squeezed to drain

½ teaspoon salt

¼ teaspoon ground nutmeg, if desired

1 jar (14 ounces) spaghetti sauce

3 tablespoons grated Parmesan cheese

Heat oven to 350°. Grease rectangular baking dish, 11 × 7 × 1½ inches. Cook and drain noodles as directed on package—except omit salt.

Mix ½ cup of the ricotta cheese, ¼ cup egg product, the mushrooms and onion. Mix remaining ¾ cup ricotta cheese, ¼ cup egg product, the spinach, salt and nutmeg. Spread ½ cup of the spaghetti sauce in baking dish. Top with 4 noodles, overlapping to fit. Layer with mushroom mixture, 3 noodles, spinach mixture, 3 noodles and remaining spaghetti sauce.

Cover loosely and bake 50 minutes. Sprinkle with Parmesan cheese. Bake uncovered about 10 minutes or until cheese is melted. Let stand 10 minutes before cutting.

1 Serving: Calories 290 (Calories from Fat 35); Fat 4g (Saturated 1g); Cholesterol 2mg; Sodium 670mg; Carbohydrate 50g (Dietary Fiber 4g); Protein 17g

Vegetable Manicotti

4 servings

PREP:
25 min

BAKE:
45 min

Betty's Success Tip

Zucchini, or "zukes," are a good source of vitamin C and also contain vitamin A. Look for firm zucchini with bright-colored skin that is free of soft spots.

8 uncooked manicotti shells

1 can (8 ounces) tomato sauce

1 teaspoon olive or vegetable oil

1 small carrot, shredded (½ cup)

1 small zucchini, shredded (½ cup)

½ cup sliced mushrooms

4 medium green onions, sliced (¼ cup)

1 clove garlic, finely chopped

1 container (15 ounces) fat-free ricotta cheese

¼ cup grated Parmesan cheese

2 tablespoons chopped fresh or 2 teaspoons dried basil leaves

¼ cup fat-free cholesterol-free egg product or 2 egg whites

½ cup shredded reduced-fat mozzarella cheese (2 ounces)

Heat oven to 350°. Spray rectangular baking dish, 11 × 7 × 1½ inches, with cooking spray. Cook and drain manicotti shells as directed on package—except omit salt. Pour ⅓ cup of the tomato sauce into baking dish.

While manicotti is cooking, heat oil in 10-inch nonstick skillet over medium-high heat. Cook carrot, zucchini, mushrooms, onions and garlic in oil, stirring frequently, until vegetables are crisp-tender. Stir in remaining ingredients except mozzarella cheese.

Fill manicotti shells with vegetable mixture; place in baking dish. Pour remaining tomato sauce over manicotti. Sprinkle with mozzarella cheese. Cover and bake 40 to 45 minutes or until hot and bubbly.

1 Serving: Calories 330 (Calories from Fat 55); Fat 6g (Saturated 3g); Cholesterol 10mg; Sodium 640mg; Carbohydrate 42g (Dietary Fiber 3g); Protein 30g

Baked Ziti and Bean Casserole

6 servings

PREP:
15 min

BAKE:
30 min

Betty's Success Tip

Ziti is a short, tubular pasta with a smooth surface. This type of pasta stands up well to thick or chunky sauces.

1 can (28 ounces) whole tomatoes, drained

1 cup fat-free ricotta cheese

¼ cup chopped red onion

1 tablespoon chopped fresh parsley

1 tablespoon chopped fresh or 1 teaspoon dried thyme leaves

½ teaspoon salt

¼ teaspoon crushed red pepper

4 cups hot cooked ziti or penne pasta

1 can (15 to 16 ounces) great Northern beans, rinsed and drained

3 slices reduced-fat mozzarella cheese, about 6½ × 4 inches

Grated Parmesan cheese, if desired

Heat oven to 400°. Spray rectangular baking dish, 11 × 7 × 1½ inches, with cooking spray. Break up tomatoes in large bowl. Stir in ricotta cheese, onion, parsley, thyme, salt and red pepper. Carefully fold in pasta and beans.

Spread pasta mixture in baking dish. Arrange mozzarella cheese on top. Bake uncovered about 30 minutes or until mixture is hot and cheese is golden brown. Sprinkle with Parmesan cheese.

1 Serving: Calories 325 (Calories from Fat 55); Fat 6g (Saturated 4g); Cholesterol 15mg; Sodium 580mg; Carbohydrate 50g (Dietary Fiber 6g); Protein 24g

Low-Fat Tortilla Casserole

6 servings

PREP:
15 min

COOK:
5 min

BAKE:
35 min

STAND:
10 min

Betty's Success Tip

The Spicy Fresh Chili Sauce also makes a great condiment for other Mexican favorites, such as tacos, burritos and enchiladas.

1 can (15 to 16 ounces) kidney beans, drained

½ cup skim milk

¼ cup fat-free cholesterol-free egg product or 2 egg whites

¼ cup chopped fresh cilantro

½ cup ready-to-serve vegetable broth

1 large onion, chopped (1 cup)

1 medium green bell pepper, chopped (1 cup)

2 cloves garlic, finely chopped

2 cans (4 ounces each) chopped mild green chile peppers, drained

4 cups reduced-fat tortilla chips

1 cup shredded reduced-fat Cheddar cheese (4 ounces)

¾ cup salsa

Reduced-fat sour cream, if desired

Heat oven to 375°. Spray 2-quart casserole with cooking spray. Mash beans and milk in medium bowl until smooth. Stir in egg product and 2 tablespoons of the cilantro; reserve.

Cook broth, onion, bell pepper, garlic and chiles in 10-inch nonstick skillet over medium heat about 5 minutes, stirring occasionally, until onion is tender. Stir in remaining 2 tablespoons cilantro.

Coarsely chop half of the chips. Place 1 cup of the chopped chips in bottom of casserole. Spread reserved bean mixture over chips. Spread vegetable mixture over bean mixture. Sprinkle with ½ cup of the cheese. Top with remaining chopped chips. Sprinkle with remaining ½ cup cheese.

Bake uncovered 30 to 35 minutes or until hot and cheese is golden brown. Serve with salsa, the remaining chips and sour cream.

1 Serving: Calories 180 (Calories from Fat 20); Fat 2g (Saturated 1g); Cholesterol 5mg; Sodium 460mg; Carbohydrate 33g (Dietary Fiber 6g); Protein 13g

Low-Fat Tomato-Corn Quiche

6 servings

PREP:
10 min

BAKE:
45 min

STAND:
10 min

Betty's Success Tip

Evaporated skimmed milk is a healthy alternative to half-and-half or whipping (heavy) cream.

1 cup evaporated skimmed milk

½ cup fat-free cholesterol-free egg product

2 tablespoons all-purpose flour

1 tablespoon chopped fresh cilantro

½ teaspoon chili powder

¼ teaspoon onion powder

¼ teaspoon salt

¼ teaspoon pepper

1 cup frozen (thawed) whole kernel corn

¾ cup shredded reduced-fat Cheddar cheese (3 ounces)

1 medium tomato, seeded and chopped (¾ cup)

Heat oven to 350°. Spray pie plate, 9 × 1¼ inches, with cooking spray. Mix all ingredients except corn, cheese and tomato in medium bowl until blended. Stir in remaining ingredients; pour into pie plate.

Bake 35 to 45 minutes or until knife inserted in center comes out clean. Let stand 10 minutes before cutting.

1 Serving: Calories 95 (Calories from Fat 10); Fat 1g (Saturated 1g); Cholesterol 5mg; Sodium 270mg; Carbohydrate 14g (Dietary Fiber 1g); Protein 9g

Savory Mushroom Strata

6 servings

PREP:
20 min

CHILL:
24 hours

BAKE:
50 min

STAND:
10 min

Betty's Success Tip

Don't throw away that day-old bread! Slightly dried-out bread slices are perfect for soaking up the wonderful flavors in this dish.

3 cups chopped mushrooms (12 ounces)

1 cup fat-free small-curd cottage cheese

2 medium green onions, chopped (2 tablespoons)

1 teaspoon chopped fresh or ½ teaspoon dried rosemary leaves

1 clove garlic, finely chopped

12 slices whole-grain or white bread

1½ cups skim milk

1 cup fat-free cholesterol-free egg product

¼ cup shredded reduced-fat Monterey Jack cheese (1 ounce)

Spray square baking pan, 9 × 9 × 2 inches, with cooking spray. Mix mushrooms, cottage cheese, onions, rosemary and garlic. Place 4 of the bread slices in pan. Spread with half of the mushroom mixture.

Beat milk and egg product until blended; pour ⅓ of the milk mixture over bread slices in pan. Spread 4 of the bread slices with remaining mushroom mixture. Place bread, mushroom sides up, in pan. Top with remaining 4 slices bread; press down gently if bread is higher than edge of dish. Pour remaining milk mixture over bread. Sprinkle with cheese. Cover and refrigerate at least 2 hours but no longer than 24 hours.

Heat oven to 325°. Bake uncovered 45 to 50 minutes or until set and top is golden brown. Let stand 10 minutes before serving.

1 Serving: Calories 215 (Calories from Fat 35); Fat 4g (Saturated 2g); Cholesterol 5mg; Sodium 550mg; Carbohydrate 33g (Dietary Fiber 5g); Protein 17g

Twice-Baked Potatoes

PREP:
20 min

BAKE:
1 hour 35 min

Betty's Success Tip

These potatoes can be put in the fridge or freezer (wrapped up tightly) before being baked again. Bake refrigerated potatoes 30 minutes; frozen potatoes about 40 minutes.

4 large baking potatoes (8 to 10 ounces each)

¼ to ½ cup milk

¼ cup butter or stick margarine, softened

¼ teaspoon salt

Dash of pepper

1 cup shredded Cheddar cheese (4 ounces)

1 tablespoon chopped fresh chives

Heat oven to 375°. Gently scrub potatoes, but do not peel them. Pierce potatoes several times with fork to allow steam to escape while potatoes bake.

Bake 1 hour to 1 hour 15 minutes or until potatoes feel tender when pierced in center with fork.

When potatoes are cool enough to handle, cut lengthwise in half; scoop out inside, leaving a thin shell. Mash potatoes in medium bowl with potato masher or electric mixer on low speed until no lumps remain. Add milk in small amounts, beating after each addition with potato masher or electric mixer on low speed (amount of milk needed to make potatoes smooth and fluffy depends on kind of potatoes used).

Add butter, salt and pepper; beat vigorously until potatoes are light and fluffy. Stir in cheese and chives. Fill potato shells with mashed potato mixture. Place on ungreased cookie sheet.

Increase oven temperature to 400°. Bake about 20 minutes or until hot.

1 Serving: Calories 180 (Calories from Fat 100); Fat 11g (Saturated 7g); Cholesterol 30mg; Sodium 210mg; Carbohydrate 16g (Dietary Fiber 1g); Protein 5g

Vegetable-Cheese Bake

6 servings

PREP:
10 min

BAKE:
30 min

Ingredient Substitution

If you're a fan of pumpernickel or light rye bread, use one of them instead of the whole wheat.

8 slices soft whole-wheat bread, cut into ½ inch cubes

2 cups shredded reduced-fat mozzarella cheese (8 ounces)

1½ cups frozen green peas or whole kernel corn

1 small onion, finely chopped (¼ cup)

1½ cups fat-free cholesterol-free egg product

1 can (12 ounces) evaporated skimmed milk

½ cup plain fat-free yogurt

1 tablespoon mustard

Heat oven to 350°. Spray square baking dish, 8 × 8 × 2 inches, with cooking spray.

Mix bread cubes, cheese, peas and onion in large bowl. Mix remaining ingredients; pour over bread mixture and stir to coat. Pour into baking dish.

Bake uncovered about 30 minutes or until golden brown and center is set.

1 Serving: Calories 295 (Calories from Fat 80); Fat 9g (Saturated 5g); Cholesterol 25mg; Sodium 610mg; Carbohydrate 33g (Dietary Fiber 6g); Protein 26g

Vegetable-Cheese Bake

Savory Potato Supper Cake

6 servings

PREP:
25 min

BAKE:
50 min

Serving Suggestion

For a delicious finishing touch, top each serving with a dollop of reduced-fat sour cream and a dusting of ground nutmeg.

1 cup fat-free ricotta cheese

½ cup soft whole-grain or white bread crumbs

1 tablespoon chopped fresh or 1 teaspoon dried marjoram leaves

½ teaspoon salt

¼ teaspoon pepper

⅓ cup fat-free cholesterol-free egg product or 3 egg whites

4 cups shredded sweet potatoes (1 pound)

4 cups shredded baking potatoes (1 pound)

¾ cup chopped onion

Pear Sauce (below) or 1 cup unsweetened applesauce

Heat oven to 375°. Spray rectangular pan, 13 × 9 × 2 inches, with cooking spray. Mix cheese, bread crumbs, marjoram, salt, pepper and egg whites in large bowl. Stir in potatoes and onion. Spread in pan.

Bake uncovered 45 to 50 minutes or until potatoes are tender and golden brown. While potato mixture is baking, prepare Pear Sauce. Cut potato mixture into squares. Serve with sauce.

Pear Sauce

3 medium Bosc pears, peeled and chopped (2 cups)

¼ cup water

2 tablespoons frozen (thawed) apple juice concentrate

1 teaspoon vanilla

½ teaspoon ground cinnamon

¼ teaspoon ground nutmeg

Cover and cook all ingredients in 1-quart saucepan over medium heat 10 minutes, stirring occasionally; reduce heat to medium-low. Cook about 30 minutes longer, stirring occasionally, until pears are very tender. Place mixture in blender or food processor. Cover and blend until chunky.

1 Serving: Calories 215 (Calories from Fat 10); Fat 1g (Saturated 0g); Cholesterol 0mg; Sodium 340mg; Carbohydrate 46g (Dietary Fiber 4g); Protein 10g

Couscous-Stuffed Tomatoes

4 servings

PREP:
15 min

BAKE:
35 min

Serving Suggestion

These savory stuffed tomatoes are nice served with a crisp green salad and breadsticks.

⅔ cup uncooked couscous

4 medium tomatoes

1 small zucchini, coarsely shredded (1 cup)

2 tablespoons grated Parmesan cheese

1 tablespoon chopped fresh or 1 teaspoon dried basil leaves

¼ teaspoon salt

¼ teaspoon pepper

Heat oven to 350°. Grease square pan, 8 × 8 × 2 inches.

Cook couscous as directed on package. Meanwhile, cut ½-inch slice from top of each tomato; scoop out pulp and reserve for other use.

Stir remaining ingredients into couscous. Spoon mixture into tomatoes. Place tomatoes in pan. Bake uncovered about 35 minutes or until tomatoes are tender.

1 Serving: Calories 145 (Calories from Fat 10); Fat 1g (Saturated 1g); Cholesterol 2mg; Sodium 190mg; Carbohydrate 30g (Dietary Fiber 2g); Protein 6g

Broccoli-Cheese Calzones

6 servings

PREP:
15 min

BAKE:
20 min

COOL:
5 min

COOK:
2 min

1 container (15 ounces) fat-free ricotta cheese

1 package (10 ounces) frozen chopped broccoli, thawed

⅓ cup grated Parmesan cheese

¼ cup fat-free cholesterol-free egg product or 2 egg whites

1 teaspoon dried basil leaves

¼ teaspoon garlic powder

1 loaf (1 pound) frozen honey-wheat or white bread dough, thawed

1 can (8 ounces) pizza sauce

Heat oven to 375°. Grease 2 cookie sheets. Mix all ingredients except bread dough and pizza sauce.

Divide bread dough into 6 equal parts. Roll each part into 7-inch circle on lightly floured surface with floured rolling pin. Top half of each dough circle with cheese mixture to within 1 inch of edge. Carefully fold dough over filling; pinch edge or press with fork to seal securely.

Place calzones on cookie sheets. Bake about 20 minutes or until golden brown. Cool 5 minutes.

While calzones are cooling, heat pizza sauce in 1-quart saucepan over medium heat about 2 minutes, stirring occasionally, until heated through. Spoon warm sauce over calzones.

1 Serving: Calories 295 (Calories from Fat 35); Fat 4g (Saturated 2g); Cholesterol 5mg; Sodium 750mg; Carbohydrate 48g (Dietary Fiber 4g); Protein 21g

Meatless Meatball Pizza

6 servings

PREP:
12 min

BAKE:
20 min

Betty's Success Tip

Do you have meat-lovers and vegetarians to please? You won't miss the sausage when you make "mini-meatballs" using Italian-flavored frozen vegetable burgers. This tastes just like Italian sausage pizza!

1 package (16 ounces) ready-to-serve pizza crust (12 to 14 inches in diameter)

2 frozen Italian-style vegetable burgers, thawed

1 can (8 ounces) pizza sauce

2 tablespoons sliced ripe olives

1 cup shredded mozzarella cheese (4 ounces)

1 cup shredded provolone cheese (4 ounces)

Heat oven to 425°.

Place pizza crust on ungreased cookie sheet. Shape burgers into ½-inch balls. Spread pizza sauce over crust. Top with burger balls and olives. Sprinkle with cheeses.

Bake 18 to 20 minutes or until cheese is melted and light golden brown.

1 Serving: Calories 425 (Calories from Fat 135); Fat 15g (Saturated 6g); Cholesterol 25mg; Sodium 990mg; Carbohydrate 55g (Dietary Fiber 3g); Protein 21g

Sweet Finales

Crunch-Topped Apple Spice Cake

15 servings

PREP:
20 min

BAKE:
45 min

⅓ cup boiling water

2 medium unpeeled cooking apples, chopped (2 cups)

1¼ cups packed brown sugar

1 cup all-purpose flour

1 cup whole-wheat flour

¾ cup fat-free cholesterol-free egg product or 5 egg whites

⅓ cup vegetable oil

1¼ teaspoons baking soda

1 teaspoon ground cinnamon

1 teaspoon vanilla

½ teaspoon ground cloves

¼ teaspoon salt

Nut Topping (below)

Heat oven to 350°. Spray rectangular pan, 13 × 9 × 2 inches, with cooking spray; dust with flour. Pour boiling water over apples in large bowl. Add remaining ingredients except Nut Topping. Beat with electric mixer on low speed 1 minute, scraping bowl constantly. Beat on medium speed 2 minutes, scraping bowl occasionally. Pour into pan.

Sprinkle Nut Topping over batter. Bake 40 to 45 minutes or until toothpick inserted in center comes out clean.

Nut Topping

⅓ cup finely chopped nuts

2 tablespoons packed brown sugar

Mix ingredients.

1 Serving: Calories 205 (Calories from Fat 60); Fat 7g (Saturated 1g); Cholesterol 0mg; Sodium 170mg; Carbohydrate 35g (Dietary Fiber 2g); Protein 3g

Apple Dumplings

6 dumplings

PREP:
55 min

COOK:
3 min

BAKE:
40 min

1 package pastry for piecrust

6 cooking apples (Golden Delicious, Braeburn, Rome), about 3 inches in diameter

3 tablespoons raisins

3 tablespoons chopped nuts

½ cup sugar

1 cup water

½ cup corn syrup

2 tablespoons butter or stick margarine

¼ teaspoon ground cinnamon

Cream or sweetened whipped cream, if desired

Heat oven to 425°. Make pastry as directed—except roll ⅔ of the pastry into 14-inch square; cut into 4 squares. Roll remaining pastry into 14 × 7-inch rectangle; cut into 2 squares. Peel and core apples. Place apple on each square.

Mix raisins and nuts. Fill apples with raisin mixture. Moisten corners of pastry squares. Bring 2 opposite corners up over apple and pinch together. Repeat with remaining corners, and pinch edges of pastry to seal. Place dumplings in ungreased rectangular baking dish, 13 × 9 × 2 inches.

Heat remaining ingredients except cream to boiling in 2-quart saucepan, stirring occasionally. Boil 3 minutes. Carefully pour around dumplings.

Bake about 40 minutes, spooning syrup over dumplings 2 or 3 times, until crust is golden and apples are tender when pierced with a small knife or toothpick. Serve warm or cool with cream.

1 Serving: Calories 680 (Calories from Fat 305); Fat 34g (Saturated 10g); Cholesterol 10mg; Sodium 450mg; Carbohydrate 93g (Dietary Fiber 4g); Protein 5g

Lemon–Poppy Seed Pound Cake

24 servings

PREP:
20 min

BAKE:
1 hour 20 min

COOL:
2 hours 20 min

2½ cups sugar

1 cup butter or stick margarine, softened

1 teaspoon lemon juice

5 large eggs

3 cups all-purpose flour

1 teaspoon baking powder

¼ teaspoon salt

1 cup milk or evaporated milk

1 tablespoon grated lemon peel

¼ cup poppy seeds

Powdered sugar, if desired

Heat oven to 350°. Grease bottom and side of angel food cake pan (tube pan), 10 × 4 inches, 12-cup Bundt cake pan or 2 loaf pans, 9 × 5 × 3 inches, with shortening; lightly flour.

Beat sugar, butter, vanilla and eggs in large bowl with electric mixer on low speed 30 seconds, scraping bowl constantly. Beat on high speed 5 minutes, scraping bowl occasionally. Mix flour, baking powder and salt. Beat flour mixture into sugar mixture alternately with milk on low speed, beating just until smooth after each addition. Fold in the lemon peel and poppy seeds. Pour into pan(s).

Bake angel food pan or Bundt cake pan 1 hour 10 minutes to 1 hour 20 minutes, loaf pans 55 to 60 minutes, or until toothpick inserted in center comes out clean. Cool 20 minutes; remove from pan(s) to wire rack. Cool completely, about 2 hours. Sprinkle with powdered sugar.

1 Serving: Calories 225 (Calories from Fat 80); Fat 9g (Saturated 5g); Cholesterol 65mg; Sodium 115mg; Carbohydrate 33g (Dietary Fiber 0g); Protein 3g

Tiramisu Toffee Dessert

12 servings

PREP:
15 min

CHILL:
24 hours

1 package (10.75 ounces) frozen pound cake, thawed and cut into 9 slices

¾ cup strong coffee

1 cup sugar

½ cup chocolate-flavored syrup

1 package (8 ounces) cream cheese, softened

2 cups whipping (heavy) cream

2 bars (1.4 ounces each) chocolate-covered toffee candy, chopped

Arrange cake slices on bottom of rectangular baking dish, 11 × 7 × 1½ inches, cutting cake slices if necessary to cover bottom of dish. Drizzle coffee over cake.

Beat sugar, chocolate syrup and cream cheese in large bowl with electric mixer on medium speed until smooth. Add whipping cream. Beat on medium speed until light and fluffy. Spread over cake. Sprinkle with candy.

Cover and refrigerate at least 1 hour, but no longer than 24 hours to set dessert and blend flavors.

1 Serving: Calories 455 (Calories from Fat 250); Fat 28g (Saturated 17g); Cholesterol 100mg; Sodium 120mg; Carbohydrate 47g (Dietary Fiber 0g); Protein 4g

Crème Brûlée

4 servings

PREP:
8 min

CHILL:
24 hours

BROIL:
3 min

Betty's Success Tips

Do not use glass custard cups or glass pie plates; they cannot withstand the heat from broiling and may break.

4 large egg yolks

3 tablespoons granulated sugar

2 cups whipping (heavy) cream

1 teaspoon vanilla

⅓ cup packed brown sugar

Beat egg yolks in medium bowl with electric mixer on high speed about 3 minutes or until thick and lemon colored. Gradually beat in granulated sugar.

Heat whipping cream in 2-quart saucepan over medium heat just until hot.

Gradually stir at least half of the hot cream into egg yolk mixture, then stir back into hot cream in saucepan. Cook over low heat 5 to 8 minutes, stirring constantly, until mixture thickens (do not boil). Stir in vanilla.

Pour custard into four 6-ounce ceramic ramekins or ungreased ceramic pie plate, 9 × 1¼ inches. Cover and refrigerate at least 2 hours but no longer than 24 hours. Custard must be completely chilled before broiling with brown sugar on top to keep custard from overheating.

Set oven control to broil. Sprinkle brown sugar evenly over custard. Broil with tops about 5 inches from heat about 3 minutes or until sugar is melted and forms a glaze. Serve immediately (mixture will be runny), or refrigerate 1 to 2 hours or until slightly firm. Store covered in refrigerator.

1 Serving: Calories 610 (Calories from Fat 380); Fat 42g (Saturated 24g); Cholesterol 340mg; Sodium 60mg; Carbohydrate 54g (Dietary Fiber 2g); Protein 6g

Turtle Cheesecake

12 servings

PREP:
30 min

BAKE:
50 min

COOL:
1 hour

CHILL:
2 hours

1½ cups finely crushed vanilla wafer cookies (about 40 cookies)

¼ cup butter or stick margarine, melted

2 packages (8 ounces each) cream cheese, softened

½ cup sugar

2 teaspoons vanilla

2 eggs

¼ cup hot fudge topping

1 cup caramel topping

½ cup coarsely chopped pecans

Heat oven to 350°. Mix cookie crumbs and butter in medium bowl. Press firmly against bottom and side of pie plate, 9 × 1¼ inches.

Beat cream cheese, sugar, vanilla and eggs in large bowl with electric mixer on low speed until smooth. Pour half of the mixture into pie plate.

Add hot fudge topping to remaining cream cheese mixture in bowl; beat on low speed until smooth. Spoon over vanilla mixture in pie plate. Swirl mixtures slightly with tip of knife.

Bake 40 to 50 minutes or until center is set. (Do not insert knife into cheesecake because the hole may cause cheesecake to crack as it cools.) Cool at room temperature 1 hour. Refrigerate at least 2 hours until chilled. Serve with caramel topping and pecans. Store covered in refrigerator.

1 Serving: Calories 440 (Calories from Fat 235); Fat 26g (Saturated 13g); Cholesterol 90mg; Sodium 340mg; Carbohydrate 46g (Dietary Fiber 1g); Protein 6g

Tips for Cheesecakes

- To check for doneness, touch the top of the cheesecake lightly, or gently shake the pan. The center may jiggle slightly, but it will set during chilling. Don't cut into the center with a knife to test for doneness because the hole could cause the cheesecake to crack.

- After baking, let the cheesecake stand at room temperature for 30 minutes or as directed before you put it in the refrigerator. Refrigerate, uncovered, 2 to 3 hours or until chilled; then cover so it doesn't dry out or pick up odors. Covering warm cheesecake may cause moisture to drip onto the cheesecake top.

- If the cheesecake has a side crust, after it has cooled for 30 minutes, run a metal spatula or table knife along the side of the crust to loosen it from the pan (if the pan has a removable side, don't remove or release it yet). Loosening the crust keeps the cheesecake from pulling away. Do this again before removing the side of the pan.

- To cut cheesecake, dip the knife into water, and clean it off after every cut. Or use a piece of dental floss! Hold a length of dental floss taut and pull the floss down through the cheesecake, making a clean cut.

Malted Milk Ball Ice-Cream Dessert

12 servings

PREP:
8 min

CHILL:
3 hours

3⅓ cups malted milk balls (10½ ounces)

1 container (12 ounces) frozen whipped topping, thawed

12 frozen rectangular ice-cream sandwiches

1 cup hot fudge sauce, warmed if desired

Place malted milk balls in resealable plastic bag. Tap with rolling pin or meat mallet until coarsely crushed. Reserve ⅓ cup.

Mix 3 cups crushed malted milk balls and whipped topping.

Arrange ice-cream sandwiches on bottom of rectangular pan, 13 × 9 × 2 inches, cutting sandwiches if necessary to cover bottom of pan. Spread whipped topping mixture over ice-cream sandwiches. Sprinkle with reserved crushed malted milk balls. Cover and freeze about 2 to 3 hours or until firm.

Cut into squares. Top with fudge sauce. Cover and freeze any remaining dessert.

1 Serving: Calories 480 (Calories from Fat 205); Fat 23g (Saturated 14g); Cholesterol 25mg; Sodium 230mg; Carbohydrate 66g (Dietary Fiber 2g); Protein 4g

Creamy Frozen Apricot Bars

16 servings

PREP:
10 min

CHILL:
2 hours

1 cup vanilla fat-free yogurt

½ cup apricot spreadable fruit

1 package (8 ounces) light cream cheese (Neufchâtel), cubed

Line square pan, 8 × 8 × 2 inches, with plastic wrap. Place all ingredients in blender or food processor. Cover and blend on high speed, stopping occasionally to scrape sides, until smooth. Carefully spread in pan. Cover and freeze about 2 hours or until firm.

Remove frozen mixture from pan, using plastic wrap to lift. Cut into 4 squares; make 2 crisscross cuts in each square to form 4 triangles.

1 Serving: Calories 65 (Calories from Fat 30); Fat 3g (Saturated 2g); Cholesterol 10mg; Sodium 65mg; Carbohydrate 8g (Dietary Fiber 1g); Protein 2g

Foiling Messy Cleanups

Some things just seem to have a thousand uses, and aluminum foil is one of those versatile items. Lining dishes or pans with foil makes cleanup quick and easy. When preparing foods with exposed bones (such as ribs) use heavy-duty foil, which won't rip or tear as easily. When the food is ready, just lift out the foil, crumple it up and toss it out—or rinse and recycle it. You can also purchase disposable aluminum pans—perfect for holiday turkeys and hams—and toss or recycle when finished. Here are more foil-friendly ideas:

- **Broiler Pans, Baking Dishes, Baking Sheets and Casseroles:** Line broiler pan with foil and spray rack with nonstick cooking spray.

- **Bars and Candy:** Line baking dish with foil, extending foil 1 to 2 inches over ends of dish. Cool completely and lift bars or candy out of pan. Another bonus of this method is bars and candy that can be cut evenly and easily!

Cherry-Berries on a Cloud

15 servings

PREP:
30 min

BAKE:
1½ hours

COOL:
2 hours

CHILL:
12 hours

6 large egg whites

½ teaspoon cream of tartar

¼ teaspoon salt

1½ cups sugar

2 cups whipping (heavy) cream

2 packages (3 ounces each) cream cheese, softened

½ cup sugar

1 teaspoon vanilla

2 cups miniature marshmallows

Cherry-Berries Topping (opposite page)

Heat oven to 275°. Butter rectangular pan, 13 × 9 × 2 inches.

Beat egg whites, cream of tartar and salt in large bowl with electric mixer on high speed until foamy. Beat in 1½ cups sugar, 1 tablespoon at a time; continue beating until stiff and glossy. Do not underbeat. Spread in pan.

Bake 1½ hours. Turn off oven; leave meringue in oven with door closed at least 2 hours.

Beat whipping cream in chilled large bowl on high speed until soft peaks form.

Beat cream cheese, ½ cup sugar and the vanilla until blended. Gently fold cream cheese mixture and marshmallows into whipped cream. Spread over meringue. Cover and refrigerate at least 12 hours. Cut into serving pieces; top with Cherry-Berries Topping. Store covered in refrigerator.

1 Serving: Calories 310 (Calories from Fat 125); Fat 14g (Saturated 9g); Cholesterol 45mg; Sodium 110mg; Carbohydrate 44g (Dietary Fiber 1g); Protein 3g

Cherry-Berries Topping

2 cups sliced strawberries or 1 bag (16 ounces) frozen strawberries, thawed and drained

1 can (21 ounces) cherry pie filling

2 teaspoons lemon juice

Mix all ingredients.

Part 3

The Very Best
Bread Machine Recipes

Nothing smells better than the aroma of fresh bread baking. With just minutes of work, your family can enjoy fresh baked bread regularly. Mastering the bread machine is simple—and convenient—as the machine handles all of the work. From kneading to baking, your bread is prepared after you've added the ingredients. So whether you have errands to run, have work to be done or would like to curl up to a great book, let your machine do the work. If you have a bread machine that gathers more dust than flour, now is the time to bring it out and surprise your family with delicious fresh baked breads. They are easier than you'd think when you follow our easy steps.

◄ **Sweet Bread Wreath**

Bread Machines Made Simple

A bread machine is easy to use after you become familiar with it. After taking a few moments to get to know the machine well, you can enjoy fresh baked goods with minimal effort. To get started, read your bread machine's use-and-care book carefully, especially the tips and hints. Be sure to assemble your machine correctly to assure proper kneading. When starting out with a new recipe, read it well so that your measurements are accurate. It's best to assemble all of the ingredients before starting; they also are best at room temperature. When you become very familiar with the machine, you may want to vary some recipes. Experiment and have fun, but be sure to only make one change at a time so you will know if it does or does not work.

Know Your Bread Ingredients

All that is needed to make bread is flour, water, yeast and sometimes a little salt. Many of us also like sweeter and richer breads and coffee cakes, so we add sugar, fat, milk and eggs to those basic ingredients. Read on to familiarize yourself with the roles of the different ingredients used to make bread.

Flour

Flour is the primary ingredient, by amount, in bread making. When wheat flour is mixed with liquid and then kneaded, the proteins in the flour go together and form sheets of gluten. Gluten is important because it allows the dough to stretch like elastic, trapping the bubbles of gas given off by the yeast.

Other grains—including corn, rye, barley, rice and millet, to name a few—can be ground into flour. They don't have enough protein to make the gluten necessary for the dough to rise. However, these grain flours can be mixed with wheat flour to make yeast doughs. We recommend using at least half wheat flour and half of a low- or no-gluten-producing flour.

Measuring Flour

All flour is sifted many times during the milling process, and some flours are labeled "presifted." If a recipe calls for sifted flour but you do not want to sift it, there is no need to adjust the amount of flour in the recipe. To obtain the most accurate measurement of flour, spoon flour into a standard dry-ingredient measuring cup and level the top with a knife or spatula.

Storing Flour

Store all flours in airtight canisters in a cool, dry place. Use all-purpose flour, unbleached flour, and bread flour within 15 months, self-rising flour within 9 months and whole wheat and wheat-blend flours within 6 to 8 months. If flour is to be kept for an extended period of time, store it in a moisture-proof bag in the refrigerator or freezer. Allow flour to come to room temperature before using it.

Because flour picks up and loses moisture over a period of time, humidity will affect the use of flour in recipes. When making a recipe, you may need to use less or more flour, but do not change the liquid measurement in the recipe. Gradually add more flour as needed, a tablespoon at a time, if the dough is too wet, or add a little more liquid, a teaspoon at a time, if it is too dry.

Yeast

Yeast is a leavening agent that is made up of thousands of tiny living plants. When given moisture, warmth and "food," yeast will grow and release tiny bubbles of carbon dioxide gas; this process makes dough rise. Yeast is very sensitive; too much heat will kill it, and cold will stunt its growth. Always check the expiration date of the yeast you are using. Basically, three forms of yeast are readily available in supermarkets for home baking.

Bread machine and quick active dry yeast are highly active strains of dry yeast that make dough rise faster than regular active dry yeast. Bread machine yeast was introduced in 1993. It is a special strain of instant yeast, packaged in jars, to end consumer confusion about what kind of yeast works best in bread machines. Because of its finer granulation, the yeast is dispersed more thoroughly during mixing and kneading. Quick active dry yeast can be purchased in premeasured packets and in jars.

Regular active dry yeast is yeast that has been dried and then packaged in a granular form. It can be purchased in premeasured packets and in jars.

These three types of dry yeast are generally interchangeable, although adjustments sometimes are required. We recommend using bread machine yeast or quick active dry yeast in the recipes in this cookbook. If you find that bread machine or quick active dry yeast makes bread rise too high for your bread machine, decrease the amount by ¼ teaspoon at a time when you make the recipe again.

Compressed cake or fresh active yeast is also available in cake form. Generally, fresh yeast is not used in bread machines because measuring it accurately is difficult.

Sweeteners

Sweeteners, including sugar, honey and molasses, provide food for the yeast to grow. They also add flavor and help the crust to brown. Sweeteners vary in flavor intensity and dissolving rate, so it is important to use the sweetener called for in the recipe.

> ### Some Like It Hot: Reheating Your Bread
>
> It is always a treat when warm bread is served at a meal. You can freshen up room-temperature bread machine loaves by heating them in the oven.
>
> For a crisper crust, place the loaf right on the oven rack. Heat it in a 300° oven about 20 minutes or until the crust is crisp and warm. For a softer crust, wrap the loaf in aluminum foil before popping into the oven. You also can heat coffee cakes in aluminum foil the same way and then frost and decorate.
>
> Bread slices and rolls can be warmed in the microwave, but you must be very careful so they don't overheat and become tough or hard.
>
> Breads heated in the microwave become dry and tough faster than bread heated in a conventional or toaster oven, so plan to eat them right away.

Some ingredients such as fruits and some vegetables contain natural sugars. Too much sugar may interfere with the development of the gluten, and the baked product could collapse. Too much sugar also can inhibit the growth of the yeast. So if you are adding fruits or vegetables to your favorite white bread, you may have to increase the amount of yeast. We don't recommend using artificial sweeteners because they do not properly "feed" the yeast.

Salt

Salt enhances the flavor of bread and strengthens the dough by tightening and improving the gluten. It also controls yeast growth, so the flavors have time to develop. Too much salt, however, can kill the yeast, so it is important to measure accurately. Salt also acts as a preservative, which helps keep the bread fresher longer. A salt-free loaf will be high and light with a coarser texture, but it will lack in flavor.

We use table salt for our recipe testing because it is a staple in most homes. Coarse or kosher salt is not used in the recipes but sometimes is used for sprinkling on top of bread doughs before baking, because it adds both flavor and a nice appearance to baked breads. We don't recommend using reduced- or low-sodium salt because it results in a poorer-quality baked product.

Fats and Oils

Fats, such as shortening, margarine, butter and oil tenderize baked goods, help bind ingredients together, aid in browning and add richness and flavor to yeast doughs.

Not all fats are created equal in texture, flavor or baking characteristics. If using a vegetable-oil spread, be sure it contains at least 65 percent fat. We do not recommend using whipped or tub products in the bread machine. Due to added air or liquid, the whipped, tub and low-fat vegetable-oil spreads are not recommended for baking bread because the results are not satisfactory.

Liquids

Liquid is used to rehydrate and activate the yeast and to blend with the flour to make a soft, elastic dough. Water and milk are the most commonly used liquids. Water gives bread a crisper crust, and milk gives bread a velvety texture and added nutrients. Buttermilk or sour milk can be substituted for fresh milk if you like a tangy flavor. Do not use delay cycles with recipes that contain fresh milk because the milk can spoil and possibly cause bacteria growth and food poisoning.

Dry milk (in its dry form) often is used in bread machine recipes so that the delay cycles can be used. Only the recipes that use dry milk and have no perishable ingredients, such as meats, eggs, dairy products or honey, can be used with the delay cycles. Dry buttermilk can be substituted for dry milk in recipes. If dry milk is not available, fresh milk can be substituted for the amount of water and dry milk called for in the recipe, but remember not to use the delay cycles.

Other than water and milk, room-temperature beer, wine and fruit and vegetables juices can also be used in bread making. And that's not the only source of liquid! Any ingredient that becomes soft or melts in the dough will add liquid, including cheese, sour cream, cream cheese and yogurt. Ingredients such as fresh fruits and vegetables also can add liquid to doughs. Ingredients that have been soaked before being added to the dough will add liquid, including raisins, dried fruit or dried mushrooms.

Eggs

Eggs are added to bread doughs for taste, richness and color. They also act as emulsifiers and will slow the staling process and help bread stay fresh a little longer. Do not use delay cycles with recipes that contain eggs because the eggs can spoil and possibly cause bacteria growth and food poisoning.

Egg washes can be made with beaten egg, egg whites or a mixture of water and egg. This is brushed on the shaped dough before baking to give bread a beautiful golden brown crust.

Keeping Bread Fresh

Homemade bread is best eaten the same day it is baked, but it will keep two or three days at room temperature.

Store bread at room temperature in a cool, dry place. Wrap the completely cooled bread in a tightly sealed paper bag if you plan to eat it within a day or two. Plastic bags keep the bread fresh but also promote molding. You might want to switch from paper to a plastic bag if there is any bread left after 2 days, because the bread will be a little drier.

Breads keep best at room temperature or for longer periods of time in the freezer, rather than in the refrigerator. The only time you may want to store the bread in the refrigerator is during hot, humid weather to help prevent mold from forming.

Freezing Bread

To freeze a loaf of bread, seal the completely cooled loaf in an airtight plastic bag or wrap for freezing. You may want to slice the bread first to save thawing time later. Also, slicing makes it easy to remove just the number of slices you need at a time. You can freeze bread up to 2 to 3 months.

To thaw the bread, loosen the wrap and let it stand at room temperature about 3 hours. If you completely unwrap it before thawing, moisture collects and can make the bread soggy. Or to thaw a frozen bread machine loaf in the oven, wrap the loaf in aluminum foil and heat in a 400° oven for 10 to 15 minutes or until thawed and warm.

Frozen bread slices can be thawed in the microwave oven. Heat each slice on High for about 15 seconds. Or pop frozen slices right into the toaster to thaw and toast in one easy step.

Coffee cakes, breadsticks and rolls also can be frozen after being cooled completely. We recommend not frosting or decorating before freezing. If you prefer to frost before freezing, be sure the frosting is dry and that a thin crust has formed so the frosting doesn't smear when being wrapped for the freezer. Seal tightly in an airtight plastic bag or wrap for freezing. You may want to slice coffee cakes before freezing so you can remove the number of slices you need, and slices will thaw more quickly. These breads will keep in the freezer for 2 to 3 months.

To thaw coffee cakes, breadsticks and rolls, let them stand loosely wrapped at room temperature 2 to 3 hours. After they have thawed, allow any moisture that may have collected on the surface to dry. Then frost or decorate as you wish.

Loaves of All Kinds

Multigrain Loaf

1 loaf, 12 servings

PREP:
10 min

CYCLE:
According to manufacturer

COOL:
10 min

Betty's Success Tip

Look for 7-grain cereal in the health-food aisle or hot-cereal section of your supermarket.

1¼ cups water

2 tablespoons butter or stick margarine, softened

1⅓ cups bread flour

1⅓ cups whole wheat flour

1 cup 7-grain or multigrain hot cereal (uncooked)

3 tablespoons packed brown sugar

1¼ teaspoons salt

2½ teaspoons bread machine yeast

Measure carefully, placing all ingredients in bread machine pan in the order recommended by the manufacturer.

Select Whole Wheat or Basic/White cycle. Use Medium or Light crust color. Remove baked bread from pan to wire rack; cool.

1 Serving: Calories 165 (Calories from Fat 25); Fat 3g (Saturated 1g); Cholesterol 5mg; Sodium 410mg; Carbohydrate 33g (Dietary Fiber 3g); Protein 5g

Whole Wheat Bread

1 loaf, 12 servings

PREP:
15 min

CYCLE:
According to manufacturer

COOL:
10 min

1 cup plus 2 tablespoons water

3 tablespoons honey

2 tablespoons butter or stick margarine

1½ cups bread flour

1½ cups whole wheat flour

¼ cup chopped walnuts, toasted, if desired

1 teaspoon salt

1½ teaspoons bread machine yeast

Measure carefully, placing all ingredients in bread machine pan in the order recommended by the manufacturer.

Select Whole Wheat or Basic/White cycle. Use Medium or Light crust color. Do not use delay cycles. Remove baked bread from pan to wire rack; cool.

1 Serving: Calories 140 (Calories from Fat 20); Fat 2g (Saturated 0g); Cholesterol 0mg; Sodium 220mg; Carbohydrate 29g (Dietary Fiber 2g); Protein 4g

If You Don't Have Bread Machine Yeast . . .

Here is how much regular active dry yeast you should use instead.

Bread Machine or Quick Active Dry Yeast	Regular Active Dry Yeast
¾ teaspoon	1 teaspoon
1 teaspoon	1½ teaspoons
1½ teaspoons	2 teaspoons

Seeded Whole Wheat Bread

1 loaf, 12 servings

PREP:
8 min

CYCLE:
According to manufacturer

COOL:
10 min

Ingredient Substitution

We selected dill, sesame and caraway seeds for this recipe, but other combinations of seeds would also work. Consider anise, fennel, celery, coriander and mustard seeds.

1 cup plus 1 tablespoon water

2 tablespoons margarine or butter, softened

1½ cups bread flour

1½ cups whole wheat flour

2 tablespoons dry milk

2 tablespoons sugar

1 teaspoon dill seeds

1½ teaspoons sesame seeds

1 teaspoon caraway seeds

1½ teaspoons salt

2 teaspoons bread machine or quick active dry yeast

Measure carefully, placing all ingredients in bread machine pan in the order recommended by the manufacturer.

Select Whole Wheat or Basic/White cycle. Use Medium or Light crust color. Remove baked bread from pan, and cool on wire rack.

1 Serving: Calories 145 (Calories from Fat 25); Fat 3g (Saturated 1g); Cholesterol 0mg; Sodium 320mg; Carbohydrate 27g (Dietary Fiber 2g); Protein 4g

Oatmeal Bread

1 loaf, 12 servings

PREP:
5 min

CYCLE:
According to manufacturer

COOL:
10 min

Ingredient Substitution

Some of us like sweet, plump raisins in our hot cooked oatmeal. If you do, you'll enjoy raisins in this oatmeal bread. Use ½ cup raisins and add them at the Raisin/Nut signal or 5 to 10 minutes before the last kneading cycle ends.

1¼ cups water

2 tablespoons margarine or butter, softened

3 cups bread flour

½ cup old-fashioned or quick-cooking oats

3 tablespoons packed brown sugar

2 tablespoons dry milk

1¼ teaspoons salt

2 teaspoons bread machine or quick active dry yeast

Measure carefully, placing all ingredients in bread machine pan in the order recommended by the manufacturer.

Select Sweet or Basic/White cycle. Use Light crust color. Remove baked bread from pan, and cool on wire rack.

1 Serving: Calories 185 (Calories from Fat 25); Fat 3g (Saturated 1g); Cholesterol 0mg; Sodium 270mg; Carbohydrate 37g (Dietary Fiber 2g); Protein 5g

Oatmeal Sunflower Bread

1 loaf, 12 servings

PREP:
10 min

CYCLE:
According to manufacturer

COOL:
10 min

Finishing Touch

If your bread machine doesn't have a Raisin/Nut signal, add the nuts 5 to 10 minutes before the last kneading cycle ends. Check your bread machine's use-and-care book to find out how long the last cycle runs.

Serving Suggestion

This nutty oatmeal bread makes a fabulous Santa Fe meat-loaf sandwich. Spread tomato jam or your favorite salsa on two slices of bread. Layer slices of cold meatloaf, Monterey Jack cheese, canned chopped green chiles, avocado slices and shredded lettuce on one slice of bread. Top with remaining slice of bread. It has a wonderfully rich, zippy flavor.

1 cup water

¼ cup honey

2 tablespoons margarine or butter, softened

3 cups bread flour

½ cup old-fashioned or quick-cooking oats

2 tablespoons dry milk

1¼ teaspoons salt

2¼ teaspoons bread machine or quick active dry yeast

½ cup sunflower nuts

Measure carefully, placing all ingredients except nuts in bread machine pan in the order recommended by the manufacturer. Add nuts at the Raisin/Nut signal.

Select Basic/White cycle. Use Medium or Light crust color. Do not use delay cycles. Remove baked bread from pan, and cool on wire rack.

1 Serving: Calories 205 (Calories from Fat 45); Fat 5g (Saturated 1g); Cholesterol 0mg; Sodium 280mg; Carbohydrate 36g (Dietary Fiber 2g); Protein 6g

Sourdough Loaf

1 loaf, 16 servings

PREP:
10 min

CYCLE:
According to manufacturer

REST:
10 min

RISE:
40 min

BAKE:
30 min

COOL:
10 min

1¼ cups Sourdough Starter (opposite page)

¼ cup water

3 cups bread flour

1 tablespoon sugar

1 teaspoon salt

1 teaspoon bread machine or quick active dry yeast

Cornmeal

Measure carefully, placing all ingredients except cornmeal in bread machine pan in the order recommended by the manufacturer.

Select Dough/Manual cycle. Do not use delay cycles.

Remove dough from pan, using lightly floured hands. Cover and let rest 10 minutes on lightly floured surface.

Grease large cookie sheet; sprinkle with cornmeal. Shape dough into round loaf, about 6 inches in diameter, on cookie sheet. Cover and let rise in warm place 35 to 40 minutes or until almost double.

Heat oven to 400°. Spray top of loaf with water. Bake 10 minutes, spraying 3 times with water. Bake 15 to 20 minutes longer or until loaf is golden brown and sounds hollow when tapped. Remove from cookie sheet to wire rack; cool.

1 Serving: Calories 175 (Calories from Fat 10); Fat 1g (Saturated 0g); Cholesterol 0mg; Sodium 210mg; Carbohydrate 37g (Dietary Fiber 1g); Protein 5g

Sourdough Starter

1 teaspoon bread machine or quick active dry yeast

¼ cup warm water (105° to 115°)

¾ cup milk

1 cup bread flour or all-purpose flour

Dissolve yeast in warm water in large glass bowl. Stir in milk. Gradually stir in flour. Beat until smooth. Cover with towel or cheesecloth; let stand in warm, draft-free place (80° to 85°) about 24 hours or until starter begins to ferment (bubbles will appear on surface of starter). If starter has not begun fermentation after 24 hours, discard and begin again.

Stir well, if fermentation has begun; cover tightly with plastic wrap and return to warm place. Let stand 2 or 3 days or until foamy. When starter has become foamy, stir well; pour into 1-quart crock or glass jar with tight-fitting cover. Store in refrigerator. When a clear liquid has risen to the top, starter is ready to use. Stir before using.

Replenish remaining starter after removing starter for bread recipe. Add ¾ cup milk and ¾ cup flour. Store uncovered at room temperature about 12 hours or until bubbles appear. Cover and refrigerate.

Classic White Bread

1 loaf, 12 servings

PREP:
7 min

CYCLE:
According to manufacturer

COOL:
10 min

Betty's Success Tip

Who doesn't like a good slice of homemade bread? This loaf may become a family favorite because it is perfect to use the delay cycle with—which means you can have fresh bread whenever you like.

1 cup plus 2 tablespoons water

2 tablespoons margarine or butter, softened

3 cups bread flour

3 tablespoons dry milk

2 tablespoons sugar

1½ teaspoons salt

2 teaspoons bread machine or quick active dry yeast

Measure carefully, placing all ingredients in bread machine pan in the order recommended by the manufacturer.

Select Basic/White cycle. Use Medium or Light crust color. Remove baked bread from pan, and cool on wire rack.

1 Serving: Calories 145 (Calories from Fat 20); Fat 2g (Saturated 0g); Cholesterol 0mg; Sodium 300mg; Carbohydrate 29g (Dietary Fiber 1g); Protein 4g

Old-World Rye Bread

1 loaf, 16 servings

PREP:
20 min

CYCLE:
According to manufacturer

REST:
10 min

SHAPE:
10 min

RISE:
45 min

BAKE:
28 min

COOL:
10 min

⅔ cup water

2 tablespoons vegetable oil

⅔ cup buttermilk

2¼ cups bread flour

1 cup rye flour

⅓ cup mashed potato mix (dry)

2 tablespoons packed brown sugar

1¼ teaspoons salt

1 teaspoon caraway seeds

2 teaspoons bread machine or quick active dry yeast

Cornmeal

Additional caraway seeds, if desired

Betty's Success Tip

If the dough keeps springing back and doesn't hold its shape when you try to roll it into a rope, cover and let it rest a few more minutes. You'll find it much easier to work with because letting it "rest" allows the gluten to relax and makes it easier to handle.

Measure carefully, placing all ingredients except cornmeal and additional caraway seeds in bread machine pan in the order recommended by the manufacturer.

Select Dough/Manual cycle. Do not use delay cycles.

Remove dough from pan, using lightly floured hands. Cover and let rest 10 minutes on lightly floured surface.

Grease large cookie sheet; sprinkle with cornmeal. Roll dough into 25-inch rope. Curl rope into coil shape; tuck end under. Place on cookie sheet. Cover and let rise in warm place 30 to 45 minutes or until double. (Dough is ready if indentation remains when touched.)

Heat oven to 400°. Brush water over loaf; sprinkle with cornmeal and additional caraway seeds. Bake 23 to 28 minutes or until loaf is golden brown and sounds hollow when tapped. Remove from cookie sheet to wire rack; cool.

1 Serving: Calories 125 (Calories from Fat 30); Fat 3g (Saturated 1g); Cholesterol 2mg; Sodium 160mg; Carbohydrate 23g (Dietary Fiber 2g); Protein 3g

Buttermilk Rye Bread

1 loaf, 12 servings

PREP:
7 min

CYCLE:
According to manufacturer

COOL:
10 min

Ingredient Substitution:

Rye flour, milled from a hardy cereal grass, is low in gluten-making protein. That is why it performs so great with bread flour, which is high in gluten-making protein. The most common type of rye flour sold in supermarkets is medium rye flour. Light and dark rye flours are available in natural foods stores or co-ops. You can use any of the three flours in this recipe.

⅔ cup water

⅔ cup buttermilk

2 tablespoons vegetable oil

⅓ cup mashed potato mix (dry)

2¼ cups bread flour

1 cup rye flour

1¼ teaspoons salt

2 tablespoons packed brown sugar

1 teaspoon caraway seeds

2 teaspoons bread machine or quick active dry yeast

Measure carefully, placing all ingredients in bread machine pan in the order recommended by the manufacturer.

Select Basic/White cycle. Use Medium or Light crust color. Do not use delay cycles. Remove baked bread from pan, and cool on wire rack.

1 Serving: Calories 155 (Calories from Fat 25); Fat 3g (Saturated 1g); Cholesterol 0mg; Sodium 260mg; Carbohydrate 30g (Dietary Fiber 2g); Protein 4g

Cutting Bread Machine Loaves

For best results when cutting warm bread loaves, we recommend using an electric knife.
Also, a sharp serrated or sawtooth bread knife works well.
There are several ways to cut bread machine loaves:

- **For square slices,** place the loaf on its side and cut down through the loaf. We find this to be the easiest way to cut loaves.
- **For rectangular slices,** place the loaf upright and cut from the top down. Slices may be cut in half, either lengthwise or crosswise.
- **For wedges,** place the loaf upright and cut down from the center into wedges. Or cut loaf in half from the top down, then place each half cut side down, and cut lengthwise into wedges.
- **For other shapes,** use your imagination! Bread slices can be cut into triangles, fingerlike strips and chunks. Or slices can be cut into other interesting shapes with cookie cutters.

Pumpernickel Bread

1 loaf, 12 servings

PREP:
10 min

CYCLE:
According to manufacturer

COOL:
10 min

Betty's Success Tip

Pumpernickel bread is a heavy dark bread. Our recipe uses both rye and whole wheat flours. The molasses, cocoa and coffee not only add flavor, but they increase the deep brown color of this bread.

Serving Suggestion

Here's your chance to make a great deli corned beef sandwich. Spread slices of pumpernickel bread with a spicy mustard. Pile high with slices of corned beef, drained canned sauerkraut and Swiss cheese, and top with another slice of bread. Serve with big, crisp kosher dill pickles.

1 cup plus 2 tablespoons water

1½ teaspoons salt

⅓ cup molasses, full flavor

2 tablespoons vegetable oil

1 cup plus 1 tablespoon rye flour

1 cup plus 2 tablespoons whole wheat flour

1½ cups bread flour

3 tablespoons baking cocoa

1½ teaspoons instant coffee granules

1 tablespoon caraway seeds

1 teaspoon bread machine or quick active dry yeast

Measure carefully, placing all ingredients in bread machine pan in the order recommended by the manufacturer.

Select Whole Wheat or Basic/White cycle. Use Medium or Light crust color. Remove baked bread from pan, and cool on wire rack.

1 Serving: Calories 170 (Calories from Fat 25); Fat 3g (Saturated 1g); Cholesterol 0mg; Sodium 270mg; Carbohydrate 35g (Dietary Fiber 3g); Protein 4g

Pumpernickel Pecan Bread

1 loaf, 12 servings

PREP:
10 min

CYCLE:
According to manufacturer

COOL:
10 min

Betty's Success Tip

If your bread machine doesn't have a Raisin/Nut signal, add the raisins and pecans 5 to 10 minutes before the last kneading cycle ends. Check your bread machine's use-and-care book to find out how long the last cycle runs.

Ingredient Substitution

The flavor of this dark bread is complemented by the sweetness of the raisins and the crunch of the nuts. Feel free to use either dark or golden raisins or substitute chopped walnuts for the pecans.

1 cup plus 2 tablespoons water

¼ cup molasses, full flavor

1 tablespoon margarine or butter, softened

2 cups bread flour

1¼ cups rye flour

2 tablespoons baking cocoa

1½ teaspoons instant coffee granules

2 teaspoons salt

2¼ teaspoons bread machine or quick active dry yeast

⅓ cup raisins

½ cup chopped pecans

Measure carefully, placing all ingredients except raisins and pecans in bread machine pan in the order recommended by the manufacturer. Add raisins and pecans at the Raisin/Nut signal.

Select Basic/White cycle. Use Medium or Light crust color. Remove baked bread from pan, and cool on wire rack.

1 Serving: Calories 190 (Calories from Fat 45); Fat 5g (Saturated 1g); Cholesterol 0mg; Sodium 410mg; Carbohydrate 35g (Dietary Fiber 3g); Protein 4g

Caraway Cheese Bread

1 loaf, 12 servings

PREP:
5 min

CYCLE:
According to manufacturer

COOL:
10 min

Betty's Success Tip

We don't recommend this recipe for bread machines that have cast-aluminum pans in a horizontal-loaf shape because our results after several tests were unsatisfactory.

Ingredient Substitution

Instead of using caraway seeds, use celery seeds in half the amount called for in the recipe. A celery seed-flavored cheese bread is excellent with sandwich fillings such as egg, tuna and chicken salad.

1 cup water

3 cups wheat flour

¾ cup shredded sharp Cheddar cheese

1½ teaspoons caraway seeds

1 tablespoon sugar

¾ teaspoon salt

1½ teaspoons bread machine or quick active dry yeast

Measure carefully, placing all ingredients in bread machine pan in the order recommended by the manufacturer.

Select Basic/White cycle. Use Medium or Light crust color. Do not use delay cycles. Remove baked bread from pan, and cool on wire rack.

1 Serving: Calories 150 (Calories from Fat 25); Fat 3g (Saturated 2g); Cholesterol 5mg; Sodium 190mg; Carbohydrate 27g (Dietary Fiber 1g); Protein 5g

Roasted Garlic Bread

1 loaf, 12 servings

PREP:
10 min

CYCLE:
According to manufacturer

COOL:
10 min

Betty's Success Tip

To be sure you will have enough roasted garlic, use at least a 2-ounce bulb of garlic for 2 tablespoons of roasted garlic and at least a 1-ounce bulb for 1 tablespoon.

Finishing Touch

If your bread machine doesn't have a Raisin/Nut signal, add the mashed garlic 5 to 10 minutes before the last kneading cycle ends. Check your bread machine's use-and-care book to find out how long the last cycle runs.

2 tablespoons mashed Roasted Garlic (below)

1 cup plus 2 tablespoons water

1 tablespoon olive or vegetable oil

3 cups bread flour

2 tablespoons sugar

1 teaspoon salt

1¼ teaspoons bread machine or quick active dry yeast

Prepare Roasted Garlic. After squeezing garlic out of cloves, slightly mash enough garlic to measure 2 or 3 tablespoons.

Measure carefully, placing all ingredients except garlic in bread machine pan in the order recommended by the manufacturer. Add mashed garlic at the Raisin/Nut signal.

Select Basic/White cycle. Use Medium or Light crust color. Do not use delay cycles. Remove baked bread from pan, and cool on wire rack.

Roasted Garlic

Heat oven to 350°. Carefully peel away paperlike skin from around garlic bulbs, leaving just enough to hold bulb intact. Trim tops of garlic bulbs about ½ inch to expose cloves. Place bulbs, stem ends down, on 12-inch square of aluminum foil. Drizzle each bulb with 2 teaspoons olive or vegetable oil. Wrap securely in foil; place in pie plate or shallow baking pan. Bake 45 to 50 minutes or until garlic is tender when pierced with toothpick or fork. Cool slightly. Gently squeeze garlic out of cloves.

1 Serving: Calories 150 (Calories from Fat 20); Fat 2g (Saturated 0g); Cholesterol 0mg; Sodium 180mg; Carbohydrate 30g (Dietary Fiber 1g); Protein 4g

Roasted Garlic Bread

Garlic Basil Bread

1 loaf, 8 servings

PREP:
5 min

CYCLE:
According to manufacturer

COOL:
10 min

Betty's Success Tip

If your bread machine has a 2-pound vertical pan, the loaf will be short but still have good texture and flavor. If your bread machine has a horizontal pan, however, there isn't enough dough to make a good loaf of baked bread.

Serving Suggestion

Here's how to make quick and easy Parmesan cheese bread-sticks. Spread toasted slices of this garlicky basil bread with margarine or butter. Sprinkle generously with grated or finely shredded Parmesan cheese. Cut each piece of toast into 1-inch sticks. Kids love them, especially for dunking into a bowl of their favorite soup for a quick lunch.

¾ cup water

2 teaspoons margarine or butter, softened

1 clove garlic, finely chopped

2 cups bread flour

1 tablespoon dry milk

1 tablespoon sugar

1 teaspoon salt

1 teaspoon dried basil leaves

1½ teaspoons bread machine or quick active dry yeast

Measure carefully, placing all ingredients in bread machine pan in the order recommended by the manufacturer.

Select Basic/White cycle. Use Medium or Light crust color. Do not use delay cycles. Remove baked bread from pan, and cool on wire rack.

1 Serving: Calories 140 (Calories from Fat 20); Fat 2g (Saturated 0g); Cholesterol 0mg; Sodium 310mg; Carbohydrate 28g (Dietary Fiber 1g); Protein 4g

Parmesan Sun-Dried-Tomato Bread

1 loaf, 12 servings

PREP:
10 min

CYCLE:
According to manufacturer

COOL:
10 min

Betty's Success Tip

If your bread machine doesn't have a Raisin/Nut signal, add the tomatoes 5 to 10 minutes before the last kneading cycle ends. Check your bread machine's use-and-care book to find out how long the last cycle runs.

1 cup plus 2 tablespoons water

3 cups bread flour

½ cup shredded Parmesan cheese

1½ cloves crushed garlic

2 tablespoons sugar

1 teaspoon salt

1½ teaspoons dried oregano leaves

2 teaspoons bread machine or quick active dry yeast

⅓ cup sun-dried tomatoes (packed in oil), drained and coarsely chopped

Measure carefully, placing all ingredients except tomatoes in bread machine pan in the order recommended by the manufacturer. Add tomatoes at the Raisin/Nut signal.

Select Basic/White cycle. Use Medium or Light crust color. Do not use delay cycles. Remove baked bread from pan, and cool on wire rack.

1 Serving: Calories 150 (Calories from Fat 20); Fat 2g (Saturated 1g); Cholesterol 5mg; Sodium 270mg; Carbohydrate 29g (Dietary Fiber 1g); Protein 5g

Mediterranean Herbed Bread

1 loaf, 12 servings

PREP:
7 min

CYCLE:
According to manufacturer

COOL:
10 min

Betty's Success Tip

Dried herbs can be used when fresh herbs aren't available. Use ½ teaspoon each of dried basil, oregano and thyme leaves.

1 cup water

1 tablespoon margarine or butter, softened

3 cups bread flour

2 tablespoons sugar

1 tablespoon dry milk

1½ teaspoons salt

1 teaspoon chopped fresh basil leaves

1 teaspoon chopped fresh oregano leaves

1 teaspoon chopped fresh thyme leaves

2¼ teaspoons bread machine or quick active dry yeast

Measure carefully, placing all ingredients in bread machine pan in the order recommended by the manufacturer.

Select Basic/White cycle. Use Medium or Light crust color. Remove baked bread from pan, and cool on wire rack.

1 Serving: Calories 135 (Calories from Fat 10); Fat 1g (Saturated 0g); Cholesterol 0mg; Sodium 300mg; Carbohydrate 29g (Dietary Fiber 1g); Protein 4g

Herb and Crunch Wheat Bread

1 loaf, 12 servings

PREP:
7 min

CYCLE:
According to manufacturer

COOL:
10 min

Finishing Touch

If your bread machine doesn't have a Raisin/Nut signal, add the nuts 5 to 10 minutes before the last kneading cycle ends. Check your bread machine's use-and-care book to find out how long the last cycle runs.

1¼ cups water

1½ cups bread flour

1½ cups whole wheat flour

2 tablespoons sugar

2 tablespoons dry milk

2 tablespoons margarine or butter, softened

1½ teaspoons salt

1½ teaspoons dried basil leaves

1 teaspoon dried thyme leaves

2 teaspoons bread machine or quick active dry yeast

½ cup dry-roasted sunflower nuts

Measure carefully, placing all ingredients except nuts in bread machine pan in the order recommended by the manufacturer. Add nuts at the Raisin/Nut signal.

Select Basic/White cycle. Use Medium or Light crust color. Remove baked bread from pan, and cool on wire rack.

1 Serving: Calories 170 (Calories from Fat 45); Fat 5g (Saturated 1g); Cholesterol 0mg; Sodium 340mg; Carbohydrate 28g (Dietary Fiber 2g); Protein 5g

Herbed Vinaigrette Bread

1 loaf, 12 servings

PREP:
5 min

CYCLE:
According to manufacturer

COOL:
10 min

Ingredient Substitution

No balsamic vinegar in the pantry? You can substitute an apple cider vinegar or red wine vinegar instead.

¾ cup plus 2 tablespoons water

1 tablespoon balsamic vinegar

⅓ cup chopped red onion

1 tablespoon vegetable oil

3 cups bread flour

1 teaspoon dried tarragon leaves

2 tablespoons sugar

¾ teaspoon salt

2 teaspoons bread machine or quick active dry yeast

Measure carefully, placing all ingredients in bread machine pan in the order recommended by the manufacturer.

Select Basic/White cycle. Use Medium or Light crust color. Do not use delay cycles. Remove baked bread from pan, and cool on wire rack.

1 Serving: Calories 145 (Calories from Fat 20); Fat 2g (Saturated 0g); Cholesterol 0mg; Sodium 150mg; Carbohydrate 29g (Dietary Fiber 1g); Protein 4g

Dill Wheat Bread

1 loaf, 12 servings

PREP:
7 min

CYCLE:
According to manufacturer

COOL:
10 min

Betty's Success Tip

Your guests will love it if you make a "dip bowl" out of a loaf of this bread. Cut off the top one-third of the loaf and put it aside. Hollow out the loaf to form a bowl. Cut the removed chunks of bread and reserved top into cubes. Fill the bowl with your favorite spinach dip or other tasty dip, and serve with the bread cubes.

1 cup water

2 tablespoons honey

2 tablespoons margarine or butter, softened

2 cups bread flour

1½ cups whole wheat flour

2 tablespoons dry milk

1 teaspoon salt

1 teaspoon dried dill weed

1 teaspoon caraway seed

2 teaspoons bread machine or quick active dry yeast

Measure carefully, placing all ingredients in bread machine pan in the order recommended by the manufacturer.

Select Whole Wheat or Basic/White cycle. Use Medium or Light crust color. Do not use delay cycles. Remove baked bread from pan, and cool on wire rack.

1 Serving: Calories 165 (Calories from Fat 25); Fat 3g (Saturated 1g); Cholesterol 0mg; Sodium 220mg; Carbohydrate 32g (Dietary Fiber 2g); Protein 5g

Greek Olive Bread

1 loaf, 8 servings

PREP:
5 min

CYCLE:
According to manufacturer

COOL:
10 min

Betty's Success Tip

If your bread machine has a 2-pound vertical pan, the loaf will be short but still have good texture and flavor. If your bread machine has a horizontal pan, however, there isn't enough dough to make a good loaf of baked bread.

Finishing Touch

If your bread machine doesn't have a Raisin/Nut signal, add the olives 5 to 10 minutes before the last kneading cycle ends. Check your bread machine's use-and-care book to find out how long the last cycle runs.

¾ cup plus 1 tablespoon water

2 teaspoons olive or vegetable oil

2 cups bread flour

1 tablespoon sugar

½ teaspoon salt

¾ teaspoon bread machine or quick active dry yeast

⅓ cup Kalamata or Greek olives, pitted and coarsely chopped

Measure carefully, placing all ingredients except olives in bread machine pan in the order recommended by the manufacturer. Add olives at the Raisin/Nut signal.

Select Basic/White cycle. Use Medium or Light crust color. Do not use delay cycles. Remove baked bread from pan, and cool on wire rack.

1 Serving: Calories 140 (Calories from Fat 20); Fat 2g (Saturated 0g); Cholesterol 0mg; Sodium 200mg; Carbohydrate 28g (Dietary Fiber 1g); Protein 4g

Cheddar Cheese and Olive Bread

1 loaf, 8 servings

PREP:
5 min

CYCLE:
According to manufacturer

COOL:
10 min

Betty's Success Tip

If your bread machine has a 2-pound vertical pan, the loaf will be short but still have good texture and flavor. If your bread machine has a horizontal pan, however, there isn't enough dough to make a good loaf of baked bread.

Finishing Touch

If your bread machine doesn't have a Raisin/Nut signal, add the olives 5 to 10 minutes before the last kneading cycle ends. Check your bread machine's use-and-care book to find out how long the last cycle runs.

¾ **cup water**

2 **cups bread flour**

¾ **cup shredded sharp Cheddar cheese**

1 **tablespoon sugar**

½ **teaspoon salt**

¾ **teaspoon bread machine or quick active dry yeast**

½ **cup small pimiento-stuffed olives, well drained**

Measure carefully, placing all ingredients except olives in bread machine pan in the order recommended by the manufacturer. Add olives at the Raisin/Nut signal.

Select Basic/White cycle. Use Medium or Light crust color. Do not use delay cycles. Remove baked bread from pan, and cool on wire rack.

1 Serving: Calories 175 (Calories from Fat 45); Fat 5g (Saturated 2g); Cholesterol 10mg; Sodium 430mg; Carbohydrate 28g (Dietary Fiber 1g); Protein 6g

Cranberry Whole Wheat Bread

1 loaf, 8 servings

PREP:
5 min

CYCLE:
According to manufacturer

COOL:
10 min

Betty's Success Tip

If your bread machine has a 2-pound vertical pan, the loaf will be short but still have good texture and flavor. If your bread machine has a horizontal pan, however, there isn't enough dough to make a good loaf of baked bread.

Finishing Touch

If your bread machine doesn't have a Raisin/Nut signal, add the cranberries 5 to 10 minutes before the last kneading cycle ends. Check your bread machine's use-and-care book to find out how long the last cycle runs.

Serving Suggestion

Spread slices of this cranberry-studded bread with cranberry relish. Stack on slices of cold turkey and Swiss cheese, and top with your favorite kind of lettuce or sprouts and gobble it up!

¾ cup water

2 tablespoons honey

1 tablespoon margarine or butter, softened

1¼ cups bread flour

¾ cup whole wheat flour

1 teaspoon salt

¼ teaspoon ground mace

1¼ teaspoons bread machine or quick active dry yeast

⅓ cup dried cranberries

Measure carefully, placing all ingredients except cranberries in bread machine pan in the order recommended by the manufacturer. Add cranberries at the Raisin/Nut signal.

Select Whole Wheat or Basic/White cycle. Use Medium or Light crust color. Do not use delay cycles. Remove baked bread from pan, and cool on wire rack.

1 Serving: Calories 155 (Calories from Fat 10); Fat 1g (Saturated 0g); Cholesterol 0mg; Sodium 300mg; Carbohydrate 34g (Dietary Fiber 4g); Protein 4g

Cranberry Whole Wheat Bread

Golden Raisin and Rosemary Wheat Bread

1 loaf, 12 servings

PREP:
10 min

CYCLE:
According to manufacturer

COOL:
10 min

Betty's Success Tip

Don't forget to crumble the dried rosemary leaves before adding them so more of the delicate flavor will be released. Also, because dried leaves are sharp, crumbling them will help eliminate larger, sharp pieces of rosemary in the bread.

Finishing Touch

If your bread machine doesn't have a Raisin/Nut signal, add the raisins 5 to 10 minutes before the last kneading cycle ends. Check your bread machine's use-and-care book to find out how long the last cycle runs.

1¼ cups water

2 tablespoons margarine or butter, softened

1½ cups bread flour

1½ cups whole wheat flour

2 tablespoons dry milk

¾ teaspoon crumbled dried rosemary leaves

2 tablespoons sugar

1½ teaspoons salt

1¾ teaspoons bread machine or quick active dry yeast

¾ cup golden raisins

Measure carefully, placing all ingredients except raisins in bread machine pan in the order recommended by the manufacturer. Add raisins at the Raisin/Nut signal.

Select Whole Wheat or Basic/White cycle. Use Medium or Light crust color. Remove baked bread from pan, and cool on wire rack.

1 Serving: Calories 160 (Calories from Fat 20); Fat 2g (Saturated 0g); Cholesterol 0mg; Sodium 320mg; Carbohydrate 34g (Dietary Fiber 3g); Protein 4g

Dilled Carrot Bread

1 loaf, 12 servings

PREP:
5 min

CYCLE:
According to manufacturer

COOL:
10 min

Ingredient Substitution

For a hint of the Mediterranean in this golden carrot bread, use the same amount of fennel seed instead of the dill weed.

1 cup plus 2 tablespoons water

½ cup shredded carrots

2 tablespoons margarine or butter, softened

2 tablespoons sugar

3 cups bread flour

1 cup Fiber One® cereal

1½ teaspoons dried dill weed

1 teaspoon salt

1½ teaspoons bread machine or quick active dry yeast

Measure carefully, placing all ingredients in bread machine pan in the order recommended by the manufacturer.

Select Basic/White cycle. Use Medium or Light crust color. Do not use delay cycles. Remove baked bread from pan, and cool on wire rack.

1 Serving: Calories 165 (Calories from Fat 25); Fat 3g (Saturated 0g); Cholesterol 0mg; Sodium 230mg; Carbohydrate 33g (Dietary Fiber 3g); Protein 4g

Potato Tarragon Bread

1 loaf, 12 servings

PREP:
7 min

CYCLE:
According to manufacturer

COOL:
10 min

Ingredient Substitution

For a delicious potato chive bread, use the same amount of freeze-dried chives or 1 tablespoon chopped fresh chives instead of the tarragon.

1 cup water

3 tablespoons margarine or butter, softened

1 egg

3 cups bread flour

¾ cup mashed potato mix (dry)

1 tablespoon sugar

1½ teaspoons salt

1½ teaspoons dried tarragon leaves

2½ teaspoons bread machine or quick active dry yeast

Measure carefully, placing all ingredients in bread machine pan in the order recommended by the manufacturer.

Select Basic/White cycle. Use Medium or Light crust color. Do not use delay cycles. Remove baked bread from pan, and cool on wire rack.

1 Serving: Calories 170 (Calories from Fat 35); Fat 4g (Saturated 1g); Cholesterol 20mg; Sodium 310mg; Carbohydrate 30g (Dietary Fiber 1g); Protein 4g

Peppery Potato and Carrot Bread

1 loaf, 12 servings

PREP:
5 min

CYCLE:
According to manufacturer

COOL:
10 min

Betty's Success Tip

Most graters have two sizes of shredders—one for small shreds and one for medium size. Be sure to use the medium-size shred for the carrots. If you use the small shred, you may have too much carrot, which will cause the dough to be too moist.

Serving Suggestion

Make your next grilled cheese a roasted garlic grilled cheese on this Peppery Potato and Carrot Bread. Make the Roasted Garlic on page 360. Spread the garlic on two slices of bread. Layer one slice of bread with slices of Monterey Jack, Muenster or provolone cheese; top with the remaining slice of bread. If you like, add some sliced avocado. Butter the outside of the sandwich, then cook over medium heat until it's golden brown and the cheese is melted, which will take about 8 minutes.

1 Serving: Calories 150 (Calories from Fat 20); Fat 2g (Saturated 1g); Cholesterol 0mg; Sodium 250mg; Carbohydrate 30g (Dietary Fiber 1g); Protein 4g

1 cup plus 2 tablespoons water

⅔ cup shredded carrots

2 tablespoons margarine or butter, softened

3 cups bread flour

½ cup mashed potato mix (dry)

1 teaspoon lemon pepper seasoning salt

1 tablespoon sugar

1 teaspoon salt

1½ teaspoons bread machine or quick active dry yeast

Measure carefully, placing all ingredients in bread machine pan in the order recommended by the manufacturer.

Select Basic/White cycle. Use Medium or Light crust color. Do not use delay cycles. Remove baked bread from pan, and cool on wire rack.

Low-Fat Jalapeño Corn Bread

1 loaf, 12 servings

PREP:
10 min

CYCLE:
According to manufacturer

COOL:
10 min

¾ cup plus 2 tablespoons water

⅔ cup frozen whole kernel corn, thawed

2 tablespoons butter or stick margarine, softened

1 tablespoon chopped seeded jalapeño chile

3¼ cups bread flour

⅓ cup cornmeal

2 tablespoons sugar

1½ teaspoons salt

2½ teaspoons bread machine or quick active dry yeast

Measure carefully, placing all ingredients in bread machine pan in the order recommended by the manufacturer.

Select Basic/White cycle. Use Medium or Light crust color. Do not use delay cycles. Remove baked bread from pan to wire rack; cool.

1 Serving: Calories 170 (Calories from Fat 20); Fat 2g (Saturated 1g); Cholesterol 5mg; Sodium 310mg; Carbohydrate 35g (Dietary Fiber 2g); Protein 5g

Zucchini Wheat Bread

1 loaf, 12 servings

PREP:
7 min

CYCLE:
According to manufacturer

COOL:
10 min

Finishing Touch

If your bread machine doesn't have a Raisin/Nut signal, add the walnuts 5 to 10 minutes before the last kneading cycle ends. Check your bread machine's use-and-care book to find out how long the last cycle runs.

¾ cup plus 1 tablespoon water

½ cup shredded zucchini

2 tablespoons margarine or butter, softened

1½ cups bread flour

1½ cups whole wheat flour

2 tablespoons dry milk

¼ cup sugar

½ teaspoon ground cinnamon

¼ teaspoon ground cloves

1 teaspoon salt

2 teaspoons bread machine or quick active dry yeast

¼ cup chopped walnuts

Measure carefully, placing all ingredients except walnuts in bread machine pan in the order recommended by the manufacturer. Add walnuts at the Raisin/Nut signal.

Select Whole Wheat or Basic/White cycle. Use Medium or Light crust color. Do not use delay cycles. Remove baked bread from pan, and cool on wire rack.

1 Serving: Calories 150 (Calories from Fat 30); Fat 4g (Saturated 1g); Cholesterol 0mg; Sodium 230mg; Carbohydrate 28g (Dietary Fiber 3g); Protein 5g

Beer Bacon Bread

1 loaf, 12 servings

PREP:
7 min

CYCLE:
According to manufacturer

COOL:
10 min

Betty's Success Tip

For flat beer, open the can or bottle and let it stand about 1 hour before using. The flat beer is necessary for a good-textured bread.

Finishing Touch

If your bread machine doesn't have a Raisin/Nut signal, add the bacon 5 to 10 minutes before the last kneading cycle ends. Check your bread machine's use-and-care book to find out how long the last cycle runs.

¾ cup flat beer or nonalcoholic beer

½ cup water

¼ cup chopped green onions

2 tablespoons mustard

1 tablespoon margarine or butter, softened

3¼ cups bread flour

1 tablespoon sugar

¾ teaspoon salt

1¾ teaspoons bread machine or quick active dry yeast

⅓ cup crumbled cooked bacon

Measure carefully, placing all ingredients except bacon in bread machine pan in the order recommended by the manufacturer. Add bacon at the Raisin/Nut signal.

Select Basic/White cycle. Use Medium or Light crust color. Do not use delay cycles. Remove baked bread from pan, and cool on wire rack.

1 Serving: Calories 165 (Calories from Fat 25); Fat 3g (Saturated 1g); Cholesterol 2mg; Sodium 210mg; Carbohydrate 30g (Dietary Fiber 1g); Protein 5g

Cheesy Mustard Pretzel Bread

1 loaf, 12 servings

PREP:
5 min

CYCLE:
According to manufacturer

COOL:
10 min

Finishing Touch

If your bread machine doesn't have a Raisin/Nut signal, add the cheese 5 to 10 minutes before the last kneading cycle ends. Check your bread machine's use-and-care book to find out how long the last cycle runs.

1 cup water

1 tablespoon vegetable oil

2 tablespoons mustard

3 cups bread flour

1 tablespoon sugar

1 teaspoon salt

2 teaspoons bread machine or quick active dry yeast

½ cup shredded sharp Cheddar cheese

Coarse salt, if desired

Measure carefully, placing all ingredients except cheese and coarse salt in bread machine pan in the order recommended by the manufacturer. Add cheese at the Raisin/Nut signal.

Select Basic/White cycle. Use Medium or Light crust color. Do not use delay cycles. Before baking cycle begins, carefully brush top of dough with water and sprinkle with coarse salt. Remove baked bread from pan, and cool on wire rack.

1 Serving: Calories 155 (Calories from Fat 30); Fat 3g (Saturated 1g); Cholesterol 5mg; Sodium 260mg; Carbohydrate 28g (Dietary Fiber 1g); Protein 5g

Rolls, Breadsticks and Focaccia

Dinner Rolls

15 rolls

PREP:
17 min

CYCLE:
According to manufacturer

RISE:
1½ hours

BAKE:
15 min

Betty's Success Tip

To make the dinner rolls ahead, cover tightly with aluminum foil after placing rolls in pan, and refrigerate 4 to 24 hours. Before baking, remove from refrigerator, remove foil and cover loosely with plastic wrap. Let rise in warm place about 2 hours or until double. If some rising has occurred in the refrigerator, rising time may be less than 2 hours. Bake as directed.

3¼ cups bread flour

¼ cup sugar

2 tablespoons butter or stick margarine, softened

1 teaspoon salt

3 teaspoons bread machine or quick active dry yeast

1 cup room-temperature water

1 large egg

Butter or stick margarine, melted, if desired

Measure carefully, placing all ingredients except melted butter in bread machine pan in the order recommended by the manufacturer.

Select Dough/Manual cycle; do not use delay cycle. Remove dough from pan.

Place dough on lightly floured surface. Knead about 5 minutes or until dough is smooth and springy. Place dough in large bowl greased with shortening, turning dough to grease all sides. Cover bowl loosely with plastic wrap, and let rise in warm place about 1 hour or until double. Dough is ready if indentation remains when touched.

Grease rectangular pan, 13 × 9 × 2 inches, with shortening.

Gently push fist into dough to deflate. Divide dough into 15 equal pieces. Shape each piece into a ball; place in pan. Brush with butter. Cover loosely with plastic wrap, and let rise in warm place about 30 minutes or until double.

Heat oven to 375°.

Bake 12 to 15 minutes or until golden brown. Serve warm or cool.

1 Roll: Calories 150 (Calories from Fat 35); Fat 4g (Saturated 2g); Cholesterol 25mg; Sodium 190mg; Carbohydrate 26g (Dietary Fiber 1g); Protein 4g

Curry Rice Dinner Rolls

10 rolls

PREP:
20 min

CYCLE:
According to manufacturer

REST:
10 min

RISE:
40 min

BAKE:
20 min

⅔ cup water

1 tablespoon vegetable oil

2 cups bread flour

½ cup cooked brown rice

1 teaspoon salt

¾ teaspoon sugar

½ teaspoon curry powder

1 teaspoon bread machine or quick active dry yeast

Margarine or butter, melted

Measure carefully, placing all ingredients except margarine in bread machine pan in the order recommended by the manufacturer.

Select Dough/Manual cycle. Do not use delay cycles.

Remove dough from pan, using lightly floured hands. Knead 5 minutes on lightly floured surface. Cover and let rest 10 minutes.

Grease large cookie sheet. Divide dough into 10 equal pieces. Shape each piece into a ball. Place 2 inches apart on cookie sheet. Brush with margarine. Cover and let rise in warm place 30 to 40 minutes or until double. (Dough is ready if indentation remains when touched.)

Heat oven to 375°. Bake 15 to 20 minutes or until golden brown. Serve warm, or cool on wire rack.

1 Roll: Calories 160 (Calories from Fat 55); Fat 6g (Saturated 1g); Cholesterol 0mg; Sodium 280mg; Carbohydrate 24g (Dietary Fiber 1g); Protein 3g

Betty's Success Tip

We found that we had better results when using cold or room-temperature rice instead of hot cooked rice. Cook the brown rice ahead and cool to room temperature or refrigerate. To cool the rice quickly, spread it out on a cookie sheet or large plate before you refrigerate it. This recipe is also a good way to use any leftover rice you might have on hand.

Curry Rice Dinner Rolls

Whole Wheat Buttermilk Rolls

24 rolls

PREP:
18 min

CYCLE:
According to manufacturer

RISE:
1 hour

BAKE:
20 min

Betty's Success Tip

We found that letting the dough rise twice—once in the bowl, then again after shaping the rolls—gave these heavenly whole wheat rolls a lighter, more tender texture.

1½ cups buttermilk

¼ cup shortening

2 tablespoons honey

2 cups whole wheat flour

1¼ cups bread flour

½ cup wheat germ

1½ teaspoons salt

2 teaspoons bread machine or quick active dry yeast

3 tablespoons margarine or butter, melted

Measure carefully, placing all ingredients except margarine in bread machine pan in the order recommended by the manufacturer.

Select Dough/Manual cycle. Do not use delay cycles.

Remove dough from pan, using lightly floured hands. Place dough in greased bowl, and turn greased side up. Cover and let rise in warm place about 30 minutes or until double. (Dough is ready if indentation remains when touched.)

Grease large cookie sheet. Punch down dough. Place dough on lightly floured surface. Divide dough into 24 equal pieces. Shape each piece into a ball. Place slightly apart on cookie sheet. Cover and let rise about 30 minutes or until double. Brush with margarine.

Heat oven to 350°. Bake 15 to 20 minutes or until golden brown. Serve warm, or cool on wire rack.

1 Roll: Calories 105 (Calories from Fat 35); Fat 4g (Saturated 1g); Cholesterol 0mg; Sodium 170mg; Carbohydrate 16g (Dietary Fiber 2g); Protein 3g

Whole Wheat Dinner Rolls

12 rolls

PREP:
17 min

CYCLE:
According to manufacturer

REST:
10 min

RISE:
40 min

BAKE:
20 min

Betty's Success Tip

We have kneaded the dough after it comes out of the bread machine to help develop the gluten, so the rolls have a nice, light texture. If the dough tends to spring back into place even after letting it rest 10 minutes, cover it again and let it rest another 5 minutes.

¾ cup water

1 tablespoon shortening

1¼ cups bread flour

1 cup whole wheat flour

2 tablespoons packed brown sugar

1 tablespoon dry milk

½ teaspoon salt

1¼ teaspoons bread machine or quick active dry yeast

Margarine or butter, melted

Measure carefully, placing all ingredients except margarine in bread machine pan in the order recommended by the manufacturer.

Select Dough/Manual cycle. Do not use delay cycles.

Remove dough from pan, using lightly floured hands. Knead **5** minutes on lightly floured surface. Cover and let rest 10 minutes.

Grease large cookie sheet. Divide dough into 12 equal pieces. Shape each piece into a ball. Place 2 inches apart on cookie sheet. Brush with margarine. Cover and let rise in warm place 30 to 40 minutes or until double. (Dough is ready if indentation remains when touched.)

Heat oven to 375°. Bake 15 to 20 minutes or until golden brown. Serve warm, or cool on wire rack.

1 Roll: Calories 135 (Calories from Fat 45); Fat 5g (Saturated 1g); Cholesterol 0mg; Sodium 150mg; Carbohydrate 21g (Dietary Fiber 2g); Protein 3g

Crescent Rolls

20 rolls

PREP:
22 min

CYCLE:
According to manufacturer

RISE:
1 hour

BAKE:
10 min

Betty's Success Tip

To make ahead of time, after you have shaped the dough into rolls and placed them on the cookie sheet, cover with plastic wrap. You can refrigerate them from 4 hours up to 48 hours. Before baking, remove the rolls from the refrigerator and re-move plastic wrap. Cover with kitchen towel and let rise in a warm place about 2 hours or until double. Bake the rolls as the recipe at right tells you.

1 Roll: Calories 195 (Calories from Fat 90); Fat 10g (Saturated 2g); Cholesterol 10mg; Sodium 280mg; Carbohydrate 24g (Dietary Fiber 1g); Protein 3g

1 egg, slightly beaten, plus enough water to equal 1⅓ cups

1 cup margarine or butter, softened

1½ teaspoons salt

¼ cup sugar

4 cups bread flour

2 teaspoons bread machine or quick active dry yeast

2 tablespoons margarine or butter, melted

Measure carefully, placing all ingredients except 2 tablespoons melted margarine in bread machine pan in the order recommended by the manufacturer.

Select Dough/Manual cycle. Do not use delay cycles.

Remove dough from pan, using lightly floured hands. Place dough in greased bowl, and turn greased side up. Cover and let rise in warm place about 30 minutes or until double. (Dough is ready if indentation remains when touched.)

Grease cookie sheet. Punch down dough. Roll dough into 20-inch circle on lightly floured surface. Brush with some of the melted mar-garine. Cut into 20 wedges. Roll up each wedge, beginning at rounded edge. Place rolls, point sides down, on cookie sheet and curve slightly. Cover and let rise in warm place 20 to 30 minutes or until almost double.

Heat oven to 375°. Brush rolls with remaining melted margarine. Bake 8 to 10 minutes or until golden brown. Serve warm, or cool on rack.

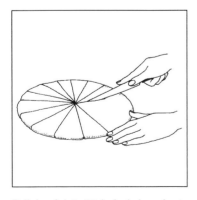

Roll dough into 20-inch circle and cut into 20 wedges.

Roll up each wedge, beginning at rounded edge.

Place roll, point side down, on cookie sheet and curve slightly.

Hit-the-Trail Breadsticks

12 breadsticks

PREP:
22 min

CYCLE:
According to manufacturer

REST:
10 min

RISE:
15 min

BAKE:
20 min

Betty's Success Tip

To make ahead, after you have shaped the dough into ropes and placed them on the cookie sheet, cover with plastic wrap. You can refrigerate them from 4 hours up to 48 hours. Before baking, remove the breadsticks from the refrigerator and remove plastic wrap. Cover with kitchen towel and let rise in a warm place about 1½ hours or until double. Bake the breadsticks as the recipe tells you.

1 cup plus 2 tablespoons water

2 tablespoons vegetable oil

3¼ cups bread flour

⅔ cup trail mix

¼ cup packed brown sugar

1 teaspoon salt

1½ teaspoons bread machine or quick active dry yeast

Measure carefully, placing all ingredients in bread machine pan in the order recommended by the manufacturer.

Select Dough/Manual cycle. Do not use delay cycles.

Remove dough from pan, using lightly floured hands. Cover and let rest 10 minutes on lightly floured surface.

Grease large cookie sheet. Divide dough into 12 equal pieces. Roll each piece into 7-inch rope. Place 1 inch apart on cookie sheet. Brush with additional vegetable oil. Cover and let rise in warm place 5 to 15 minutes or until almost double.

Heat oven to 375°. Bake 15 to 20 minutes or until golden brown. Serve warm, or cool on wire rack.

1 Breadstick: Calories 200 (Calories from Fat 45); Fat 5g (Saturated 1g); Cholesterol 0mg; Sodium 220mg; Carbohydrate 36g (Dietary Fiber 2g); Protein 5g

High Altitude

High-altitude areas (areas that are 3,500 feet or higher above sea level) will require some changes in the bread machine recipe. Air pressure is lower, so the bread will rise higher. Start by reducing the amount of yeast by ¼ teaspoon; if the loaf is still too high, reduce the yeast more the next time.

Flour dries out more quickly at high altitude, so check the dough during the kneading cycle to be sure it isn't too dry. Add water, about a teaspoon at a time, until the dough forms a smooth ball.

Check your bread machine's use-and-care book for more high-altitude adjustments, or call your local United States Department of Agriculture (USDA) Extension Service office. You will find the Extension Service office listed in the phone book under "County Government."

Cheese-Filled Breadsticks

15 breadsticks

PREP:
15 min

CYCLE:
According to manufacturer

REST:
10 min

RISE:
20 min

BAKE:
20 min

COOL:
10 min

Betty's Success Tip

Like a breadstick with a "string" attached? Use mozzarella cheese instead of Cheddar because mozzarella becomes stringy when melted. Swiss or Monterey Jack cheese would also make great-tasting breadsticks.

⅔ cup water

1 tablespoon vegetable oil

2 cups bread flour

2 teaspoons chili powder

1½ teaspoons sugar

¾ teaspoon salt

1¼ teaspoons bread machine or quick active dry yeast

1 cup shredded Cheddar cheese (4 ounces)

Measure carefully, placing all ingredients except cheese in bread machine pan in the order recommended by the manufacturer.

Select Dough/Manual cycle. Do not use delay cycles.

Remove dough from pan, using lightly floured hands. Cover and let rest 10 minutes on lightly floured surface.

Grease large cookie sheet. Roll or pat dough into 15 × 9-inch rectangle; place on cookie sheet. Sprinkle cheese over lengthwise half of rectangle. Fold dough lengthwise in half over cheese; pinch to seal edges. Cover and let rise in warm place 15 to 20 minutes or until almost double.

Heat oven to 375°. Sprinkle with additional chili powder if desired. Bake 18 to 20 minutes or until golden brown. Remove from cookie sheet to wire rack. Cool at least 10 minutes. Cut crosswise into fifteen 1-inch breadsticks.

1 Breadstick: Calories 110 (Calories from Fat 35); Fat 4g (Saturated 2g); Cholesterol 10mg; Sodium 170mg; Carbohydrate 15g (Dietary Fiber 1g); Protein 4g

Cheese-Filled Breadsticks

Classic Focaccia

2 focaccia, 12 servings each

PREP:
20 min

CYCLE:
According to manufacturer

RISE:
30 min

BAKE:
20 min

Betty's Success Tip

To make caramelized onion focaccia, make dough as directed at right, except omit rosemary, 2 tablespoons oil and Parmesan cheese. To make onion topping, heat ⅓ cup olive or vegetable oil in nonstick 10-inch skillet over medium heat. Stir in 4 cups thinly sliced onions (4 medium onions) and 4 cloves garlic, finely chopped, to coat with oil. Cook uncovered 10 minutes, stirring every 3 to 4 minutes. Reduce heat to medium-low. Cook 30 to 40 minutes longer, stirring well every 5 minutes, until onions are light golden brown (onions will shrink during cooking). Continue as directed at right, except do not brush dough with oil; after second rising, carefully spread onion mixture over breads. Bake as directed.

3 cups bread flour

2 tablespoons chopped fresh or 1 tablespoon dried rosemary leaves, crumbled

1 tablespoon sugar

1 teaspoon salt

1 package bread machine or quick active dry yeast (2¼ teaspoons)

3 tablespoons olive or vegetable oil

1 cup room-temperature water

2 tablespoons olive or vegetable oil

¼ cup grated Parmesan cheese

Measure carefully, placing all ingredients except 2 tablespoons olive oil and the Parmesan cheese in bread machine pan in the order recommended by the manufacturer.

Select Dough/Manual cycle. Remove dough from pan.

Grease 2 cookie sheets or 12-inch pizza pans with small amount of oil.

Gently push fist into dough to deflate. Divide dough in half. Shape each half into a flattened 10-inch round on cookie sheet. Cover loosely with plastic wrap lightly sprayed with cooking spray, and let rise in warm place about 30 minutes or until double.

Heat oven to 400°. Gently make depressions about 2 inches apart in dough with fingertips. Carefully brush with 2 tablespoons oil; sprinkle with cheese. Bake 15 to 20 minutes or until golden brown. Serve warm or cool.

1 Serving: Calories 80 (Calories from Fat 25); Fat 3g (Saturated 1g); Cholesterol 0mg; Sodium 115mg; Carbohydrate 11g (Dietary Fiber 0g); Protein 2g

Classic Focaccia

Roasted Pepper Focaccia

1 focaccia, 12 servings

PREP:
15 min

CYCLE:
According to manufacturer

REST:
10 min

RISE:
40 min

BAKE:
20 min

Betty's Success Tip

If your bread machine doesn't have a Raisin/Nut signal, add the bell peppers and artichokes 5 to 10 minutes before the last kneading cycle ends. Check your bread machine's use-and-care book to find out how long the last cycle runs.

1 cup water

1 tablespoon margarine or butter, softened

3 cups bread flour

1 tablespoon sugar

1 teaspoon garlic powder

¾ teaspoon salt

1½ teaspoons bread machine yeast or quick active dry yeast

½ cup roasted red bell peppers (from 12-ounce jar), drained and chopped

⅓ cup quartered marinated artichoke hearts (from 6-ounce jar), drained

Cornmeal

1 tablespoon olive or vegetable oil

Coarse salt, if desired

Measure carefully, placing all ingredients except bell peppers, artichokes, cornmeal, oil and coarse salt in bread machine pan in the order recommended by the manufacturer. Add bell peppers and artichokes at the Raisin/Nut signal.

Select Dough/Manual cycle. Do not use delay cycles.

Remove dough from pan, using lightly floured hands. Cover and let rest 10 minutes on lightly floured surface.

Grease large cookie sheet; sprinkle with cornmeal. Pat dough into 15 × 12-inch rectangle on cookie sheet. Cover and let rise in warm place 35 to 40 minutes or until almost double.

Heat oven to 400°. Make deep depressions in dough at 1-inch intervals with fingertips. Drizzle or brush with oil. Sprinkle with coarse salt. Bake 18 to 20 minutes or until golden brown. Serve warm, or cool on wire rack.

1 Serving: Calories 135 (Calories from Fat 10); Fat 1g (Saturated 0g); Cholesterol 0mg; Sodium 180mg; Carbohydrate 28g (Dietary Fiber 1g); Protein 4g

Rosemary Focaccia

1 focaccia, 8 servings

PREP:
12 min

CYCLE:
According to manufacturer

REST:
10 min

RISE:
30 min

BAKE:
18 min

¾ cup water

2 tablespoons olive or vegetable oil

2 cups bread flour

1 tablespoon sugar

1 teaspoon salt

1½ teaspoons bread machine or quick active dry yeast

3 tablespoons olive or vegetable oil

2 to 3 tablespoons chopped fresh rosemary leaves

Coarse salt, if desired

Measure carefully, placing all ingredients except the 3 tablespoons oil, rosemary and coarse salt in bread machine pan in the order recommended by the manufacturer.

Select Dough/Manual cycle. Do not use delay cycles.

Remove dough from pan, using lightly floured hands. Cover and let rest on lightly floured surface 10 minutes.

Grease large cookie sheet. Roll or pat dough into 12-inch circle on cookie sheet. Cover and let rise in warm place about 30 minutes or until almost double.

Heat oven to 400°. Make depressions in dough at 1-inch intervals with fingertips. Drizzle with 3 tablespoons oil. Sprinkle with rosemary and coarse salt. Bake 15 to 18 minutes or until golden brown. Serve warm, or cool on wire rack.

1 Serving: Calories 205 (Calories from Fat 80); Fat 9g (Saturated 1g); Cholesterol 0mg; Sodium 270mg; Carbohydrate 28g (Dietary Fiber 1g); Protein 4g

Betty's Success Tip

Be sure to chop the rosemary leaves instead of leaving them whole. They can become dry quickly during baking, which makes them sharper and more unsafe to swallow.

Crusty Mustard Focaccia

1 focaccia, 8 servings

PREP:
15 min

CYCLE:
According to manufacturer

REST:
10 min

RISE:
10 min

BAKE:
18 min

⅔ cup water

1 tablespoon olive or vegetable oil

2 tablespoons spicy mustard

2¼ cups bread flour

1 tablespoon sugar

1 teaspoon salt

1½ teaspoons bread machine or quick active dry yeast

3 tablespoons olive or vegetable oil

Coarse salt, if desired

Measure carefully, placing all ingredients except the 3 tablespoons oil and the coarse salt in bread machine pan in the order recommended by the manufacturer.

Select Dough/Manual cycle. Do not use delay cycles.

Remove dough from pan, using lightly floured hands. Knead 5 minutes on lightly floured surface (if necessary, knead in enough flour to make dough easy to handle). Cover and let rest 10 minutes.

Grease large cookie sheet. Roll or pat dough into 12-inch circle on cookie sheet. Cover and let rise in warm place about 10 minutes or until almost double.

Heat oven to 400°. Prick dough with fork at 1-inch intervals, or make deep depressions in dough with fingertips. Brush with 3 tablespoons oil. Sprinkle with coarse salt. Bake 15 to 18 minutes or until golden brown. Serve warm, or cool on wire rack.

1 Serving: Calories 160 (Calories from Fat 20); Fat 2g (Saturated 0g); Cholesterol 0mg; Sodium 340mg; Carbohydrate 32g (Dietary Fiber 1g); Protein 4g

Crusty Mustard Focaccia

Greek Olive Focaccia

1 focaccia, 8 servings

PREP:
12 min

CYCLE:
According to manufacturer

REST:
10 min

RISE:
30 min

BAKE:
18 min

Betty's Success Tip

If your bread machine doesn't have a Raisin/Nut signal, add the olives 5 to 10 minutes before the last kneading cycle ends. Check your bread machine's use-and-care book to find out how long the last cycle runs.

¾ cup water

1 small onion, chopped (¼ cup)

2 tablespoons olive or vegetable oil

3 cups bread flour

2 tablespoons sugar

1 teaspoon salt

1 teaspoon dried rosemary leaves

1¾ teaspoons bread machine or quick active dry yeast

⅓ cup Kalamata or Greek olives, pitted

1 tablespoon olive or vegetable oil

1 teaspoon dried rosemary leaves, if desired

Measure carefully, placing all ingredients except olives, the 1 table-spoon oil and 1 teaspoon rosemary in bread machine pan in the order recommended by the manufacturer. Add olives at the Raisin/Nut signal.

Select Dough/Manual cycle. Do not use delay cycles.

Remove dough from pan, using lightly floured hands. Cover and let rest 10 minutes on lightly floured surface.

Grease cookie sheet. Pat dough into 12-inch circle on cookie sheet. Cover and let rise in warm place about 30 minutes or until almost double.

Heat oven to 400°. Make deep depressions in dough at 1-inch intervals with fingertips. Drizzle with 1 tablespoon oil. Sprinkle with 1 teaspoon rosemary. Bake 15 to 18 minutes or until edge is golden brown. Serve warm, or cool on wire rack.

1 Serving: Calories 235 (Calories from Fat 45); Fat 5g (Saturated 1g); Cholesterol 0mg; Sodium 340mg; Carbohydrate 43g (Dietary Fiber 2g); Protein 6g

French Baguettes

2 baguettes, 12 servings each

PREP:
20 min

CYCLE:
According to manufacturer

RISE:
1 hour 10 min

BAKE:
25 min

1 cup water

2¾ cups bread flour

1 tablespoon sugar

1 teaspoon salt

1½ teaspoons bread machine or quick active dry yeast

1 egg yolk

1 tablespoon water

Measure carefully, placing all ingredients except egg yolk and the 1 tablespoon water in bread machine pan in the order recommended by the manufacturer.

Select Dough/Manual cycle. Do not use delay cycles.

Remove dough from pan, using lightly floured hands. Place dough in greased bowl, turning to coat all sides. Cover and let rise in warm place about 30 minutes or until double. (Dough is ready if indentation remains when touched.)

Grease cookie sheet. Punch down dough. Roll dough into 16 × 12-inch rectangle on lightly floured surface. Cut dough crosswise in half to make two 8 × 12 pieces. Roll up each half of dough tightly, beginning at 12-inch side. Pinch edge of dough into roll to seal. Gently roll back and forth to taper ends.

Place loaves 3 inches apart on cookie sheet. Make 3 or 4 diagonal slashes across tops of loaves, using sharp knife, or make 1 lengthwise slash on each loaf. Cover and let rise in warm place 30 to 40 minutes or until double.

Heat oven to 375°. Mix egg yolk and 1 tablespoon water; brush over tops of loaves. Bake 20 to 25 minutes or until golden brown. Serve warm, or cool on wire rack.

1 Serving: Calories 60 (Calories from Fat 0); Fat 0g (Saturated 0g); Cholesterol 10mg; Sodium 100mg; Carbohydrate 13g (Dietary Fiber 0g); Protein 2g

Roasted Pepper and Artichoke Baguettes

2 baguettes, 12 servings each

PREP:
22 min

CYCLE:
According to manufacturer

REST:
10 min

RISE:
40 min

BAKE:
25 min

Betty's Success Tip

To make ahead, after you have patted the dough into a rectangle on the cookie sheet, cover it with plastic wrap. You can refrigerate it from 4 hours up to 48 hours. Before baking, remove the dough from the refrigerator and remove plastic wrap. Cover with kitchen towel and let rise in a warm place about 2 hours or until it is almost double. Then continue as the recipe tells you.

½ cup water

½ cup roasted red bell peppers (from 12-ounce jar), drained and chopped

⅓ cup marinated artichoke hearts (from 6-ounce jar), well drained

1 tablespoon margarine or butter, softened

3¼ cups bread flour

1 tablespoon sugar

1 teaspoon garlic powder

¾ teaspoon salt

1½ teaspoons bread machine or quick active dry yeast

1 egg, slightly beaten

Measure carefully, placing all ingredients except egg in bread machine pan in the order recommended by the manufacturer.

Select Dough/Manual cycle. Do not use delay cycles.

Remove dough from pan, using lightly floured hands. Knead 10 times on lightly floured surface. Cover and let rest 10 minutes.

Grease large cookie sheet. Roll dough into 16 × 12-inch rectangle on lightly floured surface. Cut dough crosswise in half to make two 8 × 12 pieces. Roll up each half tightly, beginning at 12-inch side. Pinch edge of dough into roll to seal. Gently roll back and forth to taper ends.

Place loaves 3 inches apart on cookie sheet. Make 3 or 4 diagonal slashes across tops of loaves, using sharp knife, or make 1 lengthwise slash on each loaf. Cover and let rise in warm place 30 to 40 minutes or until double. (Dough is ready if indentation remains when touched.)

Heat oven to 375°. Brush egg over tops of loaves. Bake 20 to 25 minutes or until golden brown. Serve warm, or cool on wire rack.

1 Serving: Calories 75 (Calories from Fat 10); Fat 1g (Saturated 0g); Cholesterol 10mg; Sodium 90mg; Carbohydrate 15g (Dietary Fiber 1g); Protein 2g

Zesty Pesto Tomato Baguettes

2 baguettes, 8 servings each

PREP:
22 min

CYCLE:
According to manufacturer

REST:
10 min

RISE:
40 min

BAKE:
25 min

Betty's Success Tip

If your bread machine doesn't have a Raisin/Nut signal, add the tomatoes 5 to 10 minutes before the last kneading cycle ends. Check your bread machine's use-and-care book to find out how long the last cycle runs.

1 cup plus 2 tablespoons water

⅓ cup pesto

3 cups bread flour

2 tablespoons sugar

1½ teaspoons salt

1¼ teaspoons bread machine or quick active dry yeast

⅓ cup coarsely chopped sun-dried tomatoes (packed in oil), drained

1 egg, beaten

Shredded Asiago or Parmesan cheese, if desired

Measure carefully, placing all ingredients except tomatoes, egg and cheese in bread machine pan in the order recommended by the manufacturer. Add tomatoes at the Raisin/Nut signal.

Select Dough/Manual cycle. Do not use delay cycles.

Remove dough from pan, using lightly floured hands. Cover and let rest 10 minutes on lightly floured surface.

Grease large cookie sheet. Roll dough into 16 × 12-inch rectangle on lightly floured surface. Cut dough crosswise in half. Roll up each half of dough tightly, beginning at 12-inch side. Pinch edge of dough into roll to seal. Gently roll back and forth to taper ends.

Place loaves 3 inches apart on cookie sheet. Make 3 or 4 diagonal slashes across tops of loaves, using sharp knife, or make 1 lengthwise slash on each loaf. Cover and let rise in warm place 30 to 40 minutes or until double. (Dough is ready if indentation remains when touched.)

Heat oven to 375°. Brush egg over tops of loaves. Sprinkle with cheese. Bake 20 to 25 minutes or until golden brown. Serve warm, or cool on wire rack.

1 Serving: Calories 115 (Calories from Fat 30); Fat 4g (Saturated 1g); Cholesterol 1mg; Sodium 250mg; Carbohydrate 20g (Dietary Fiber 1g); Protein 3g

Crusty Homemade Bread Bowls

6 servings

PREP:
20 min

CYCLE:
According to manufacturer

REST:
10 min

RISE:
20 min

BAKE:
22 min

COOL:
15 min

1 cup water

2¾ cups bread flour

1 tablespoon sugar

1 teaspoon salt

1½ teaspoons bread machine or quick active dry yeast

1 egg yolk

1 tablespoon water

Measure carefully, placing all ingredients except egg yolk and the 1 tablespoon water in bread machine pan in the order recommended by the manufacturer.

Select Dough/Manual cycle. Do not use delay cycles.

Remove dough from pan, using lightly floured hands. Cover and let rest 10 minutes on lightly floured surface.

Grease outsides of six 10-ounce custard cups. Place cups upside down on ungreased cookie sheet. Divide dough into 6 equal pieces. Roll or pat each piece into 7-inch circle on lightly floured surface. Shape dough circles over outsides of cups. Cover and let rise in warm place 15 to 20 minutes or until slightly puffy.

Heat oven to 375°. Mix egg yolk and 1 tablespoon water; brush gently over bread bowls. Bake 18 to 22 minutes or until golden brown. Carefully lift bread bowls from custard cups—bread and cups will be hot. Cool bread bowls upright on wire rack.

1 Serving: Calories 240 (Calories from Fat 20); Fat 2g (Saturated 0g); Cholesterol 35mg; Sodium 360mg; Carbohydrate 50g (Dietary Fiber 2g); Protein 7g

Betty's Success Tip

When placing the dough circle over the cup, don't let the dough curl under the edge of the cup. It will bake onto the edge of the cup and be difficult to remove. If some of the dough should bake onto the edge, use the point of a paring knife to carefully separate it from the cup.

Serving Suggestions

These bread bowls are not only fun to use but are also great to eat. Fill the bowl with a crisp green salad and serve as a side dish. Or fill it with a thick, chunky stew or your favorite main-dish salad.

Crusty Homemade Bread Bowls

Coffee Cakes
and Sweet Breads

Honey-Walnut Coffee Cake

12 servings

PREP:
27 min

CYCLE:
According to manufacturer

REST:
10 min

RISE:
1 hour

BAKE:
25 min

¼ cup water

⅔ cup sour cream

2 tablespoons margarine or butter, softened

1 egg

3 cups bread flour

2 tablespoons granulated sugar

1 teaspoon salt

2 teaspoons bread machine or quick active dry yeast

Honey-Walnut Filling (below)

¼ cup margarine or butter, melted

⅓ cup packed brown sugar

¼ cup honey

Measure carefully, placing all ingredients except Honey-Walnut Filling, ¼ cup margarine, the brown sugar and honey in bread machine pan in the order recommended by the manufacturer.

Select Dough/Manual cycle. Do not use delay cycles.

Remove dough from pan, using lightly floured hands. Cover and let rest 10 minutes on lightly floured surface. Prepare Honey-Walnut Filling; set aside. Mix ¼ cup margarine, the brown sugar and honey in ungreased rectangular pan, 13 × 9 × 2 inches; spread evenly in pan.

Roll or pat dough into 24 × 9-inch rectangle. Spread filling crosswise over half of the rectangle to within ¼ inch of edges of dough; fold dough crosswise in half over filling; seal edges. Cut rectangle crosswise into six 2-inch strips. Twist each strip loosely; place strips crosswise in pan. Cover and let rise in warm place about 1 hour or until double.

Heat oven to 375°. Bake 20 to 25 minutes or until golden brown. Immediately turn pan upside down onto heatproof serving platter. Let pan remain over coffee cake 1 minute; remove pan. Serve warm.

Honey-Walnut Filling

½ cup chopped walnuts

⅓ cup margarine or butter, softened

¼ cup honey

Mix all ingredients.

1 Serving: Calories 365 (Calories from Fat 170); Fat 19g (Saturated 5g); Cholesterol 30mg; Sodium 350mg; Carbohydrate 45g (Dietary Fiber 1g); Protein 5g

Easy Apple Coffee Cake

10 servings

PREP:
20 min

CYCLE:
According to manufacturer

REST:
10 min

RISE:
45 min

BAKE:
35 min

COOL:
15 min

Ingredient Substitution

You can use any flavored filling you like in this easy fruit-filled cake. Use cherry, blueberry, peach or apricot pie filling. Or try a canned poppy seed filling or lemon curd.

⅔ cup water

3 tablespoons margarine or butter, softened

2 cups bread machine flour

3 tablespoons granulated sugar

1 teaspoon salt

1½ teaspoons bread machine or quick active dry yeast

1 cup canned apple pie filling

Powdered sugar, if desired

Measure carefully, placing all ingredients except pie filling and powdered sugar in bread machine pan in the order recommended by the manufacturer.

Select Dough/Manual cycle. Do not use delay cycles.

Remove dough from pan, using lightly floured hands. Cover and let rest 10 minutes on lightly floured surface.

Grease large cookie sheet. Roll dough into 13 × 8-inch rectangle on lightly floured surface. Place on cookie sheet. Spoon pie filling lengthwise down center third of rectangle. On each 13-inch side, make cuts from filling to edge of dough at 1-inch intervals, using sharp knife. Fold ends up over filling. Fold strips diagonally over filling, alternating sides and overlapping in center. Cover and let rise in warm place 30 to 45 minutes or until double. (Dough is ready if indentation remains when touched.)

Heat oven to 375°. Bake 30 to 35 minutes or until golden brown. Remove from cookie sheet to wire rack; cool. Sprinkle with powdered sugar.

1 Serving: Calories 160 (Calories from Fat 35); Fat 4g (Saturated 1g); Cholesterol 0mg; Sodium 280mg; Carbohydrate 29g (Dietary Fiber 1g); Protein 3g

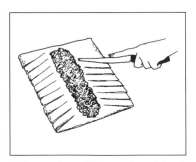

Make cuts from filling to edge of dough at 1-inch intervals.

Fold strips diagonally over filling, alternating sides and overlapping in center.

Easy Apple Coffee Cake

Apricot Cream Cheese Ring

10 servings

PREP:
20 min

CYCLE:
According to manufacturer

REST:
10 min

RISE:
50 min

BAKE:
35 min

COOL:
30 min

⅓ cup water

2 tablespoons margarine or butter, softened

1 egg

2 cups bread flour

2 tablespoons sugar

½ teaspoon salt

1¾ teaspoons bread machine or quick active dry yeast

1 package (3 ounces) cream cheese, softened

1½ tablespoons bread flour

¼ to ⅓ cup apricot preserves

1 egg, beaten, if desired

2 tablespoons sliced almonds

Measure carefully, placing all ingredients except cream cheese, the 1½ tablespoons flour, preserves, the beaten egg and almonds in bread machine pan in the order recommended by the manufacturer.

Select Dough/Manual cycle. Do not use delay cycles.

Remove dough from pan, using lightly floured hands. Cover and let rest 10 minutes on lightly floured surface. Mix cream cheese and 1½ tablespoons flour.

Grease round pan, 9 × 1½ inches. Roll dough into 15-inch circle. Place in pan, letting side of dough hang over edge of pan. Spread cream cheese mixture over dough in pan; spoon apricot preserves onto cream cheese mixture. Make cuts along edge of dough at 1-inch intervals to about ½ inch from cream cheese mixture. Twist pairs of dough strips and fold over cream cheese mixture. Cover and let rise in warm place 40 to 50 minutes or until almost double.

Heat oven to 375°. Brush beaten egg over dough. Sprinkle with almonds. Bake 30 to 35 minutes or until golden brown. Cool at least 30 minutes before cutting.

1 Serving: Calories 170 (Calories from Fat 65); Fat 7g (Saturated 3g); Cholesterol 30mg; Sodium 180mg; Carbohydrate 24g (Dietary Fiber 1g); Protein 4g

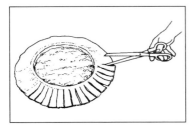

Make cuts along edge of dough at 1-inch intervals to about ½ inch from cream cheese mixture.

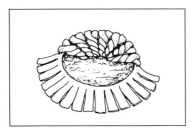

Twist pairs of dough strips and fold over cream cheese mixture.

Apricot Cream Cheese Ring

Cherry and White-Chocolate Almond Twist

16 servings

PREP:
32 min

CYCLE:
According to manufacturer

REST:
10 min

RISE:
45 min

BAKE:
35 min

COOL:
15 min

Betty's Success Tip

Be sure to use a sharp knife or kitchen scissors when cutting the roll lengthwise in half. This will help prevent the filling from pulling on the knife during cutting.

½ cup maraschino cherries

¾ cup plus 2 tablespoons water

1 teaspoon almond extract

2 tablespoons margarine or butter

3¼ cups bread flour

2 tablespoons sugar

1 teaspoon salt

2 teaspoons bread machine or quick active dry yeast

White Chocolate Almond Topping (opposite page))

2 tablespoons margarine or butter, softened

¼ cup maraschino cherries, well drained

Cherry Glaze (opposite page), if desired

Drain ½ cup cherries thoroughly; reserve 2 to 4 teaspoons cherry juice for Cherry Glaze.

Measure carefully, placing ½ cup cherries and remaining ingredients except White-Chocolate Almond Topping, 2 tablespoons margarine, the ¼ cup cherries and Cherry Glaze in bread machine pan in the order recommended by the manufacturer.

Select Dough/Manual cycle. Do not use delay cycles.

Remove dough from pan, using lightly floured hands. Cover and let rest 10 minutes on lightly floured surface. Prepare White-Chocolate Almond Topping.

Grease large cookie sheet. Roll dough into 15 × 10-inch rectangle. Spread 2 tablespoons margarine over dough. Sprinkle with topping and ¼ cup cherries; press into dough. Roll up dough, beginning at 15-inch side. Place on cookie sheet.

Cut roll lengthwise in half. Place halves, filling side up and side by side, on cookie sheet; twist together gently and loosely. Pinch ends to fasten. Cover and let rise in warm place about 45 minutes or until double.

Heat oven to 350°. Bake 30 to 35 minutes or until golden brown. Remove from sheet to wire rack. Cool. Drizzle with Cherry Glaze.

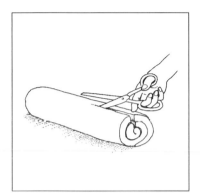

Cut roll lengthwise in half.

Place halves, filling side up and side by side, on cookie sheet; twist together gently and loosely.

White-Chocolate Almond Topping

½ cup chopped white baking chips

⅓ cup chopped slivered almonds

2 tablespoons sugar

Mix all ingredients.

Cherry Glaze

½ cup powdered sugar

2 to 4 teaspoons reserved maraschino cherry juice

Mix ingredients until smooth and thin enough to drizzle.

1 Serving: Calories 200 (Calories from Fat 55); Fat 6g (Saturated 2g); Cholesterol 0mg; Sodium 190mg; Carbohydrate 34g (Dietary Fiber 1g); Protein 4g

Sweet Bread Wreath

24 servings

PREP:
20 min

CYCLE:
According to manufacturer

REST:
10 min

RISE:
50 min

BAKE:
30 min

COOL:
15 min

Betty's Success Tip

Braid the ropes together loosely to keep the dough from stretching and so the wreath will have a nice, round shape. Be sure to pinch the ends together tightly when forming the circle so they won't separate during rising or baking.

¼ cup water

¾ cup sour cream

1 egg

3 cups bread flour

3 tablespoons sugar

1 teaspoon salt

2 teaspoons bread machine or quick active dry yeast

1 egg, beaten

3 tablespoons sugar

¼ teaspoon ground cinnamon

¼ teaspoon ground anise or ground cloves

¼ teaspoon freshly grated or ground nutmeg

Measure carefully, placing all ingredients except beaten egg, 3 tablespoons sugar, the cinnamon, anise and nutmeg in bread machine pan in the order recommended by the manufacturer.

Select Dough/Manual cycle. Do not use delay cycles.

Remove dough from pan, using lightly floured hands. Cover and let rest 10 minutes on lightly floured surface.

Grease large cookie sheet. Divide dough into thirds. Roll each third into 26-inch rope. Place ropes side by side; braid together gently and loosely. Pinch ends to fasten. Shape braid into circle on cookie sheet; pinch ends together. Cover and let rise in warm place 45 to 50 minutes or until double. (Dough is ready if indentation remains when touched.)

Heat oven to 350°. Brush beaten egg over dough. Mix 3 tablespoons sugar, cinnamon, anise and nutmeg; sprinkle over dough. Bake 25 to 30 minutes or until golden brown.

1 Serving: Calories 80 (Calories from Fat 20); Fat 2g (Saturated 1g); Cholesterol 20mg; Sodium 105mg; Carbohydrate 14g (Dietary Fiber 0g); Protein 2g

Sweet Bread Wreath

Swedish Coffee Ring

16 servings

PREP:
25 min

CYCLE:
According to manufacturer

REST:
10 min

RISE:
1 hour

BAKE:
25 min

COOL:
10 min

Betty's Success Tip

If your bread machine doesn't have a Raisin/Nut signal, add the citron, almonds and lemon peel 5 to 10 minutes before the last kneading cycle ends. Check your bread machine's use-and-care book to find out how long the last cycle runs.

¾ cup water

2 eggs

¼ cup margarine or butter, softened

Pinch of saffron, crushed

4 cups bread flour

⅓ cup sugar

1 teaspoon salt

4 teaspoons bread machine or quick active dry yeast

⅓ cup chopped citron or candied mixed fruit

¼ cup chopped blanched almonds

2 teaspoons grated lemon peel

Vanilla Glaze (below)

Green and red candied cherries, if desired

Measure all ingredients except citron, almonds, lemon peel, Vanilla Glaze and cherries in bread machine pan in the order recommended by the manufacturer. Add citron, almonds and peel at the Raisin/Nut signal.

Select Dough/Manual cycle. Do not use delay cycles.

Remove dough from pan, using lightly floured hands. Cover and let rest 10 minutes on lightly floured surface.

Grease large cookie sheet. Divide dough in half. Roll each half into 30-inch rope. Place ropes side by side on cookie sheet; twist together gently and loosely. Pinch ends to fasten. Shape twist into a circle on cookie sheet; pinch ends together. Cover and let rise in warm place 45 to 60 minutes or until double.

Heat oven to 375°. Bake 20 to 25 minutes or until golden brown. Remove from cookie sheet. Cool. Drizzle with glaze. Top with cherries.

Vanilla Glaze

1 cup powdered sugar

About 1 tablespoon water

¼ teaspoon vanilla

Mix ingredients until smooth and thin enough to drizzle.

1 Serving: Calories 230 (Calories from Fat 45); Fat 5g (Saturated 1g); Cholesterol 25mg; Sodium 109mg; Carbohydrate 43g (Dietary Fiber 2g); Protein 5g

Raisin Cinnamon Bread

12 servings

PREP:
5 min

CYCLE:
According to manufacturer

COOL:
10 min

Betty's Success Tip

If your bread machine doesn't have a Raisin/Nut signal, add the raisins 5 to 10 minutes before the last kneading cycle ends. Check your bread machine's use-and-care book to find out how long the last cycle runs.

1 cup plus 2 tablespoons water

2 tablespoons margarine or butter, softened

3 cups bread flour

3 tablespoons sugar

1½ teaspoons salt

1 teaspoon ground cinnamon

2½ teaspoons bread machine or quick active dry yeast

¾ cup raisins

Measure carefully, placing all ingredients except raisins in bread machine pan in the order recommended by the manufacturer. Add raisins at the Raisin/Nut signal.

Select Sweet or Basic/White cycle. Use Medium or Light crust color. Remove baked bread from pan, and cool on wire rack.

1 Serving: Calories 175 (Calories from Fat 20); Fat 2g (Saturated 0g); Cholesterol 0mg; Sodium 290mg; Carbohydrate 37g (Dietary Fiber 2g); Protein 4g

Honey Lemon Bread

12 servings

PREP:
7 min

CYCLE:
According to manufacturer

COOL:
10 min

Ingredient Substitution

For a flavor change, use grated orange peel instead of the lemon peel to make Orange Honey Bread. The zip of the orange in the bread makes it great for French toast, topped with sliced bananas or blueberries, a drizzle of warm honey and a sprinkle of cinnamon.

¾ cup plus 2 tablespoons water

3 tablespoons honey

2 tablespoons margarine or butter, softened

3 cups bread flour

2 tablespoons dry milk

1½ teaspoons grated lemon peel

1 teaspoon salt

2 teaspoons bread machine or quick active dry yeast

Measure carefully, placing all ingredients in bread machine pan in the order recommended by the manufacturer.

Select Sweet or Basic/White cycle. Use Medium or Light crust color. Do not use delay cycles. Remove baked bread from pan, and cool on wire rack.

1 Serving: Calories 145 (Calories from Fat 20); Fat 2g (Saturated 0g); Cholesterol 0mg; Sodium 220mg; Carbohydrate 29g (Dietary Fiber 1g); Protein 4g

Honey Lemon Bread

Chocolate Walnut Bread

12 servings

7 min

CYCLE:
According to manufacturer

COOL:
10 min

Betty's Success Tip

Because you will add the chocolate chips with all the other ingredients, they will break up during kneading and will melt during baking, so you will have a chocolate bread, not a chocolate chip bread.

Ingredient Substitution

Mint-chocolate chips or milk chocolate chips will give you a different flavor of chocolate bread. Not in the mood for chocolate? Try the same amount of butterscotch-flavored chips.

1 egg plus enough water to equal ¾ cup plus 2 tablespoons

½ teaspoon salt

3 tablespoons sugar

1 tablespoon margarine or butter, softened

½ teaspoon vanilla

2¼ cups bread flour

1 tablespoon dry milk

¾ cup semisweet chocolate chips

¼ cup walnut halves

1 teaspoon bread machine or quick active dry yeast

Measure carefully, placing all ingredients in bread machine pan in the order recommended by the manufacturer.

Select Sweet or Basic/White cycle. Use Medium or Light crust color. Do not use delay cycles. Remove baked bread from pan, and cool on wire rack.

1 Serving: Calories 180 (Calories from Fat 55); Fat 6g (Saturated 2g); Cholesterol 20mg; Sodium 110mg; Carbohydrate 30g (Dietary Fiber 2g); Protein 4g

416   **www.bettycrocker.com**

Peach Maple Bread

12 servings

PREP:
5 min

CYCLE:
According to manufacturer

COOL:
10 min

Betty's Success Tip

If your bread machine doesn't have a Raisin/Nut signal, add the peaches 5 to 10 minutes before the last kneading cycle ends. Check your bread machine's use-and-care book to find out how long the last cycle runs.

Ingredient Substitution

Can't find dried peaches? Dried apricots also would taste good because their flavor goes so well with the hint of maple flavoring and nutmeg found in this bread.

¾ cup plus 2 tablespoons water

¼ cup maple-flavored syrup

1 tablespoon margarine or butter, softened

3 cups bread flour

2 tablespoons packed brown sugar

¼ teaspoon ground nutmeg

1¼ teaspoons salt

2¼ teaspoons bread machine or quick active dry yeast

½ cup cut-up dried peaches

Measure carefully, placing all ingredients except peaches in bread machine pan in the order recommended by the manufacturer. Add peaches at the Raisin/Nut signal.

Select Sweet or Basic/White cycle. Use Light crust color. Remove baked bread from pan, and cool on wire rack.

1 Serving: Calories 170 (Calories from Fat 10); Fat 1g (Saturated 0g); Cholesterol 0mg; Sodium 260mg; Carbohydrate 37g (Dietary Fiber 1g); Protein 4g

Maple Sweet Potato Bread

12 servings

PREP:
7 min

CYCLE:
According to manufacturer

COOL:
10 min

Betty's Success Tip

Be sure to use vacuum-packed sweet potatoes because they are drier than regular canned sweet potatoes. The extra liquid in the regular canned sweet potatoes makes the dough too moist, which will cause the loaf to be gummy and possibly make it collapse after baking.

¾ cup canned vacuum-packed sweet potatoes, drained and mashed

½ cup water

3 tablespoons sour cream

1 teaspoon maple extract

3 cups bread flour

¼ cup sugar

½ teaspoon ground cinnamon

1 teaspoon salt

2 teaspoons bread machine or quick active dry yeast

Measure carefully, placing all ingredients in bread machine pan in the order recommended by the manufacturer.

Select Sweet or Basic/White cycle. Use Medium or Light crust color. Do not use delay cycles. Remove baked bread from pan, and cool on wire rack.

1 Serving: Calories 155 (Calories from Fat 10); Fat 1g (Saturated 1g); Cholesterol 5mg; Sodium 210mg; Carbohydrate 33g (Dietary Fiber 1g); Protein 4g

Maple Sweet Potato Bread

Sweet Orange Bread

12 servings

PREP:
11 min

CYCLE:
According to manufacturer

COOL:
10 min

Betty's Success Tip

Dividing a raw egg in half isn't hard! To do it, slightly beat the egg with a fork or wire whisk just until it is mixed. Then measure 2 tablespoons of the beaten egg, which is equal to half a large egg.

¾ cup minus 3 tablespoons water

3 tablespoons frozen orange juice concentrate, thawed

1½ eggs (see Betty's Success Tip)

3 cups bread flour

½ teaspoon grated orange peel

¼ cup sugar

2 tablespoons dry milk

1½ tablespoons margarine or butter, softened

1¼ teaspoons salt

2 teaspoons bread machine or quick active dry yeast

Orange Glaze (below), if desired

Measure carefully, placing all ingredients except Orange Glaze in bread machine pan in the order recommended by the manufacturer.

Select Sweet or Basic/White cycle. Use Medium or Light crust color. Do not use delay cycles. Remove baked bread from pan, and cool on wire rack. Drizzle with Orange Glaze.

Orange Glaze

½ cup powdered sugar

⅛ teaspoon grated orange peel, if desired

1 to 2 teaspoons orange juice

Mix all ingredients until smooth and thin enough to drizzle.

1 Serving: Calories 165 (Calories from Fat 20); Fat 2g (Saturated 0g); Cholesterol 25mg; Sodium 250mg; Carbohydrate 33g (Dietary Fiber 1g); Protein 5g

Panettone

12 servings

PREP:
7 min

CYCLE:
According to manufacturer

COOL:
10 min

Betty's Success Tip

If your bread machine doesn't have a Raisin/Nut signal, add the pineapple and citron 5 to 10 minutes before the last kneading cycle ends. Check your bread machine's use-and-care book to find out how long the last cycle runs.

¾ cup plus 2 tablespoons milk

1 egg

2 tablespoons margarine or butter, softened

1 teaspoon salt

3 cups bread flour

1½ teaspoons anise seeds, crushed

2 teaspoons bread machine or quick active dry yeast

⅓ cup coarsely chopped dried or candied pineapple

⅓ cup chopped candied citron, drained

Measure carefully, placing all ingredients except pineapple and citron in bread machine pan in the order recommended by the manufacturer. Add pineapple and citron at the Raisin/Nut signal.

Select Basic/White cycle. Use Medium or Light crust color. Do not use delay cycles. Remove baked bread from pan, and cool on wire rack.

1 Serving: Calories 170 (Calories from Fat 25); Fat 3g (Saturated 1g); Cholesterol 20mg; Sodium 250mg; Carbohydrate 33g (Dietary Fiber 2g); Protein 5g

Hot Cross Buns

16 buns

PREP:
27 min

CYCLE:
According to manufacturer

REST:
10 min

RISE:
40 min

BAKE:
20 min

COOL:
10 min

Betty's Success Tip

If your bread machine doesn't have a Raisin/Nut signal, add the raisins 5 to 10 minutes before the last kneading cycle ends. Check your bread machine's use-and-care book for how long the last cycle runs.

2 eggs plus enough water to equal 1⅓ cups

½ cup butter, softened

4 cups bread flour

¾ teaspoon ground cinnamon

¼ teaspoon ground nutmeg

1½ teaspoons salt

2 tablespoons sugar

1½ teaspoons bread machine or quick active dry yeast

½ cup dark raisins

½ cup golden raisins

1 egg

2 tablespoons cold water

White Icing (below)

Measure carefully, placing all ingredients except raisins, 1 egg, the cold water and White Icing in bread machine pan in the order recommended by the manufacturer. Add raisins at the Raisin/Nut signal.

Select Dough/Manual cycle. Do not use delay cycles.

Remove dough from pan, using lightly floured hands. Cover and let rest 10 minutes on lightly floured surface.

Grease cookie sheet or 2 round pans, 9 × 1½ inches. Divide dough in half. Divide each half into 8 equal pieces. Shape each piece into a smooth ball. Place about 2 inches apart on cookie sheet or 1 inch apart in pans. Snip a cross shape in top of each ball, using scissors. Cover and let rise in warm place about 40 minutes or until double.

Heat oven to 375°. Beat egg and cold water slightly; brush on buns. Bake 18 to 20 minutes or until golden brown. Remove from cookie sheet to rack. Cool slightly. Make a cross on bun with White Icing.

White Icing

1 cup powdered sugar

1 tablespoon milk or water

½ teaspoon vanilla

Mix all ingredients until smooth and spreadable.

1 Bun: Calories 245 (Calories from Fat 65); Fat 7g (Saturated 4g); Cholesterol 30mg; Sodium 240mg; Carbohydrate 43g (Dietary Fiber 1g); Protein 4g

COMPLIMENTS
of
Betty's B&B

Hot Cross Buns

Raisin Brioche

12 rolls

PREP:
25 min

CYCLE:
According to manufacturer

REST:
25 min

REFRIGERATE:
2 hours

RISE:
45 min

BAKE:
26 min

¼ cup milk

3 tablespoons water

⅓ cup margarine or butter, softened

2 egg yolks

2 cups bread flour

⅓ cup sugar

1 teaspoon ground cinnamon

½ teaspoon salt

3 teaspoons bread machine or quick active dry yeast

1 cup golden raisins

1 egg, beaten

Measure carefully, placing all ingredients except raisins and beaten egg in bread machine pan in the order recommended by the manufacturer. Add raisins at the Raisin/Nut signal. If your bread machine doesn't have a Raisin/Nut signal, add the raisins 5 to 10 minutes before the last kneading cycle ends. Check your bread machine's use-and-care book for how long the last cycle runs.

Select Dough/Manual cycle. Do not use delay cycles.

Remove dough from pan, using lightly floured hands. Cover and let rest 10 minutes on lightly floured surface.

Grease 12 large muffin cups, 3 × 1½ inches. Divide dough into 16 equal pieces. Shape each piece into a ball, using floured hands. Cut 4 balls into 3 pieces each; roll into small cone-shaped balls. Place the 12 large balls in muffin cups. Make indentation in center of each large ball with thumb. Place 1 small ball in each indentation. Cover and refrigerate 2 hours.

Remove rolls from refrigerator. Let rise covered in warm place 40 to 45 minutes or until almost double.

Heat oven to 350°. Brush beaten egg over rolls. Bake 22 to 26 minutes or until golden brown. Immediately remove from pan. Serve warm, or cool on wire rack.

1 Roll: Calories 205 (Calories from Fat 65); Fat 7g (Saturated 2g); Cholesterol 55mg; Sodium 180mg; Carbohydrate 33g (Dietary Fiber 1g); Protein 4g

Raisin Brioche

Orange Pecan Buns

12 buns

PREP:
25 min

CYCLE:
According to manufacturer

REST:
10 min

RISE:
45 min

BAKE:
20 min

Betty's Success Tip

To make ahead, after you have shaped the dough into buns and placed them on the cookie sheet, cover with plastic wrap. You can refrigerate them from 4 hours up to 48 hours. Before baking, remove the buns from the refrigerator and remove plastic wrap. Cover with kitchen towel and let rise in a warm place about 2 hours or until double. Then brush the buns and bake as the recipe tells you.

1 cup milk

¼ cup sour cream

1 tablespoon orange marmalade

3 cups bread flour

1 tablespoon sugar

1 teaspoon salt

2 teaspoons bread machine or quick active dry yeast

½ cup orange marmalade

⅓ cup chopped pecans, toasted

1 egg, beaten

Vanilla Glaze (below), if desired

Measure carefully, placing all ingredients except ½ cup marmalade, the pecans, egg and Vanilla Glaze in bread machine pan in the order recommended by the manufacturer.

Select Dough/Manual cycle. Do not use delay cycles.

Remove dough from pan, using lightly floured hands. Cover and let rest 10 minutes on lightly floured surface.

Grease large cookie sheet. Mix ½ cup marmalade and the pecans; set aside. Divide dough into 12 equal pieces. Flatten each piece into a 3½-inch circle. Place 1 rounded teaspoon marmalade mixture on center of each circle. Bring edges of dough up over filling; pinch edges to seal. Place buns, pinched sides down and about 2 inches apart, on cookie sheet. Cover and let rise in warm place 30 to 45 minutes or until double. (Dough is ready if indentation remains when touched.)

Heat oven to 350°. Brush egg over buns. Bake 15 to 20 minutes or until golden brown. Drizzle Vanilla Glaze over warm rolls. Serve warm.

Vanilla Glaze

1 cup powdered sugar

About 1 tablespoon water

¼ teaspoon vanilla

Mix ingredients until smooth and thin enough to drizzle.

1 Bun: Calories 185 (Calories from Fat 35); Fat 4g (Saturated 1g); Cholesterol 20mg; Sodium 220mg; Carbohydrate 33g (Dietary Fiber 1g); Protein 5g

Chocolate S'mores Buns

12 buns

PREP:
30 min

CYCLE:
According to manufacturer

REST:
10 min

RISE:
40 min

BAKE:
25 min

COOL:
20 min

1 cup water

2 tablespoons margarine or butter, softened

2¾ cups bread flour

⅔ cup miniature semisweet chocolate chips

¼ cup sugar

1 teaspoon salt

2¼ teaspoons bread machine or quick active dry yeast

S'mores Filling (below)

12 large marshmallows

¼ cup miniature semisweet chocolate chips or white baking chips, melted, if desired

Betty's Success Tip

When you bring the dough up over the marshmallow, be careful not to stretch the dough too thin or to make holes in the dough, or the filling will bubble out during baking. Not only will you lose the great chocolate and marshmallow filling, but the muffin pan will be a mess to clean.

Measure carefully, placing all ingredients except S'mores Filling, marshmallows and ¼ cup melted chocolate chips in bread machine pan in the order recommended by the manufacturer.

Select Dough/Manual cycle. Do not use delay cycles.

Remove dough from pan, using lightly floured hands. Cover and let rest 10 minutes on lightly floured surface. Prepare S'mores Filling.

Grease 12 medium muffin cups, 2½ × 1¼ inches. Divide dough into 12 equal pieces. Pat each piece into a 3½-inch circle. Place 1 tablespoon filling and 1 marshmallow on center of each circle. Bring edges of dough up over marshmallow; pinch edges to seal. Place pinched sides down in muffin cups. Cover and let rise in warm place 35 to 40 minutes or until almost double.

Heat oven to 375°. Bake 20 to 25 minutes or until buns sound hollow when tapped. Remove from pan to wire rack. Cool completely. Drizzle with melted chocolate chips.

S'mores Filling

⅓ cup miniature semisweet chocolate chips

⅓ cup graham cracker crumbs

2 tablespoons margarine or butter, melted

Mix all ingredients.

1 Bun: Calories 260 (Calories from Fat 80); Fat 9g (Saturated 4g); Cholesterol 0mg; Sodium 260mg; Carbohydrate 43g (Dietary Fiber 2g); Protein 4g

Maple Walnut Twists

16 twists

PREP:
30 min

CYCLE:
According to manufacturer

REST:
10 min

RISE:
1 hour

BAKE:
40 min

Betty's Success Tip

To make ahead, after you have placed the twists in the pan, cover with plastic wrap. You can refrigerate them from 4 hours up to 48 hours. Before baking, remove the twists from the refrigerator and remove plastic wrap. Cover with kitchen towel and let rise in a warm place about 2 hours or until double. Bake the twists as the recipe tells you at right.

1 cup water

¼ cup margarine or butter, softened

1 egg

3½ cups bread flour

⅓ cup sugar

1 teaspoon salt

1½ teaspoons bread machine or quick active dry yeast

Walnut Filling (opposite page)

Maple Icing (opposite page)

Measure carefully, placing all ingredients except Walnut Filling and Maple Icing in bread machine pan in the order recommended by the manufacturer.

Select Dough/Manual cycle. Do not use delay cycles.

Remove dough from pan, using lightly floured hands. Cover and let rest 10 minutes on lightly floured surface. Prepare Walnut Filling.

Grease rectangular pan, 13 × 9 × 2 inches. Roll or pat dough into 16 × 10-inch rectangle on lightly floured surface. Spread half of the filling lengthwise down center third of rectangle. Fold one outer third of dough over filling; spread remaining filling over folded dough. Fold remaining third of dough over filling; pinch edge to seal.

Cut crosswise into 16 1-inch strips. Holding a strip at each end, twist in opposite directions. Place strips about 1 inch apart in pan, forming 2 rows of 8 strips each. Cover and let rise in warm place 50 to 60 minutes or until double. (Dough is ready if indentation remains when touched.)

Heat oven to 350°. Bake 35 to 40 minutes or until golden brown. Drizzle Maple Icing over warm twists. Serve warm.

Spread filling lengthwise down center third of rectangle.

Fold one outer third of dough over filling; spread remaining filling over folded dough.

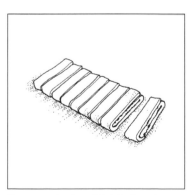

Cut crosswise into 16 1-inch strips. Holding a strip at each end, twist in opposite directions.

Walnut Filling

¼ cup finely chopped walnuts

2 tablespoons maple-flavored syrup

2 tablespoons margarine or butter, softened

½ teaspoon ground cinnamon

Mix all ingredients.

Maple Icing

1 cup powdered sugar

½ teaspoon maple extract

About 1 tablespoon milk

Mix all ingredients until smooth and thin enough to drizzle.

1 Twist: Calories 190 (Calories from Fat 55); Fat 6g (Saturated 1g); Cholesterol 15mg; Sodium 230mg; Carbohydrate 32g (Dietary Fiber 1g); Protein 3g

Caramel Sticky Rolls

15 rolls

PREP:
30 min

CYCLE:
According to manufacturer

RISE:
30 min

BAKE:
35 min

Betty's Success Tip

To make ahead, after placing slices in pan, cover tightly with plastic wrap or aluminum foil and refrigerate 4 to 24 hours. Before baking, remove from refrigerator; remove plastic wrap or foil and cover loosely with plastic wrap. Let rise in warm place about 2 hours or until double. If some rising has occurred in the refrigerator, rising time may be less than 2 hours. Bake as directed.

Ingredient Substitution

For cinnamon rolls, omit Caramel Topping and pecan halves. Grease bottom and sides of rectangular pan, 13 × 9 × 2 inches, with shortening. Place dough slices in pan. Let rise and bake as directed at right, except do not turn pan upside down. Remove rolls from pan to wire rack. Cool 10 minutes. Drizzle rolls with Vanilla Glaze (page 426) if desired.

3½ cups bread flour

⅓ cup sugar

1 teaspoon salt

1½ teaspoons bread machine or quick active dry yeast

1 cup room-temperature water

¼ cup butter or stick margarine, softened

1 large egg

Caramel Topping (opposite page)

1 cup pecan halves (4 ounces), if desired

Filling (opposite page)

2 tablespoons butter or stick margarine, softened

Measure carefully, placing all ingredients except Caramel Topping, pecan halves, Filling and 2 tablespoons softened butter in bread machine pan in the order recommended by the manufacturer

Select Dough/Manual cycle; do not use delay cycle. Remove dough from pan.

Make Caramel Topping. Pour into ungreased rectangular pan, 13 × 9 × 2 inches. Sprinkle with pecan halves. Make Filling.

Gently push fist into dough to deflate. Flatten dough with hands or rolling pin into 15 × 10-inch rectangle on lightly floured surface. Spread with 2 tablespoons butter; sprinkle with Filling. Roll rectangle up tightly, beginning at 15-inch side. Pinch edge of dough into roll to seal. Stretch and shape until even. Cut roll into 15 1-inch slices with dental floss or a sharp serrated knife. Place slightly apart in pan. Cover loosely with plastic wrap and let rise in warm place about 30 minutes or until double.

Heat oven to 350°.

Bake 30 to 35 minutes or until golden brown. Let stand 2 to 3 minutes; immediately turn upside down onto heatproof tray or serving plate. Let stand 1 minute so caramel can drizzle over rolls; remove pan. Serve warm.

Roll up dough; pinch edge of dough into roll to seal.

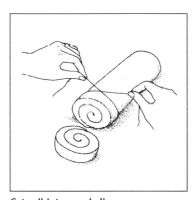

Cut roll into equal slices.

Caramel Topping

1 cup packed brown sugar

½ cup butter or stick margarine, softened

¼ cup corn syrup

Heat brown sugar and butter to boiling in 2-quart saucepan, stirring constantly; remove from heat. Stir in corn syrup.

Filling

½ cup chopped pecans or raisins, if desired

¼ cup granulated or packed brown sugar

1 teaspoon ground cinnamon

Mix all ingredients.

1 Roll: Calories 335 (Calories from Fat 115); Fat 13g (Saturated 6g); Cholesterol 40mg; Sodium 240mg; Carbohydrate 51g (Dietary Fiber 1g); Protein 5g

Festive Raspberry Rolls

12 rolls

PREP:
30 min

CYCLE:
According to manufacturer

REST:
10 min

RISE:
25 min

BAKE:
20 min

Betty's Success Tip

To make ahead, after you have snipped each slice and opened the dough pieces, cover with plastic wrap. You can refrigerate the rolls from 4 hours up to 48 hours. Before baking, remove the rolls from the refrigerator and remove plastic wrap. Cover with kitchen towel and let rise **in a warm** place about 2 hours or until double. Bake the rolls as the recipe tells you.

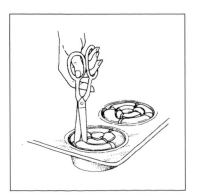

Place slices, cut sides up, in muffin cups. Snip through each slice twice, cutting into fourths, using kitchen scissors.

⅓ cup milk

⅓ cup water

3 tablespoons margarine or butter, softened

1 egg

2 cups bread flour

⅓ cup sugar

½ teaspoon salt

1¾ teaspoons bread machine or quick active dry yeast

3 tablespoons raspberry preserves

Measure carefully, placing all ingredients except preserves in bread machine pan in the order recommended by the manufacturer.

Select Dough/Manual cycle. Do not use delay cycles.

Remove dough from pan, using lightly floured hands. Cover and let rest 10 minutes on lightly floured surface.

Grease 12 medium muffin cups, 2½ × 1¼ inches. Roll or pat dough into 15 × 10-inch rectangle. Spread preserves over dough to within ¼ inch of edges. Roll up dough, beginning at 15-inch side; pinch edge of dough into roll to seal (see page 431). Stretch and shape roll to make even.

Cut roll into 12 equal slices (see page 431). Place slices, cut sides up, in muffin cups. Snip through each slice twice, cutting into fourths, using kitchen scissors. Gently spread dough pieces open. Cover and let rise in warm place about 25 minutes or until double. (Dough is ready if indentation remains when touched.)

Heat oven to 375°. Bake 15 to 20 minutes or until golden brown. Immediately remove from pan to wire rack. Serve warm, or cool on wire rack.

1 Roll: Calories 145 (Calories from Fat 35); Fat 4g (Saturated 1g); Cholesterol 20mg; Sodium 140mg; Carbohydrate 25g (Dietary Fiber 1g); Protein 3g

Festive Raspberry Rolls

Sugared Doughnuts

20 doughnuts

PREP:
25 min

CYCLE:
According to manufacturer

REST:
10 min

RISE:
45 min

BAKE/FRY:
30 min

Betty's Success Tip

Use a deep-fat frying thermometer to be sure the oil temperature is correct. If the oil is too hot, the doughnuts will be golden brown but will not be cooked inside. If the oil is not hot enough, the doughnuts will absorb too much oil and be greasy.

Serving Suggestion

If you don't have a doughnut cutter, you still can make great doughnuts. Roll the dough out into a rectangle until it is ⅜ inch thick. Cut the dough into 20 squares. With your fingers, form a hole about an inch wide in the center of each square. The hole will help the doughnut fry evenly, so the center will not be undercooked and doughy. Try covering these square doughnuts with powdered sugar and a touch of cinnamon. Yum!

⅔ cup milk

¼ cup water

¼ cup margarine or butter, softened

1 egg

3 cups bread flour

¼ cup sugar

1 teaspoon salt

2½ teaspoons bread machine or quick active dry yeast

Vegetable oil

Additional sugar, if desired

Measure carefully, placing all ingredients except vegetable oil and additional sugar in bread machine pan in the order recommended by the manufacturer.

Select Dough/Manual cycle. Do not use delay cycles.

Remove dough from pan, using lightly floured hands. Cover and let rest 10 minutes on lightly floured board.

Roll dough ⅜ inch thick on lightly floured board. Cut with floured doughnut cutter. Cover and let rise on board 35 to 45 minutes or until slightly raised.

Heat 2 to 3 inches oil in deep fryer or heavy Dutch oven to 375°. Fry 2 or 3 doughnuts at a time 2 to 3 minutes, turning as they rise to the surface, until golden brown. Remove from oil with long fork or slotted spoon. Drain on wire rack. Roll warm doughnuts in sugar.

1 Doughnut: Calories 185 (Calories from Fat 100); Fat 11g (Saturated 2g); Cholesterol 10mg; Sodium 140mg; Carbohydrate 19g (Dietary Fiber 1g); Protein 3g

Metric Conversion Guide

Volume

U.S. Units	Canadian Metric	Australian Metric
1/4 teaspoon	1 mL	1 ml
1/2 teaspoon	2 mL	2 ml
1 teaspoon	5 mL	5 ml
1 tablespoon	15 mL	20 ml
1/4 cup	50 mL	60 ml
1/3 cup	75 mL	80 ml
1/2 cup	125 mL	125 ml
2/3 cup	150 mL	170 ml
3/4 cup	175 mL	190 ml
1 cup	250 mL	250 ml
1 quart	1 liter	1 liter
1 1/2 quarts	1.5 liters	1.5 liters
2 quarts	2 liters	2 liters
2 1/2 quarts	2.5 liters	2.5 liters
3 quarts	3 liters	3 liters
4 quarts	4 liters	4 liters

Weight

U.S. Units	Canadian Metric	Australian Metric
1 ounce	30 grams	30 grams
2 ounces	55 grams	60 grams
3 ounces	85 grams	90 grams
4 ounces (1/4 pound)	115 grams	125 grams
8 ounces (1/2 pound)	225 grams	225 grams
16 ounces (1 pound)	455 grams	500 grams
1 pound	455 grams	1/2 kilogram

Measurements

Inches	Centimeters
1	2.5
2	5.0
3	7.5
4	10.0
5	12.5
6	15.0
7	17.5
8	20.5
9	23.0
10	25.5
11	28.0
12	30.5
13	33.0

Temperatures

Fahrenheit	Celsius
32°	0°
212°	100°
250°	120°
275°	140°
300°	150°
325°	160°
350°	180°
375°	190°
400°	200°
425°	220°
450°	230°
475°	240°
500°	260°

Note: The recipes in this cookbook have not been developed or tested using metric measures. When converting recipes to metric, some variations in quality may be noted.

Index

Note: <u>Underscored</u> page references indicate boxed text or sidebars. **Boldfaced** page references indicate photographs.